A Canadian Bankclerk

Rhonda Mohammed

colourting
CLASSICS

Contents

Preface

The story herein told is true to life; true, the greater part of it, to my own life. Also, I am convinced that my experience in a Canadian Bank was but mildly exciting as compared with that of many others.

My object in publishing "Evan Nelson's" history is to enlighten the public concerning life behind the wicket and thus pave the way for the legitimate organization of bank clerks into a fraternal association, for their financial and social (including moral) betterment.

Bank officials, I trust, will see to it that my misrepresentations are exposed.

To mothers of bank clerks who attach overmuch importance to the gentility of their Boy's avocation; to fathers who think that because the bank is rich its employees must necessarily become so in time; to friends who criticize the bank clerks of their acquaintance for not settling down—this story is addressed.

To the men of our banks who are dissatisfied with the business they have chosen, or someone else has chosen for them; to Old Country clerks who come out to Canada under the impression that Five Dollars is as good as One Pound; to bank employees in the United States, and to office men everywhere—I am telling my tale.

Finally, I appeal to "the girls we have known." Be sure you study the subject thoroughly before accusing that inscrutable, proud and procrastinating clerk of yours of inconstancy.

THE AUTHOR.

1

Our Banker

The Ontario village of Hometon rested. It had been doing for so many years. There, in days gone by, pioneers with bushy beards—now long out-of-date, but threatening to sprout again—had fearlessly faced the wolf-haunted forests, relying, no doubt, upon the ferocity of their own appearance to frighten off the devourer.

A few old elm trees still remained in the village, to protect it from the summer sun; and still lived also an occasional pioneer, gnarled and rugged like the old elms, to sigh and shake his head at the new civilization, and shelter whom he might from the power of its stroke.

One of these ancient fathers meandered across the main street and into a grocery store. He plucked a semi-petrified prune from its sticky environment and drew a stool up to the counter.

"Well, Dad," greeted the grocer, "what's new in the old town?"

The old gentleman worried the stolen morsel into one cheek and replied:

"Our boys keep a-leavin' on us, John; keep a-goin'."

While the grocer stood wondering whether the "keep a-goin'" referred to himself or "our boys," a customer entered.

"How d'you do, Mrs. Arling," he smiled, leaving the old man to his quid-like mouthful.

But, in the case of a lady shopper, where business interferes with the telling of a story—or anything—postpone business.

"Ah yes, Grandpa Newman," she sighed, "the town will soon be deserted."

The grey-haired man looked at her as much as to ask: "Pray, how did you manage to overhear what I was saying?" What he did ask was:

"How does his mother feel, Mrs. Arling?"

"I'm just on my way there now," replied the lady-shopper; "give me a can of pork-and-beans, will you, John?"

The grocer, whom almost everyone in town called by his first name, climbed nimbly up the side of his store and fished out the desired article. Meanwhile Mrs. Arling winked at the old man and whispered:

"He looks like a boy, Grandpa, the way he scales that shelf; but he's past forty!"

"Aye, so he is, Mary; but you both seem like chits to me."

Grandpa Newman smiled when "Mary" had gone, then shook his head and sighed. The grocer proceeded to wheedle more news out of the village information bureau.

"Who's leaving us now, Dad?" he asked.

"Young Nelson; he's goin' away out here to Mt. Alban to j'in one of them banks."

"You don't say!"

"Yes," drawled the grandsire, "it beats the Old Scratch how these youngsters have got new-fangled idears into their heads. Now, when I was a boy—"

But the observation Mrs. Arling was, a few minutes later, making to Mrs. Nelson, is more to the point:

"My dear Caroline, I just dropped in to tell you how sorry and how glad I am."

Mrs. Arling was fair, round and vivacious. The woman to whom she talked was dark and slender, but also vivacious. The latter smiled.

"It is lonesome, Mary; but you know we can't keep them home forever."

"No, indeed," agreed Mrs. Arling, "that's what I tell my silly old man when he gets to worrying about our boy, who's only twelve. Let them go—they'll be glad to come back."

"It's all very well for you to sit there and act brave," laughed Mrs. Nelson, "but wait till the day arrives."

The force of the argument told on Mrs. Arling.

"Maybe you're right, Caroline," she admitted. "But it must be a great consolation to see Evan enter such a splendid business."

"That is what consoles me, Mary. Banking is such a respectable, genteel occupation!"

The dark woman's eyes were bright; she spoke with great pride.

"You're right, Caroline, it is genteel. Bank boys get into such nice society. And they can always—you know—look so nice!"

"You know, Mary," rejoined the slender woman, "his pa almost repented giving him permission to quit school. Evan was getting along so well. He would have taken both his matric. and his second this summer; but he *would* go in a bank, and when a vacancy occurred so near home we thought perhaps it would be as well to let him go, in case he should not get so good a chance again."

Mrs. Arling sat in thought.

"Caroline," she said at length, "do you think Evan ever cared much about our girl?"

Mrs. Nelson blushed before one who had been a school-chum.

"I was going to mention that," she said, bashfully.

"You think there is something between them, then?"

"Why, Mary, they are only children. And yet, I often wish that Evan would some day get serious."

"Wouldn't it be lovely!"

The conversation drifted, like ocean-tide, into many fissures and along innumerable channels. The May afternoon ebbed away.

"I really must be going," said Mrs. Arling, suddenly. "Let us know how he gets along. I'm sure the whole town misses Evan, and is proud of him."

Mrs. Nelson smiled fondly.

"And we, too, are proud of Our Banker."

It was the second day of "our banker's" apprenticeship. According to the chronology of homesickness he had been in the banking business about a year. He stood at a high desk in the back end of a dark office, gazing blankly on a heap of letters addressed, or to be addressed, everywhere. An open copying-book lay at his elbow, the pages of which were smeared with indelible streaks. Clerical experts had invented that book for the purpose of recording letters, but Nelson had applied too much water, and the result of his labors was chaos; worse—oblivion.

"Just gaze on that!" cried the teller-accountant, Alfred Castle.

While Alfred gazed a pencil artist might have made a good sketch of him—if the artist, of course, had been any good. The sketch, to be perfect, would need to portray a tall, slim, blonde person with feminine features. But no crayon could convey an idea of the squeaky voice and the supercilious manner.

"I can't understand how anyone could ball things up like that," he continued.

But assertions seemed incapable of rousing Evan from his stupid lethargy. A question might help.

"Why didn't you stop before you had spoiled the whole bunch?" asked the teller sharply.

Evan swallowed.

"I kept thinking," he stammered, "that each one—"

Castle turned away impatiently, refusing to hear the speaker out. He entered his cage and closed the door, leaving Evan to his nightmare. The manager strolled back through the office.

"Where's Perry?" he asked the new junior.

"Out with the drafts, sir," replied Evan, weakly.

The manager was worthy of description also. He was short, heavy of shoulders and slightly knock-kneed. He was perhaps forty years old, his hair was getting thin, and his dark eyes snapped behind a pair of glasses. Just now, instead of snapping, his eyes twinkled.

"What in thunder have you been trying to do?" he exclaimed.

As he leafed over the pages of the copying-book his mirth came nearer and nearer the surface, until at last he was laughing aloud and with much enjoyment.

"Cheer up," he said, seeing the expression of Evan's face, "we'll let them go this time without re-writing."

Then he showed the young clerk how to copy a letter without spoiling both the letter and the tissue-paper pages.

"Thank you, Mr. Robb," said Evan, earnestly.

While the dainty teller fretted in his cage, like a rare species of wild animal, the manager dug Nelson out of his mess and tried to make light of the disaster.

"We all have to learn," he said kindly.

Sam Robb might have been either a diplomat or merely a good-hearted human being. At any rate, Evan Nelson resolved, after the tone of Robb's words had penetrated, that he would always do his utmost to please the manager.

The return of Porter Perry, alias the "Bonehead," was heralded by loud scuffling over by the ledgers. A string of oaths escaped ("escaped" is hardly the way to express it) the ledger-keeper, William Watson, as Porter approached.

"You ——! why didn't you get back here sooner?"

The teller raised his blonde head.

"Enough of that profanity, Watson," he said, peremptorily.

Perry, also called "the porter," dodged Watson, and, muttering a savage growl, shot across the office to the collection desk.

"Here, you," said Mr. Robb, "get busy on this mail. Where have you been—playing checkers in the library or shooting craps on the sidewalk?"

Porter still had his hat on. He took the hint when the manager said, half-mischievously, "Judging by the size of the mail, don't you think you had better stay a while?"

The remainder of the day's work meant confusion and headaches for Evan. Before going to his boarding-house for supper he took a walk by himself along one of the back streets of Mt. Alban. A song his sister used to sing seemed to dwell in the very air about him. It associated itself with home memories and sent a thrill through him.

Mt. Alban was only thirty miles from Hometon, and yet Evan felt that he was gone from home forever. So he was—if he continued to work in the bank. He knew that he would be able to get home only for an occasional week-end; nor were the Hometon trains convenient to bank hours. There was no branch of the bank in Hometon, and he would, consequently, never be located there. When the first move came it would take him still further away.

Evan sauntered, with his thoughts, past comfortable homes fronted with lawns and shaded by weeping willows. There is a peculiar melancholia about a May day; it had an effect on the young bankclerk. He walked by hedges beyond the end of Mt. Alban's asphalt out into the suburbs. Spring birds sang their thanks to Nature, and to the homesick heart a bird's singing is sadness. It is natural for such a heart to seek quiet. Evan had no desire for company. He wanted to think, all by himself. His mind travelled in the one circle, the arcs of which were home, school and the bank. Yes, and Frankie Arling!

Although only seventeen he had a tenacious way of liking a girl; and Frankie had always appealed to him. He thought of her as he walked by the hedges. It was she, indeed, who helped him, more than anything else, to forget the ordeal of his first few days' clerkship. He shuddered when he thought of the hundred and one inscrutable books in the office, so well known to the teller and Watson, and a shiver accompanied thought of mail and copying-books; but he viewed matters from a different angle when Frankie came forward in his mind. How worldly-wise he would be when he went home, and what a hit he would make with his own money in the ice-cream places of Hometon! Wouldn't Frankie be proud of him!

Exclamation marks hardly do justice to Evan's enthusiasm as he allowed himself to speculate on the future. Being "good stuff" at bottom, he forced himself, finally, on this May-day walk, to look at the sunlight on the lawns and trees; and when he doubled back to the boarding-house it was with a good imitation of his old football energy. At table he spoke blithely to the guests, and was quite gay during soup. Cold roast beef brought a slight chill with it. Cake had something of a sour flavor. He drank his tea in silence.

In the evening he declined an invitation to a party, extended to him over the telephone, at the bank. After sweeping out the office he perched himself on a stool and wrote a long letter home. Before daylight had quite disappeared he "wound" the vault combination, seriously, faithfully, and crept up the back stairs to his bed above the bank's treasure. He soberly inspected a heavy revolver, placed it on a chair beside the bed, and retired with a sound not unlike a groan.

Perry came in late and raised a dreadful hubbub. He smoked cigarettes in the room, whistled the raggiest rags and tried his best to make things uncomfortable for the new man. Nelson ground his teeth beneath the sheets and wished he had been born strong.

The first official question Evan was asked the following morning concerned the winding of the combination.

"Never forget that," enjoined Watson.

"Mr. Nelson," called the teller from his cage, "come here." Evan obeyed the summons.

"Go over to the B—— Bank and ask them for their general ledger."

"All right, sir," said Nelson, meekly, and taking his cap from a peg went out to execute the commission.

He had hardly disappeared when Watson walked to the phone and called up the B——Bank, informing them of Nelson's mission and asking them to send him on to some other bank. It was half an hour before the junior returned; he had been all over town; the report he brought with him was this:

"I found out it had just been sent back here."

Now the general ledger of a bank contains a summary of all business done. It would not do for one bank to see the general ledger of another. Neither the branches nor the clerks of one bank may have business secrets in common with another bank; of course it is all right for head offices and general managers to get their heads together in such small matters as keeping down the rate of interest and curtailing loans—but then all competitors should unite against that great enemy, the public.

Evan was given a copy of "Rules and Regulations" to study while waiting for the "Bonehead" to get his drafts ready for delivery. He was pointed to the clause on secrecy and commanded to memorize it forthwith.

The new junior soon discovered that Porter Perry was something of a joke among Mt. Alban merchants. The "Bonehead" had sometime and somewhere earned the dignity of his title. The way he approached customers about a draft was ridiculous even to Evan—and it meant something for Evan to have a definite idea about anything these apprenticeship days. Remarks passed between store clerks, and the giggles and smirks of girls behind counters, did not relieve the embarrassment Nelson felt at being sub-associated with Perry, and worse still, the compulsory recipient of loudly bawled pointers. In proportion as Nelson felt humiliated did Perry feel dignified and important.

The Bonehead had a wonderful faculty for calling people by their first names on the street. This, he doubtless argued, would impress the new "swipe" with a sense of his (Porter's) popularity. It does not take long for boys in a bank to conceive a high and mighty regard for position.

Back to the office from their morning round, Perry took it upon himself to teach Evan the mysteries of the Collection Register. After half an hour's faithful instruction the teller came along and inspected the work. Two dozen drafts had been entered wrong; "Drawer" was mixed up with "Endorser," dates of issue were confused with dates of maturity, and everything but the amounts was topsy-turvy.

"You are, without a doubt," said Castle, turning away, as was his habit, without trying to pull the boys through their trouble, "the worst mess I ever came across." His remarks were addressed to Perry, particularly.

Evan went flat. It is thrillingly unpleasant to find yourself an incompetent in the routine of an office when you could with ease recite Hugo's verses in French and write a long treatise on the Punic Wars. Evan inwardly shuddered. Perry stood beside him grinning and muttering imprecations on the teller.

"What difference does it make how you enter them?" he said, and grabbing a handful of drafts, stamped them at random with the bank's endorsement stamp and the "C" stamp.

Evan stood looking out of the back window. A robin, digging for food on a grassy plot, raised his bright little eyes to the bankclerk, as much as to say:

"Come on out, old chap. You'll never find anything to eat in that dark, musty place!"

As he gazed on the gay bird Evan remembered lessons from his childhood reader. His mind persisted in flying back to school-days. Why? Did he still crave knowledge? Was he hungry for something he knew the bank would never give him?

Years later Evan knew why his mind had dwelt upon the dear days of school life. At school he had had scope for his imagination and his genius, in the writings of poet and historian, inventor and novelist. He could drink as deeply as he would of the fountain of learning, and still the springs would be there for him, soothing, refreshing.

Not so in the bank. Although he knew little or nothing of the business as yet, something told him that here was a shorn pasture. He could find plenty of work for his hands, and bewildering, tiring work for his head; but where was there occupation and recreation for the mind?

Perhaps the fact that he was associated with a boy of Perry's calibre made the contrast between school and office wider. He recalled examination-days when he had sat before a long paper with a feeling of power and security. His pen could not travel fast enough, so familiar was he with French and Latin vocabulary and construction, Ancient History, Modern Literature, English Grammar, and other subjects. But here in the bank he stumbled over a sight draft for $4.17 drawn by a grocery firm and accepted by one Jerry Tangle.

Of course Evan exaggerated matters. Everyone who is homesick paints home in beautiful colors and daubs every other place with mud-grey. He forgot lamplight hours when he had wrested groans from Virgil and provoked the shade of Euclid, and remembered only the good old friends and the favorite studies of school-days. He did not know that Time would bring familiarity with bank routine and that he would learn to like the brainless labors of a clerk. He only knew that he felt hungry, empty; that he had given up something illimitable for a mathematical thing hedged about with paltry figures.

Evan was roused from his reverie by the feminine voice of Castle.

"Here you, get me ten three-dollar bills."

The teller handed him six fives. Evan was, for a moment, doubtful of the existence of the denomination asked for, but he reasoned that Castle would not give him the thirty dollars and look so serious if it were only a joke. He went around among the banks on a wild-goose-chase for the second time that day. A sympathizing junior from another bank met him on the street.

"Say, Bo," he said, grinning; "don't let 'em kid you any more."

Evan's eyes suddenly opened. He made a confidant of this fellow and asked him about the initiation tricks of bankclerks. He was warned against winding combinations, ringing up fictitious numbers on the telephone, and other misleaders.

Evan did not smile when he handed the six fives back to the teller. He said nothing in reply to Castle's question, until the teller grew intolerable; then he growled:

"Go to hell!"

Evan was not a profane individual, as a rule, but there were times when drastic measures seemed justifiable.

Castle looked at him with real anger, and came out of his cage.

"You darn young pup!" he exclaimed menacingly.

Watson raised his voice in a loud laugh, and drew the teller's attention to the new man. Mr. Robb came back to the cage for some change,—and the storm did not mature.

Evan was not relieved. He wanted to have a row with Castle. But it was not the teller he worried about back at his own desk: it was himself. He was ignorant! With all his high-school education and his big marks in languages he did not know that combinations should not be wound, or that three-dollar bills were not somewhere in circulation. There *was* knowledge for him in the bank, after all!

And he decided to make that knowledge his. He applied himself to the office books, after that, and fought against the desire to quit and go back to school. He would ask questions about everything and know all there was to know.

2

Swipe Days

When Nelson was able to take out the collections Porter found himself in line for the savings ledger. It never occurred to the Bonehead that elevation was apt to bring added responsibilities; he thought only of the promotion. Nothing now mattered except the fact that J. Porter Perry was a ledger keeper. He managed to drop the information in every store on his last trip round with the bills, and proclaimed his successor in a tone that was very irritating to the new "swipe."

Evan ground his teeth—but thought of Frankie. He spoke respectfully to all the bank's customers, and tried to act like a gentleman, on the street. In a week's time he knew every merchant in town well enough to speak to him, and had overcome the giggles and whisperings of counter girls.

Mornings were always bright enough to him. When he first wakened a kind of pall usually settled about his lonesome crib, but the May sunlight soon helped him forget that he was "out in the world alone." He knew that his father would gladly send him money and stand by him no matter what happened. This was great consolation, although Evan did not admit to himself that it was. He wanted to be an independent man, as his forefathers had been; he was unwilling to have his father support him any longer by store-labor. When he reflected that soon he would be able to keep himself and make little gifts to his mother and sister he took courage and forged through whatever difficulty happened to be in the way.

Evan had seen college boys fritter away their time, miss examinations repeatedly and get into trouble that cost their fathers dearly. He determined that he would keep clear of youthful mixups and try to save his money, to show his parents that he appreciated what they had done for him, and to repay them, as well as he could, for what they had given him. Sometimes he thought he had made a mistake in going into a bank, but he felt, at that, that it was a brave and unselfish thing to do, and he thought he saw wherein banking had many advantages over school life. He could get an education behind the wicket and the iron railing that would make him self-reliant. This idea fixed itself firmly in his mind.

Homesickness still bothered him, of course. It made itself most strongly felt after meals, like a species of gout. A youth, especially a bankclerk, usually enjoys a good appetite; there is considerable excitement about satisfying it. But when bodily hunger is appeased the mind has leisure to satisfy itself or to feel dissatisfied. Evan could not throw off the gloom that settled on him in the afternoons and evenings. He saw and heard constantly that which reminded him of home and those he loved best. But he did not succumb to the torture. He faced his trials and resolved to make good.

While Nelson was battling against foes seen and unseen, Perry was engaged in gladiatorial combat with a savings ledger. In the space of a week he had developed a singularly profane vocabulary. Probably the contiguity of Watson had something to do with it. He was under the special tutelage of Watson, and the handling he received was anything but gentle. It surely did require patience to instill anything into that head of Porter's. His instructor would stand over him and tell him in a dozen words just exactly what entries to make in a customer's passbook. Porter would stare into oblivion during the lesson and when it was done make a dab at his ink-pot, enter up a cheque as credit, cross it out and make it a debit, then reverse the entry—all before Watson could interfere. The Bonehead was not slow; in fact, he was too rapid—but his swiftness was a serious detriment since the direction taken was usually wrong. Porter acted on impulses, and they seemed destined forever to be senseless. A swift inspiration came to him, he made a slash with his heavily inked pen, there was a blot, a figure with heavy lines drawn crookedly through it, an exclamation of despair—and then the blank look. The vacant expression seemed to be behind all his woes, and an empty mind was undoubtedly behind that.

"You missed your calling, Port," said Bill Watson on one occasion; "you should have been a sign painter. Those aren't figures you are making, you know."

Perry looked hopelessly at his work and then into the ledger keeper's face. Watson indulged in a spasm of mirth.

"I can hardly wait till balance day," he stammered, with difficulty controlling himself; "that nut of yours will crack—and I don't think there'll be enough kernel to excite a squirrel."

"Aw, cut it out and show me this," grumbled the savings-man.

"Yes," interrupted the teller, in his mandatory way, "don't be kidding him all the time, Watson."

The ledger keeper looked at Castle through the wire of the cage.

"Oh, hello, Clarice," he said, "when did you get back?"

The teller reddened, but made no reply. He was not accustomed to impudence, for he was a near relative of Inspector Castle's. This time, though, he could not find words to support his dignity, so he remained silent.

Evan heard him speaking to the manager about it, later.

"I simply won't stand it, Mr. Robb," he was saying; "they've got to show respect."

"Well, you know, Alf," said the manager carelessly, "they're only boys. Don't be too hard on them.... By the way, how do you like Nelson?"

"Oh, he's no worse than the general run," replied Castle impatiently; "I suppose he'll get there in time."

"Yes," said Robb, reflectively, "like the rest of us.... You know, I rather like the boy; he seems anxious to do his best."

Castle made no reply, but left the manager's office suddenly, as though disgusted at not having found satisfaction there. The manager sighed, deeply enough for Evan to hear, and murmured audibly:

"Mollycoddles, all of us!"

With that he slammed down his desk-top and reached for his hat with one hand and a half-smoked cigar with the other. When the front door closed behind him Watson and Perry engaged in a rough-and-tumble. A heavy ruler rolled to the floor with a bang, Porter's big boot struck a fixture, and various other accidents contributed to the hubbub.

"My ——, cut it out!" shrieked the helpless teller, glowing with wrath.

Watson made a grab for him, but he rushed into his cage and locked the door. The combatants were puffing too hard to speak, or one of them at least would probably have vented some sarcasm. Evan eyed the proceedings approvingly; it was a relief to witness a little disorder where the orderly teller-accountant ruled. Porter, with all his boneheadedness, was a match for any man in the office, including the manager, when it came to the primitive way of "managing" affairs; Evan was compelled to admire his physique and the tenacity with which he clung to an opponent. After all "the porter" possessed certain qualities not to be despised. But Watson hit the point uppermost in Nelson's mind.

"Port," he said gasping, "if you would wrestle with your job as gallantly as you do with an antagonist you'd soon be chief inspector."

Perry grinned.

"Come on, Bill," he coaxed, "put me next to this dope."

Bill bent over him and laid down the law. Evan finished his mail. The teller brushed the office from him with a whisk, and, adjusting his tie and hat to a nicety, walked out into the streets to be admired by the female population of Mt. Alban.

An hour later the "swipe" was diligently dusting the front office, his back to the door, when someone entered the bank. Thinking it was Porter he did not look up, but went on with his work. There was a sickening dusty smell in the office: the aftermath of a broom.

"Hello, there," said Robb; "do you work all the time, Nelson?"

Evan looked up with an apologetic smile, and, hurriedly dusting the manager's chair, made as though to leave the sanctum.

"Don't run away, my boy," said the manager; "I came in on purpose to see you. Sit down."

The junior obeyed.

"How do you like banking by this time?"

"Pretty well, sir, thank you," said Evan timidly.

Mr. Robb looked at him disconcertingly during a pause.

"Who advised you to join a bank staff, Nelson?" he asked, slowly.

"It was my own idea, Mr. Robb. I felt as though I had gone to school long enough at my father's expense. He earns his bread hard and I began to feel it was up to me to do something for myself."

"Oh, I see," said the manager, pensively. Again he was silent.

"Did you say you wanted to see me about something?" ventured the new junior.

"Well—I—I was just wondering, Nelson, if you had taken up with the bank just as a sort of notion, and if you had I was going to discourage you."

"Don't you think it's a good business, Mr. Robb?"

"Sure—sure—it's all right. That is, for certain ones. You'll probably be quitting it when you get older."

Evan did not reply immediately. He was trying to figure out what the manager meant.

"I hope I'll get along well," he said, finally.

"I hope so, Nelson; you deserve it; I'll do all I can for you. But the bank is rather uncertain, you know. We are all—well, more or less servants. Even I get my call-downs regularly. You didn't know that, eh? Well, you'll get wise to a whole lot of things as time goes on. However, I don't want to discourage you. Do your best wherever you are."

Mr. Robb puffed his cigar into life before continuing.

"Don't take things too seriously, though. Now Mr. Castle, for instance—anything he says just swallow it with a few grains of salt. He's got bank blue-blood in his veins, you know.

And this sweeping and dusting—don't be so particular. You should be out playing ball or tennis. I must get a woman to clean up from now on. The last manager here started this business, but I'm going to stop it. I didn't say anything while Perry was on the job because it helped break him in to the habit of discipline—but you don't need a schoolmaster; in fact, you need a sporting coach.... Here, do you smoke?"

Evan declined the cigar with thanks.

"You're right," said Robb, "it's a poor habit.... Was there nothing in your home town that attracted you?" he asked suddenly.

"What do you mean—a business?"

"Yes."

"No, sir. There doesn't seem to be anything so good as the bank for a young fellow."

"That's right," smiled the manager; "there doesn't seem to be. The only thing some people in this country can see is the bank."

The junior looked surprised. Robb smiled satirically.

"A little of it won't do you any harm though, Nelson. Stay with it for a while, since you have left school for good, and something else will come along.... How do you like your boarding-house?"

"All right, sir."

When the manager had gone Nelson sat submerged in thought. He came to the conclusion that Mr. Robb had "some kick coming" or he would not give the banking business such cheap mention. He was swayed by the prejudice of his boyhood days when the bank boys of Hometon were the big dogs; and by the well-remembered expectations of his dear mother: "We're going to have a banker in our family!"

The same evening Evan was perched on a stool stamping a pad of "forms" when Watson entered.

"Hello, Nelson," casually. "There wasn't a phone call for me, was there?"

"No, I didn't hear any, Mr. Watson."

Bill turned his face and grinned. By and by he focused his black eyes on the new "swipe."

"How do you like banking by this time?" he asked soberly.

"I'm beginning to like it better," said Evan.

After a pause: "You know, they're apt to move a fellow any time; even you might be moved. You've got along a whole lot better than most juniors, and I wouldn't be sur——"

The ledger keeper broke off—the telephone was ringing. He took down the receiver and began to talk loudly enough for Evan to hear.

"Yes, long distance. Where? Toronto! All right. Hello. Yes, this is the S—— Bank, Mt. Alban. Yes, this is one of the clerks. Who? ..."

Watson put his hand over the mouthpiece and whispered excitedly to the staring junior:

"It's the inspector!" Then he continued to speak: "Yes, sir, we have two junior men here. Yes, sir, one of them is here now. Three weeks. Yes, he's pretty good. You want to speak to him, sir?"

Watson turned to Evan.

"Inspector wants you," he said in a businesslike way.

Evan felt his knees weaken. He stared at the ledger keeper despairingly, but bucked up when Watson said:

"Don't keep him waiting—remember he's the inspector."

"Hello," said Nelson, feebly. "Yes, sir. I—I suppose so, sir, if the b-bank wants me to. Report there at once?—all right, sir, I'll try—I mean I'll report—"

He hung up the receiver and murmured: "Berne!"

"Well," said Watson, like one who had been waiting in suspense for the news, "does he want to move you?"

The ledger keeper laughed very hard and called it a good joke.

"But it will mean more money for me, won't it?" asked Evan, anxiously.

"Sure, your salary will probably be doubled. They may put you on the cash there. It's an out-of-the-way place, you know, and you're practically an experienced man by now."

A few minutes later two of the boys from another Mt. Alban bank came to the front door and were admitted by Watson. They formed a semicircle around the latest man of the hour in bank moves, and plied him with questions. They appeared to enjoy the thought of his being moved to a remote quarter of the province. The thing finally struck Evan himself as funny, and they all indulged in a very satisfactory laugh. It developed later, but not before Evan had telegraphed the exciting news home to his mother, that only three out of the four had known what they were laughing at.

Soon after a boy enters the bank he begins to look for something exciting, in the form of promotion, or a move. He is given to understand that many interesting and profitable changes await every bankclerk; he knows not the day nor the hour when he may be transferred to far-off green fields, filled with strange girls and other "things" to make life pleasant. It is this ever-growing expectancy which gives banking a fascination for young men, especially country boys. They cannot see the day of weariness and monotony that is coming, the day of poverty and celibacy, because between that time and the present there is a golden glamor, a flame of luring light. This flame is fanned by the windy tongues of reckless clerks and fed with the "oxygen" that escapes from head office envelopes.

Evan believed it possible for his reputation to reach the ears of the inspector after three weeks' service, and, although he was surprised for the moment, he considered it reasonable enough that one of the high-up officials should communicate with him over the telephone. All night he counted cash in a nightmare and saw himself signing letters to head office as "pro-accountant." Early the following morning he packed his trunk and mentally bade his room good-bye. On his way to the telegraph office, before eight o'clock, he was surprised to meet Mr. Castle, the teller.

"I heard about it, Nelson," said Castle, stopping him on the street, "and came down to inform you. This funny work has got to stop."

The teller-accountant was partial to verbs of command.

"What's that?" said Evan, bewilderedly.

Then Castle explained the frame-up, and, leaving the junior to console himself on his first big disappointment, went up town to breakfast. "Long distance" had meant across the street in a competitive bank.

The feelings of humiliation and chagrin experienced by the poor "swipe" were exactly those that come to all bankboys in the days of their initiation. It was the beginning of wisdom for Evan: though the end was a long way off. Just as he had fallen from the position of pro-accountant to junior, and from $400 to $200, in one minute, would he tumble off many another pinnacle, on his way to solid ground.

It was a week before the Berne sensation died out in the "banking circles" of Mt. Alban. It expired one balance night, the end of the month of May. Everything but work must be forgotten in a bank when balance day comes.

The manager was back at his desk by seven o'clock, the teller in his cage a few minutes later, Watson turned up about seven-thirty—the savings-man had taken no nourishment at all. With a pair of red ears and a mouth full of indelible he sat propped up to his savings ledger, the picture of idiocy. His lips moved unintelligibly as he slowly crawled up a long row of figures, smearing the sheet en route. At regular intervals he stopped in the middle of a column, muttered profane repetitions, and started at the bottom again. Watson cast a twinkling eye on poor Perry.

"Hadn't you better graze, Port?"

No reply. This was a fight to the finish with Porter. His opponent had him throttled, but still he was game. The current-account ledgerman laughed ecstatically to himself. Castle was annoyed.

"Don't laugh, Watson," he said, again using his favorite imperative, "you'll have to balance the savings yourself anyway."

Bill Watson squinted through the wire at his fellow-clerk.

"The 'Rules and Regulations' put that up to the accountant," he said, still smiling. Castle ripped a blotted sheet out of his "blotter," but made no answer.

Evan had hurried through with his mail and his supper, and was now intensely occupied in adding the interest table. He was shown an out-of-date table with figures at the bottom of each page, and told that every month the junior had to add those stereotyped columns. Like all bank beginners, Nelson did not use his brains. Juniors are taught (1) to obey, (2) to work, (3) to ask no foolish questions. No matter how absurd a task appears, perform it without a kick. The happy-go-lucky boys take a chance and ask questions rather than do what seems to be unnecessary work; but Evan was the conscientious kind, the kind that obeys unquestioningly and never lets up until fully convinced of error. There is a noble six hundred in the bank, as well as the army; but in the bank the number is greater than six hundred.

Perry was working hard this balance-night, but not from a sense of duty—he wanted to show the management that he could balance that savings ledger. Porter was a bulldog; Evan more like a sleigh-dog.

The manager and the teller-accountant left the office about eleven o'clock. Watson was "out" a small amount in the current ledgers, but had left them to take down a new set of balances for Porter. Yawning hopelessly, Perry leaned against the desk, wondering how on earth he had ever managed to be out $396,492.11 in a ledger with deposits of only $400,000.....

The town of Mt. Alban was silent. The main street was in darkness, except for the gleam that came from the windows of three bank buildings. It was past midnight, but out of twenty bankboys in the town, fifteen were still working.

In one of the banks a young clerk slept, with his head on his hands and his hands on an interest table. The ledger-keeper found him thus.

"Too dang bad," he said to Perry; "I forgot all about him.... Hey, Nelson, it's morning!"

Evan raised his head and opened his eyes. Watson smiled good-naturedly.

"It's a shame to kid you," he said. "This was another bum steer. But the practice in adding won't hurt you, eh?"

Nelson stumbled up the back stairs and fell asleep on his bed to the tune of an adding-machine, run by Porter. In his dreams he stood at the foot of a mighty column—of figures. It reached to the clouds. A ghostly friend of Jack-in-the-Beanstalk's whispered to him that he must climb that column if he would reach Success. Evan began the ascent.

3

A Man of the World

Miraculous as it seemed to Evan, the ledgers were finally made to balance. Porter lengthened his stride a foot and walked once more well back on his heels—just as if his bad work had not been responsible for a three days' dizzy mixup. A certain Saturday afternoon came round.

"I guess we can do without you till Monday noon," said the manager, over Nelson's shoulder, as the latter pondered over an unwritten money-order.

It was welcome news to Evan. He had come to feel, however, that his presence was indispensable to the well-being of the collection register and other books of record. It appeared to him that in one afternoon and a forenoon the hand of any other but himself must irrevocably "ball" the junior post.

"You mean you don't want me to drive back Sunday night?" he asked Mr. Robb, doubtingly.

"That's what. You'd better take all the holidays you can get now, Nelson; you'll be tied tighter than wax-end before you're in the business long."

Evan seemed still perplexed.

"Who'll take out the drafts Monday morning, Mr. Robb?" he asked, seriously.

The manager looked at him with an expression half humor and half pity.

"Do you suppose," he said with a grin, "that the merchants will be very badly offended at not getting these bills at the earliest moment?"

Evan smiled. Robb still stood beside him.

"Evan! ....."

He looked up, surprised to hear himself addressed so familiarly by the manager; but the latter was speaking:

".... Remember this: extra holidays never save you labor. The work is always waiting for your return, piling up through every hour of your pleasure."

Mr. Robb sighed and walked into his office, leaving the new junior to absorb another impression. The words spoken did impress Nelson. He sat gazing before him at the wall, wondering why the manager was so friendly toward him and so cynical on matters of business. From looking at nothingness his eyes gradually focused on a calendar, and at an "X" mark in pencil thereon. The mark indicated the day when he would make a trip home to tell about "the world": that day had come.

With a smile he laid aside the money-order he had been examining and began straightening up his desk, whistling as he did so. Castle, out in his cash, was annoyed.

"Will you kindly stop that whistling," he commanded in his high tones.

"Excuse me," said the junior quickly, "I wasn't thinking."

"Well you want to think," returned Castle.

"No you don't," called Watson; "you'll get h—l if you dare to think. As the hymn says, 'Trust and obey'—but for heaven's sake don't think. Now *I* think—"

"Shut up, Bill," interposed Perry, "I've been up this column twice already."

Bill opened his eyes and leered down on the savings man.

"Look who's here," he said, facetiously. "Why, it's the new ledger keeper; the great-grandson of Burroughs, and inventor of the new system of adding—the system which says: Go up a column three times and if the totals agree there is something wrong; mistrust them; get the other man to add it."

Porter scowled. Castle could scarcely repress a smile, but he dug his nose into a bunch of dirty money, and managed to turn his thoughts to microbes and other sober subjects.

Evan, his grip packed, stood apologetically behind the cage, waiting for the teller to turn around.

"What do *you* want?" said Castle.

"Cash this cheque, will you, please?"

A smile wavered on Watson's lip. Porter felt in his pockets. The teller grinned.

"Hardly worth while keeping that in an account," he said, with the intention of joking. It was a wonder, too, for he seldom tried to be funny with inferiors.

"I wouldn't have even that," replied Evan, "if it weren't for the account."

Bill haw-hawed.

"You're no humorist, Castle," he said.

The teller was red and white in an instant. The ledger keeper never had shown him any respect; he had called him Mister but a few times, and that was just after Bill had come from another branch. Castle was smaller than Watson and possessed an inferior personality. Bill was big and humorous—and reckless. It was the joy of his life to torment the teller; and yet he was not mean; he was not even obstreperous; he got along splendidly with the manager, and showed him respect.

The teller's anger exhausted itself inwardly. Evan still stood with his grip in his hand looking at the boys working behind their desks. He felt that he ought to bid them good-bye, but he did not like to do it individually, and it was almost as hard to say a general farewell.

"Good-bye," he called faintly from the front door. Castle did not raise his head. Porter and Bill lifted theirs, but only to grin. The manager stepped out of his office and extended his hand with a smile.

"Have a good time," he said, and whispered: "Monday night will do, if your mother kicks very hard."

"Thank you, Mr. Robb, I——"

"That's all right."

On the train Evan rejoiced. He thought of the sad day he had landed at the station of Mt. Alban with lonesomeness and misgivings; of the thrills of discouragement and homesickness that had tortured him for the first two weeks; of the blank explanations of "the porter," and ensuing jumbles of figures and bills; and of his first look at that bed above the vault. It all seemed to have happened at a remote period in his life—probably in the pre-existent land; even balance day, but three days past, was remote.

It was not in these seemingly ancient memories that Evan had his rejoicing, but in the realization that they were memories. As the train carried him buoyantly toward Hometon he recounted the accomplishments he had acquired in four or five weeks. He could add twice as rapidly as any high-school student in the average collegiate; he knew the collection register and diary; he could enter up a savings-bank passbook better than Perry—with a clearer hand and a much clearer comprehension; he could draw a draft, reckon dates of maturity without a calendar; and so on. But, what he prized most, he was familiar with a host of technical terms, used in the banking business the world over. And after buying his ticket and purchasing a hat-pin for his sister, Lou, he had two dollars of his own money in his pocket. That would buy up most of the ice-cream in Hometon, for one evening anyway.

Such thoughts and reflections as these kept Evan interested until the brakeman shouted "Hometon next!" Then a lofty and exulting happiness took the place of interest. He looked on the approaching spires and humble cupolas of his home town with an expression possibly similar to that of an eagle in flight over a settlement of earthy creatures. He felt a sudden loyalty for Mt. Alban, and suspected that it would be part of his professionalism to maintain the honor of his business-town in Hometon.

The bankclerk straightened his back and marched down the aisle of the train. Alfred Castle and the interest table seemed a thousand miles away. Two happy faces smiled at him from the station platform. Frankie Arling and Sister Lou ran up to him.

"Gee, but isn't he a sport?" said Lou, sweeping him in from tip to toe, and addressing herself to her companion.

"Yes, indeed," laughed Frankie, taking his raincoat from his arm, and throwing it over her own. Lou seized his suitcase.

He submitted to the hold-up with a kind of dignity; looked about him with the air of a tourist; and paid less attention to the questions of the girls than he might have done.

"The old town's just the same," he soliloquized aloud.

Lou was speaking to a passer-by and did not hear the remark. Frankie had been paying better attention. She smiled and looked into his face coyly.

"Does it seem so very long since you left, Evan?"

"Well—I don't know, Frank." He regarded her critically. Lou was attending now.

"I expected to find you with a moustache," she said.

The remark fitted so well into Frankie's thoughts it amused her very much. Both girls laughed to each other without restraint. In fact, they were not very sedate for the main street of Hometon.

Mrs. Nelson had the house as clean and cheerful as mother and a summer's day can make a home. She sat on the front verandah with the material for a pair of pyjamas on her white-aproned lap. Long before the three youngsters were within hailing distance she waved the light flannelette above her head.

Evan's kiss made the mother blush. There never had been much demonstration of affection in the family: there had been no excuse for it. But now matters were different. Evan, too, was a trifle embarrassed.

"Well, I like that," said Lou; "he never kissed me, mother!"

He caught his sister and bestowed a gentle bite on her cheek; she squirmed and would not let him away without a conventional kiss. When he had satisfied her, Lou glanced at the brother and then at Frankie.

"Someone else to be smacked," she said, stopping Frankie's flight by winding her arms around the twisting waist.

Evan was ready to turn the whole affair into a joke, and shouting "I'm game," he caught Frankie and pressed his lips to hers.

Again Mrs. Nelson blushed. So did Miss Arling.

"Gee!" cried Lou; "I just thought that's what the bank did for fellows."

Evan was thus acknowledged a regular bankclerk, and the laugh he vented was well tinctured with exultation.

Then began a series of questions and answers, recitations and interruptions, commendations and exaggerations. For two hours the mother, the son and the two wide-eyed girls listened and looked, or asked and received. The expressions Evan used puzzled them, but he shook his head deprecatingly when they asked for definitions which he knew would be unintelligible to them. He had not been talking with them long before he discovered how to interest them—by saying mysterious things. From the moment of his discovery he revelled in the clerical technical phrases that he had picked up at the Mt. Alban office, and the women justified the assertion of that circus man who said: "Humanity likes to be humbugged."

Lou, with a new and sudden affection for housework, insisted on getting the supper. Mrs. Nelson, of course, could not consent to it on this the night of her banker's return; nobody's hands but her own must lay the cloth and mix the salad. But Lou was strangely insistent, and the upshot of the competition was co-operation. Evan was left on the verandah with Frankie.

No doubt there is a time for everything. That was the time for Evan to tell how lonesome he had been.... And this is the time to make a brief sketch of Miss Arling. Her face was sweet, then it was thoughtful; her eyes were blue-green, bright. She looked not unlike Love's incarnation. She bore a strong resemblance to a baby. In short, she was—what her best friends called her—a dear.

"You don't know how I have missed you, Frank," said Evan, and when she gave him a scrutinizing look, he hurriedly added: "a fellow gets so lonesome, you know."

"Do you like the bank, Evan?" she asked, fencing.

"You bet. A fellow gets such a good insight into—things."

"You were a dandy at school," she observed seriously.

He eyed her suspiciously. He was no longer a school-boy. He repeated a remark he had heard in the office:

"If a fellow goes to school all his life he misses the education of business. That's how it is so many professional men fall down when it comes to collecting accounts."

Frankie regarded him with a smile in which considerable admiration shone. She was just a girl of seventeen.

"I suppose it must be nice to make your own living," she said, and, after thinking a moment, "awfully nice!"

"You bet. I got tired of seeing Dad come home for meals all tuckered out, to find me playing ball on the lawn or reading literature on the verandah."

He cast his eyes toward Main Street. The village bell announced the evening meal, and a familiar figure walked toward the home of George Nelson, village merchant.

"There he comes, Frankie," said Evan, unconsciously sighing; "that step will always remind me of summer evenings and studious noon hours."

The bankclerk felt a sudden desire to work hard and repay his father for the consideration shown him at school. The village merchant would have been willing to help his boy through any college in the country, and the boy knew it. He felt proud of his start in business, of the paltry two dollars in his pocket, as he watched his father approach.

Mr. Nelson waved his hat when he saw Evan on the verandah; and when he came up,—

"Hey," he laughed, "it's a wonder you wouldn't call into a fellow's store and say good-day."

Evan shook hands heartily, smiling into the blue eyes that had more than once cowed him with a glance, when he was performing some ridiculous feat of boyhood.

"I understand," said the father, before Evan could make an excuse; "it's up to Ma. I'm surprised she leaves you alone out here with a young lady."

Perceiving the effect of his remark on Frankie, George Nelson laughed merrily and pinched the girl's cheek.

Soon the glad family was seated at a supper table, Mrs. Nelson's table—that is description enough. Frankie knew she was not an intruder. She was there as Lou's companion, not as Evan's sweetheart. She knew Evan wanted her to be there, her mother knew it, his mother knew it, everybody knew it. The whole town knew it. Things might as well be done in the open, in Hometon, for they would out anyway.

"How's business, Dad?" asked Evan, in quite a business tone.

"Oh, just the same. We continue to buy butter for twenty-five cents and sell it retail at twenty-three cents. Joe breaks about the same number of eggs a day, and John is still good opposition. Well—how do you like the bank?"

"Fine," said Evan immediately; "the manager says he is going to push me along."

"Isn't that just splendid," exclaimed the mother, joyously.

"That depends," said Mr. Nelson, mischievously, "what is meant by being pushed along. If it means a move some hundreds of miles away——"

Mrs. Nelson sighed after vainly trying to smile. She was singularly quiet for a while. Her husband was enjoying himself immensely. He was an optimist, his wife inclined to pessimism. George Nelson believed in making the best of things that had already happened and making nothing of things to come until they came. Caroline, his wife, lived a great many of her troubles in advance. At the same time, the father was as "sentimental" as the mother in the teeth of happenings. He could suffer as much beneath a smile as she could behind tears. Encouraging the boy, however, was making the best of matters, and

Mr. Nelson was going to do his part.

"Perhaps it's just as well you did quit school, Evan," he said cheerfully; "they say the new principal isn't up to much."

After that the conversation alternated between school and the bank, and Evan was enabled to gather valuable material for the institution of comparisons. He launched out in the direction of a bank and kicked back-water schoolward. He managed so well no one had the heart to duck him; his friends had compassion on him in his young enthusiasm. But in spite of the consent silence is supposed to lend, Evan felt that he was scarcely convincing. An atmosphere of good old days was thrown about him; Frankie seemed to be dropping suggestions continually that took him back to the classroom, where Literature and History charmed, or upon the ball field, where Mike Malone swung his long leg and his barnyard boot. A little opposition would have given the bankclerk a keener interest in the conversation; the reiteration of "yes" seemed to make him doubt his own arguments.

But Evan was not to be disheartened by imaginings. He used more of his technical talk on the "Dad," though with less effect than he had observed on the women, and, as a sort of clincher, divulged a little of the bank's business. The father took an interest there.

"Do you mean to say they've got deposits amounting to that?" he said, postponing a bite.

Mrs. Nelson lighted up. Evan was coming out.

"Isn't it grand," she cried, "to think your bank is so strong, Evan. Just think of all those deposits."

"Humph!" grunted the father, "and a fellow can't get a loan to save his neck."

He stole a look at his son, but Evan was not familiar with loans, yet. His first business in that direction was going to be done with Watson, a few days later. Mr. Nelson's hint affecting the management of a bank passed over Evan's head, for Evan was a clerk, not a banker. When it came to actual banking the father knew much more than our banker did, but his knowledge was not comprehensible to the boy, much less to Mrs. Nelson. The "Dad" could only eat his baked potato, look at his dish of strawberries—and trust to the future.

Saturday evening was a small triumph for Evan. He walked up and down the village street with Frankie and Lou, ravaged the refreshment parlors, chatted at every crossing with a bevy of old schoolmates, and spent an enjoyable and typically "village" night.

Sunday morning was bright, and the Nelson family was gay. The word "bank" reverberated throughout the kitchen, the dining-room and parlor, floated around the verandah, tinkled among the Chinese jingles clinking in the breeze, and bounced like a ball on the lawn. Evan was happy all forenoon. And he talked a great deal at dinner.

After dinner, though, Our Banker's mind took a business turn. He thought of what the manager had said to him about work piling up and waiting for the clerk. While he sat for a few moments alone on the verandah he mentally sorted over a bunch of bills, entered them up wrong, heard Castle's squawking voice, and eventually yawned over a heap of mail. He found several envelopes returned from wrong banks and was (still mentally) expecting a memo from head office about them.

His father came quietly out of the house and took a chair beside him, driving away his routine ruminations.

"Evan," he said seriously, "I had a talk with your old teacher not long ago and he said it was a shame for you to quit school just when you did. He said you should have got your matric. at least, so that if ever you tired of the bank you could jump right into college. Now, if ever you feel like quitting, remember I'll be only too glad to send you back to school."

Those words had an effect exactly the contrary to what was intended. Evan felt the force of his father's generosity and unselfishness; he was strengthened in his resolve to be independent; not only independent, but a help to his father.

"No, Dad," he said; "I'm very fond of bank work, and I know I'll succeed."

Both encouragement and discouragement had the effect of spurring Evan on. There was no hope for him: he must go in and play the game—or, rather, fight the fight—to a finish.

Then he would know what others knew but could not tell him; what Sam Robb knew and would have been happy to make every prospective bankclerk understand.

In spite of himself and his surroundings Evan felt the old homesickness creeping over him Sunday night. He had decided to take the first train on Monday back to work; he told himself that the hardest way was the best way, and he sought a short cut to success. After church Frankie found it difficult to elicit cheerful words from him.

The two strolled along a side street. Those dear old Ontario villages and towns where the boys and girls walk on Sunday nights along tree-darkened ways, how long will they listen to the repetitions of lovers? Evan's and Frankie's parents had said the same "foolish" things to each other that Evan and Frankie were now saying, and on the very same street. History repeats, but not with the accuracy of Love.

"Some day I'll come home a manager, Frankie," he was saying, "and then you and I will get married."

"Oh, I hope so," she answered.

She went to bed that night with a happy young heart, and Evan retired feeling sure he loved and would some day marry Frankie Arling.

4

Being a Sport

A sickening sensation took possession of Evan as he boarded the train Monday forenoon for Mt. Alban. He found it hard to banish from his thoughts the invitation his father had given him, to return to school and the pleasant experiences that made up a school education.

The two young girls waved him good-bye from the platform of Hometon station, and it afterwards became known that a tear had stood for a second in the bankclerk's eye.

"You needn't have come till night," said the manager, as Evan walked solemnly into the office.

The words made Evan more homesick than ever. One characteristic of the disease known as homesickness is a strong tendency toward a relapse. One may imagine himself cured, he goes out of his environment,—and comes back with a new attack.

Because of the pain occasioned by visiting home Evan decided he would stay away several months before making another excursion among home-folk. In this resolve he was unintentionally selfish; his mother and his other friends loved to see his face, if it were but for an hour. But young men are always inconsiderate of their loved ones' affections. They probably fear that in humoring their parents and kin they will humor themselves to the point of losing their grit. What Evan considered self-preservation was, from the standpoint of the folk at home, something resembling neglect or indifference. When his mother received a note from him saying he would not be home till fall, she had a "good" cry. Mr. Nelson smiled, while the women-folk were looking, and sighed later.

"Let him go it," he said, cheerily; "it takes these things to make a man, you know."

Mrs. Nelson was more resigned after that; she was most anxious to see her son "a man."

Frankie was also notified of the rigid resolve. She felt chilly while reading the letter, and postponed an answer for two weeks. The letter she wrote was as follows:

Dear Evan,

I don't see why you should make yourself any further away than you really are. It may not be very much pleasure for you to come back to this little burg, but it is nice for us.

I wrote off my Latin and German papers to-day; to-morrow it's French and Literature. Do you remember how you used to help me guess the passages for memorization? You surely were a lucky guesser.

If you are dead certain you don't want to come home for all those months, you will at least write occasionally and tell us how you are getting along. Mother is calling me now, and I must close. I hope you won't be offended at this letter.

Sincerely,

FRANK

When Evan received the note from "his" girl he was much excited. Perry had been moved, a new junior had come, and the old junior was promoted to savings bank. Not only was he excited, he was confused. Besides having to actually wait on customers he was obliged to break in the new "swipe"; and the latter, sad to tell, was about Porter's speed.

The reply Evan sent Frankie was busy. It was rushed off to convey the good news of promotion, and must necessarily have a business ring. In spite of its brevity, however, it contained two or three new bank idioms.

Real work began for Nelson. Not to say that a juniorship is a sinecure: some swipes earn their salaries several times over. One was once known to write the inspector as follows:

Dear Sir,

I could make more money sawing wood than I can banking.

The following reply came back, through the manager, of course:

Tell M-he could earn more money at the job he mentions, but that it would not take him so long to learn wood-sawing as it will to learn banking.

The inspector might have gone one step further and got to the truth of the matter. One requires no education to saw wood, and no intellect; but both education and a certain degree of intelligence must appertain to him who would make successful application to a bank; and education itself requires an expenditure of time and money. The ability a young man possesses has cost him something and has cost his father or widowed mother a great deal. What right has the bank to use it without paying what it is worth? It ought to be worth a bare living, at least—like wood-sawing.

Time flew, for Evan, on his new post. There is certain excitement about bank work, just as there is in playing checkers. It is said of both occupations that they develop the faculties. Counting the stars also strengthens certain brain-tissues. In fact, there are many educational agencies in the world and the universe: it is no trouble to find one or a thousand—the difficulty comes in selecting. He who can choose, with open eyes, the factors that shall enter into his education, is going to be among the fittest. But few boys of seventeen know where to look; certainly Evan Nelson did not. He was naturally a specialist; that is, he was one to put his whole heart into anything. If he had been left to the moulding influence of a university he would have fastened upon literature or science and created something for the world; but, unfortunately, he was thrown headlong into a counting-house, and, being an enthusiast, began to dig among musty books with an energy that was, in great measure, wasted—except, to the beneficiaries of the concern.

The life he had led at home had given Evan scope for his imagination. The life he now led made no demand on his creative powers, with the result that his imagination turned away from great things and concentrated on little things—like pleasure.

It was the old story, the story that Sam Robb and others knew. With Nelson it began later than usual, but came with a rush in the following way:

One night in his room above the vault he sat reading in French a story from De Maupassant, a dictionary beside him. Bill Watson walked into the room and sat down with a grunt, and a cigarette. He lounged back in a chair, well-dressed and glossy-looking, and puffed white rings upward toward the ceiling.

"Why don't you go out a little, Evan?" he said, casually.

The ledger keepers had become pretty well acquainted by now. Evan's sincerity and energy were telling on the books, too. Even Castle had spoken nicely to him one day.

"Out where?" asked Evan, looking away from the French fiction.

"To parties. Where did you think I meant—out in the back yard?"

"I don't know many people yet," replied the savings man.

"You never will, either, unless you make a break. Say, kid, there's a party on to-night. I can get you a pass. Will you come?"

"It's too late," parried Evan.

Bill regarded him with a look of pity.

"Don't ever make a break like that to a girl in this town," he said, smiling, "or she'll take you for a greeny. People don't go to dances at eight o'clock, you know—not in Mt. Alban."

Nelson felt embarrassed. Watson was talking on:

"It helps business, you know. Customers like to know the fellows who are looking after their money. They like to think you take an interest in them."

Evan closed his book quickly.

"I'm not afraid to go to the hanged party," he said suddenly.

"That's talking, Nelsy. Get busy, then. You've got nothing to shave, so it shouldn't take you long to get ready."

Before long the new savings man presented himself dressed for the dance. Bill regarded him with concealed amusement.

"Say, Evan," he said softly, "could you lend us a dollar? I think there's something in my account, but I forgot to draw it this afternoon."

Evan knew there was nothing in Bill's account, but he could not refuse the trifling loan. He wondered how Watson could spend eight dollars a week, when his board only cost him three dollars and a half.

In return for the loan Bill did his best to make Evan feel comfortable at the dance. Now the savings man knew nothing about dancing, and he was equally ignorant of cards. He found girls at the party anxious to teach him the former, and married ladies ready to give him "a hand." With thought of Watson's recently delivered words fresh in his mind, he began to learn new ways of making himself valuable to the bank. He would ingratiate himself with the customers.

Two members of the party were particularly agreeable "customers." Evan discovered that there were some very interesting girls in Mt. Alban. One of the two belles paid Watson great attention and the other seemed partial to Evan himself; both treated him exceedingly well.

"She's a bird, isn't she, Nelson?" observed Watson, when the two bankclerks were alone for a moment.

"You bet. That dark hair of hers is mighty becoming."

Watson laughed.

"I mean the other, you jackass. Mine."

"Oh," said Nelson, absently.

The following day Julia Watersea came into the bank and deposited some money with the teller. Evan felt his face fill up when he saw the red passbook—it meant she would have to face him before the transaction was finished.

"How are you to-day?" he asked, working hard on the book and trying to look professional.

"Very well, thank you, Mr. Nelson. By the way, do you like picnics?"

Bill kicked him from behind.

"Yes—yes, indeed," said Evan, quickly.

"Well, we girls are getting one up for Saturday afternoon. Could you and Mr. Watson come?"

Bill rushed up to the savings wicket.

"Could we?" he cried, smiling at the dark-haired girl. "Can we?"

"All right," said Julia, with color; "we're going to meet at our place."

De Maupassant and the dictionary were doomed. Bill warmed up to the junior ledgerman now that the latter was growing sociable. He periodically forgot to put a cheque through during bank hours, preferring to do his business through Evan.

Miss Watersea's picnic happened, and it was a good one. Evan enjoyed himself so well he forgot to write Frankie her weekly letter. He would have had to mention Julia in it, anyway, and perhaps it was as well to omit writing altogether.

The girl Bill called his was something like Lou Nelson. Evan felt at home in her company, but she did not attract him in the same way Julia did. Hazel Morton had more fire in her than either Lou or Julia—that, Evan said to himself, was how it was she held Bill Watson. Bill was not at all easy to hold.

In the day when Evan Nelson was a savings ledgerman, bankclerks in Eastern towns were nicknamed "village idols." The title was quite appropriate, too. Even yet bankboys are looked for and looked after in those towns. It is quite natural that they should be, for they are a good class of fellows. The worst that can be said about them, as a rule, concerns their prospects; and it is to the credit of young women that they do not take a man's means into account when they want to fancy him.

After the picnic Bill and Evan were alone above the vault. The current-account man was moody.

"Kid," he said, impulsively, "it's —— to be poor, isn't it? Why don't you kick once in a while? The only decent kicker we have around this dump is Robb. He's all right."

Evan smiled pensively.

"—— it," continued Watson, "I don't see why a fellow can't earn enough to—to—"

"Get married on?" suggested Evan, who was, at the same moment thinking of an ideal composed of Frankie Arling and Julia Watersea.

"Sure! Why not?"

"Would you really like to get married, Bill?"

"Yes, I would."

"So would I."

Watson was forced to laugh. He was twenty—that was bad enough. But Nelson was not yet eighteen. Bill continued to gaze at the serious face of his companion until his own countenance changed. Instead of speaking or sighing he lighted a cigarette.

"Will you have one, Nelsy?"

Evan shook his head.

"Do you think Julia would object?"

"What's she got to do with me?" challenged Nelson.

"Why, she's your girl, man. Sailors have sweethearts in every port, you know, and bankers in every town."

Evan tried to connect sailors and sweethearts with cigarettes, but just at that time was unable to establish anything but a far-fetched relationship. Later in life, on the Bowery, he thought he saw the connection.

In the midst of parties and picnics balance day loomed up. Castle's frame of mind, like a special make of barometer, registered the event a day or so in advance.

"Have you got your ledger proved up?" he asked Evan.

"Pretty well, I think."

Under Bill's tutelage, Evan had dropped the "sir" when speaking to Castle.

"Remember, the interest has to be computed this month. Watson, it will be up to you to check it."

"I'm not the accountant," said Bill, chewing gum with a smacking noise. "I'll help him make it up, though."

Mr. Robb came to the cage door for some change, and the teller referred the matter to him.

"Oh, do your best with it, boys," he said. "I'm strong for co-operation. There isn't enough of it among the staff."

Castle turned away with a sneer.

"I've got the liability," he said, sulkingly.

"I'll take charge of that this time," returned Robb; "give the boys a hand at the savings, Alf. And say, Watson, get the cash book written up early so that I can post the general, will you?"

"All right, sir," said Bill, cheerily.

Evan experienced a thrill as these orders were passed around. He felt that he was part of a great system. The names of ledgers and balance-books sounded pleasant to him, for he was daily learning considerable about them. Their puzzles were solving and their mysteries dissolving before his constant gaze. He felt like an engineer lately on the job, or a new chauffeur, only more mighty.

His sense of greatness waned, though, toward midnight on balance day. The savings ledger was out an ugly amount. Bill was also in straits.

"It's a wonder to me," he growled, as the two plodded along alone in the semi-darkness, "that bankclerks don't go nutty."

Evan was scaling a column and did not answer. Watson continued, keeping time with the adding machine.

"Work, work, work; doggone them, it's a wonder they wouldn't ask for a few more particulars on this ledger-sheet. Why, in heaven's name, do they want the names of customers down at head office? They don't know these ginks here, and never will. If they don't believe our totals, why don't they come and look over the books? Oh, ——!"

"Hurrah!" shouted Nelson, cavorting around his desk.

Bill knew the savings man must have struck a balance, but he was too sorely irritated to show enthusiasm.

"Why don't you pat me on the back, Bill?"

"Shut up. Anybody could balance that passbook of a ledger."

Evan cooled down and remained quiet a while. Bill, thinking he had offended his companion, soon looked across with an apologetic smile. Nelson was staring wildly at his totals.

"What's the matter?" asked Watson, well acquainted with vacant looks in bankclerk faces on balance night.

"I—I thought I was balanced. It seems to be one cent out."

The reaction struck Bill as funny, because it duplicated experiences he had had and seen, but he made an effort to suppress his mirth. He laughed silently upon his own unbalanced return-sheet until his nervous system was satisfied, then he spoke.

"Evan."

"What do you want?" sourly.

"Did you ever hear the story about the maid who counted her chickens before they were?"

Evan scowled and raced up and down his columns in search of the stray cent. He did not find it. Bill took pity, seeing that he would not have to go past the units column, and proved Evan's totals. But the cent still hid.

"I'll bet it's in the calling," he said, grinning. "Do you know what that means?"

"No."

"It means you will have to tick off a whole month's work. And remember, we've got the interest to make up, too. No parties this week, kiddo. No more Julias for yours. She'll have another fancier by the time you're unearthed from this junk-heap."

Nelson wondered how Watson could make light of so gloomy a matter. He took his own work very seriously, as most bankboys have to. Bill often worried, but not about his work. When he changed pillows it was a question of finance.

"Cheer up, Nelsy," he said, carelessly, "things always turn up. Remember the old motto: 'It took Noah six hundred years to learn how to build an ark; don't lose your grit.' I'll fish you out if you get too far under water."

Evan was not fond of the idea of being fished out. He wanted to swim unaided.

But he failed. All next day he worried over his "difference," giving a start whenever one cent detached itself from an amount. In the evening Bill called off the ledger to him. When they were nearing the end he called an amount one cent wrong.

"What's that, what's that?" Evan repeated, excitedly.

Bill called it again, but rightly. He chuckled quietly for a little space, greatly to Nelson's aggravation.

It was midnight the first of the month. The savings man struggled alone with his balance; the desks swam around the office and figures danced like devils before him.

"D—!" he muttered.

That was one of his first legitimate swear-words at Mt. Alban—but others would come.

The recording angel up above might as well open an account first as last, for one more human being had entered a bank.

The front door jarred and some of the bankboys entered. Bill was not quite sober, and one of his companions had, what he himself insisted was, "about half a bun."

"Don't work all night, Nelsy," said Watson, "th-there's another d-day coming."

"Sure, lots 'em," said the half-intoxicated one.

A teller from one of the other Mt. Alban banks extended a box of cigarettes toward Nelson.

"No thanks!"

"By heck, it helps a fellow a whole lot when he's tired," said the teller; "come on—just one."

Even felt fagged from hours of bootless labor. He hesitated, almost stupidly, and the bankclerk pushed the box rapidly into his hand. He figured it would be childish to refuse after that—and accepted his first cigarette.

It did help him, for the moment. After a few puffs he began to be amused at Bill's words and actions.

"Close up shop," said Bill, recklessly; "to —— with honest endeavor."

"How much are you out?" asked the alien teller.

"One dirty little copper," said Bill, answering for his desk-mate.

"Let's have a look," said the teller. "This is against the rules, I know—"

"Aw, bury the rules," cried Watson.

While the teller looked Evan's difference loomed up as big as a mountain. The tired savings clerk had stumbled over it many times.

"By Jove!" he shouted, "give us another cigarette!"

A moment later he was sorry he had asked for it, but he was obliged to smoke it. It brought him such pleasant sensations he decided it would be a good medicine to take in crises of hard work.

Immediately after Nelson's difference was found, the boys planned a dance. They had been treated well by the girls of Mt. Alban, and it was up to them to reciprocate.

"Don't you think so?" asked the semi-drunk.

"Sure," said Evan, choking on an inhale.

"Who'll start the fund?" asked Bill.

"I will," responded Nelson, producing a five-dollar bill—all he had.

"That's the kind of a sport," said the foreign teller. "Gee! I haven't seen a real five outside my cage for a month."

"I wish I was on the cash like you, Jack," grinned Watson.

"What would you do?"

"Why, borrow a little occasionally. You didn't get me wrong, I hope?"

"No chance, Bill; we know you're honest."

The dance given by the bankboys of Mt. Alban was a success—in all but a financial way. The thing did not pay for itself, and there was an extra draft on each banker for two dollars. Even wrote home for a loan of five dollars. He also hinted that he needed a new suit, that he felt shabby at parties beside the private banker's son and the haberdasher's nephew. A cheque came signed "George Nelson"; it was twenty-five dollars high. Evan sighed. Then he slowly folded the cheque into his wallet.

He ordered a suit from one of the town tailors and paid ten dollars down.

Bill Watson usually wrote the cash book and the cash items. He saw the cheque from Hometon and made mental note of it. A day or two later he asked Evan for a loan to pay the bank guarantee premium, and got five dollars.

When his suit was finished Nelson was a few dollars short. He went on the tailor's books. The same night Julia Watersea called him up and asked him down. He felt obliged to take some candy along.

"How much should I spend for a box of chocolates, Bill?" he asked.

"Nothing less than a buck, kid," replied Bill, almost rendering his speech ambiguous.

Evan's salary was still two hundred a year—dollars, not pounds. The box of candy he bought consumed almost two days' earnings.

5

MOVED

While Evan and Julia ate their candy and put their digestive organs out of tune, Frankie Arling sat reading stray poems from her French reader. She repeated to herself, in the little nook she called her study, a verse of De Musset's:

J'ai perdu ma force et ma vie,

Et mes amis et ma gaieté;

J'ai perdu jusqu'à, la fierté

Qui faisait croire à mon genie.

That was about how she felt. She had cried considerably when Our Banker first went away. Now she did not yield to the temptation of tears, but she was miserably lonesome and sad—the more so since his letters grew less and less frequent and less intimate.

Frankie was a girl of seventeen and as romantic as those young creatures are made. She had always been Evan's "school girl," and he had always been her juvenile hero. Perhaps theirs was the commonest form of love-affair, but the character of the affection could never rightly be called "common." Incompatibility makes affection commonplace and mean, but Frankie and Evan were suited to each other. They both knew they were, and that knowledge made them feel sure of the ideals they cherished.

Because she clung to her ideals so tenaciously Frankie was often very wretched; she was so on the night of Evan's visit to the Waterseas with the box of candy. Not that she knew about it—but she began to doubt the impossibility of such happenings. His letters had gradually fed a suspicion in her mind.

An idea occurred to Frankie. She would call up Mr. Dunlap, the Hometon teller, and invite him up to spend the evening; then she would question him concerning the fickleness of bankclerks.

Dunlap answered her telephone call with the words: "Well, Miss Arling, I'm working to-night—but I'll gladly postpone work for *you*." He accepted the invitation with alacrity and seemed quite pleased with the verandah welcome he received. Mrs. Arling was out, and he could not occupy the parlor alone with the daughter; but still he had reason to be thankful.

"How is Evan getting along?" was one of the first questions the bankclerk asked.

"Very well, I think," answered Frankie; then, settling immediately to business: "Tell me, Mr. Dunlap, is bank work very exciting?"

"Oh, I don't know. There are some things about it that keep up your spirits. Not so much the bank work itself as the associations."

"What do you mean by 'associations'?"

"Well—when a fellow gets moved, for instance, he meets new—"

"Girls?" suggested Frankie, smiling faintly.

"Yes—like you."

Miss Arling did not recognize the attempt at gallantry.

"I suppose you have been moved pretty often, haven't you, Mr. Dunlap?"

"Six times in four years."

"Have you a girl in every place where you lived?"

"Not exactly," he laughed. "Of course, I write an odd letter to somebody in every one of those towns."

The school-girl had found out what she wanted to know. If Dunlap had come to visit her with any idea that she had forgotten her school-"fellow," Nelson, he could not have cherished the illusion long, for she seemed to lose interest in everything, all very suddenly, and when he suggested that he probably ought to go back and balance the ledger-keeper's books she encouraged him in so generous an undertaking. A man with six girls knows when he is wanted.

Frankie went in to her piano and played "Sleep and Forget." That was a strange selection for a young school-girl to choose; but young girls are born dramatists. Darkness had fallen and the stars were beginning to peep. She was on the verandah again, looking at the evening sky, wondering why people left home and loved ones for the other things, wealth, fame, pleasure, change. The night had sadness in its countenance—which it reflected to the girl's. She was quite like a summer's evening. She should have been, perhaps, more like a summer morning.

While the Hometon girl stood on her father's verandah, gazing and philosophizing, Evan stood on the Watersea verandah at Mt. Alban, gazing also, but not reflecting. He was looking into the eyes of Julia, rather steadily for a lad of less than eighteen, and talking.

"Mighty good of you to take in a stranger like me," he was saying.

"My dear boy" (Julia was past nineteen), "we just love to have your company. Come any time you can."

He had a sudden impulse to take her hand, but she seemed to detect it, and subdued him with a powerful smile.

"Miss Wat—"

"Call me 'Julia,' won't you?"

"All right, I will." (But he didn't.) "I think you are a good sport."

"Oh, Mr.—"

"Call me 'Evan,' will you?"

"What a nice name," she smiled; "it's odd. All right, Evan, but you mustn't call me a 'sport.'"

He had thought it was going to be considerable of a compliment.

"You know what I mean, Miss—Julia!"

"Oh, don't call me 'Miss Julia,'" she laughed; "that sounds like a maiden aunt."

He colored; his breaks were coming too thickly.

They wandered down the lawn-walk to the gate, and there Nelson bade her good-night by shaking hands. He knew she would be in the bank next day, but handshakes are always in order after nine o'clock p.m.

As he walked along Mt. Alban's quietest and prettiest street toward the bank a peculiar sense of loneliness and guilt possessed him. He suggested to himself that he only regarded Julia as a friend, and that knowing people like the Waterseas was necessary to his success as a banker. Of course he intended to pay his way along; he would always give Julia candy and take her out, in return for her kindness to him. The thought that he might be involving her in one of those attachments more easily made than broken did not enter Evan's head. He was too inexperienced to worry over such matters. Others were too experienced.

Telepathic waves reached him from Hometon. He saw Frankie's face clearly outlined inside the Little Dipper. He remembered his words to her, words containing a promise. Yes, indeed, he would be true—

But still he felt the warmth of Julia's hand. Why had he taken it in his, and why had he felt buoyant when she blushed?

He was vaguely conscious of a conflict in his heart. Yet he swore to himself that everything would be all right. Young men are usually quite sure that nothing unpleasant can come of anything.

Bill Watson was sitting in the manager's office when Evan entered. He greeted the savings man with a puff of smoke followed by no words.

"Something new for you to be in so early, Bill," said Evan.

Bill opened his mouth in the shape of a cave, and kept the white smoke revolving within it—like some sort of mysterious and legendary white fleece.

"How did she like the chocolates?" he said suddenly.

"They seemed to go all right."

Bill puffed a while.

"Shame to blow good coin like that," he said, musingly.

"Why?"

"Well, when a fellow thinks of the blots he makes earning a bean he should be gentle with it."

Nelson laughed derisively.

"You're not getting economical, are you, Bill?"

"No, but, I'm sore on myself to-night. About once a month I take a night off to repent."

Evan pinched his pal's knee-cap.

"A fellow can't be a piker, Bill," he said, with the air of a profligate young millionaire escapading in the columns of the press. "You can't go to parties and things without spending money."

Watson looked at his desk-mate.

"Evan," he said, thoughtfully, "in about two years more you'll be just where I am."

"Where's that?"

"In debt, and a spendthrift—if you can call me a spendthrift for getting away with $400 a year."

Nelson sighed. It was unusual for Watson to turn monitor. What he said was all the more effective on that account.

The Hometon boy thought of his tailor's account. He would have to be writing home for more money before long—unless he could borrow it. The very caution Bill had sounded suggested to Nelson a way out. He would borrow from a stranger. He could pay his father back the cheque, and also he could settle the tailor's bill. Just how he would settle the real debt itself was not for present consideration. It never is. It is the humanest thing in the world to borrow money.

Evan turned the light on his desk and wrote a letter to his father. It thanked the merchant for his loan, in rather a businesslike manner, and assured him he would get the money back. This was the letter of an ostensibly self-made son to his merchant father, reversing the title of a well-known story.

Another letter Evan wrote—to Frankie Arling. This one was as follows:

Dear Frank,

It is quite a while since I wrote you. I hope you have not been accusing me of negligence. I am pretty busy, you know.

The people up here are mighty kind to us bank-fellows. There is one family in particular that uses us white. Miss Watersea—that is the daughter—told me last night I was to come up as often as I could. They have a magnificent home. I wish I were making more money so that I could take Julia (that's her name) out more.

How are you getting along at school? It's surprising how soon a person forgets those lessons you are now learning. Bill is calling me—I must close for this time.

Yours, as before,

EVAN

If he had known the comments Frankie would make on a conspicuous sentence of one of his paragraphs, Evan would have made the letter still shorter than it was. It was natural that he should refer to Julia. One should never write a letter to anyone when someone else is on his mind, unless the third party is a mutual friend. Letters, like young children just able to talk, have a habit of telling tales. Often we say to a sheet of paper what we would scarcely tell by word of mouth to the one to whom it is addressed; and yet the letter is mailed and forgotten with the profoundest nonchalance.

The following day a long envelope came from head office to the Mt. Alban office. It contained the "increases."

Castle's salary was raised from $650 to $800. Watson got $100; Evan a raise of $50. The junior did not expect any, and he was not disappointed in his expectations. Nevertheless he was disappointed.

Mr. Robb was snubbed! He said nothing. Bill emulated the manager's stoicism—another two dollars per week made little difference to Bill; it would all have to go out in debts, anyway.

Castle "took" his increase with dignity, making no comments and voicing no rapture. Bill watched him from his ledger.

"Say, Alf," he said at last, under a growing deviltry, "you seem to be a favorite. Now I don't think you're worth eight hundred dollars a year—honestly, do you?"

The teller's delicate skin became pink.

"I don't blame you for being sore, Watson," he retorted, gingerly for him, "when head office shows discrimination; it hurts, I suppose."

Watson grinned. He rarely lost his temper. He sighed comically.

"I can't help if my name isn't Castle," he said, coolly.

The teller opened the door of his cage and rushed into the manager's room.

"Mr. Robb," he cried, in his tenor tones, "I'm not going to stand for the insults of Watson any longer."

"What's the matter now?" asked Robb, not encouragingly.

"Watson's talking of favoritism and that sort of rot. He knows I earn all I get from head office."

"That's right enough, Alf," said Robb, calmly. "You earn what you get, but you also get what you earn. The rest of us don't."

The teller was dumfounded. The way the manager spoke would have halted him even had he considered the words unjust—which he could not. But Castle's sense of dignity was too great to endure argument at that moment; he flushed with humiliation and withdrew unceremoniously from Robb's office.

Robb would not give his teller the satisfaction of calling Watson on the carpet, but when Castle had quit work for the day, the manager accosted Bill.

"Were you rubbing it into Alf to-day?" he asked, leaning against the ledger desk.

"Just a little," said Bill, smiling.

"You want to go easy, Watson. Some day Alf will be an inspector or something, and then he'll remember thee."

Bill looked up from his work quickly.

"Surely we don't have to curry the favor of a brat like that!" Then, in a moment, "His preaching against me to-day didn't seem to get him in very strong with the manager, Mr. Robb?"

Robb made a face.

"Oh, I don't pay much attention to him. Sometimes I feel sorry for him, and then again I can't help despising him. He's got bank aristocracy in him, and that makes it hard for him among us common fellows. I think I insulted him this afternoon—"

Bill interrupted with:

"Wouldn't be surprised if he squealed it to the Big Eye."

The boys called Inspector I. Castle the "Big Eye," because of his initial and of his facility for seeing things; also for other reasons.

"Oh, no," said the manager, sceptically, "I don't think he's that much of a cad."

"Well, you know, Mr. Robb, he'd soothe his poor little conscience with the thought that it is a fellow's duty to report any treason against head office. That's the policy the bank itself pursues. Why should Castle have any more honor than he is taught to have?"

Evan pretended to be busy, but he was listening.

Mr. Robb laughed.

"I'm ashamed of you, Watson," he said, and still smiling, walked away. Once inside his office, however, his face straightened and he looked steadily at a corner of the ceiling.

When Castle left the bank, about four-thirty, he walked soberly up town to the Coign Hotel and ascended to his room. It was a nice room for the teller of a town bank to occupy, boasting a wicker chair, a leather couch and a brass bed. A couple of rather pretentious pictures hung on the walls, otherwise decorated with pennants. The pennants were all Alfred knew about colleges. A desk filled one corner of the room, and there was the atmosphere of an office over all. The wonder is that Alf didn't have his bed encaged.

To his desk the nifty bankman turned his eyes. After washing his hands and adjusting his tie, he sat down to write.

Twenty-four hours after the letter he had written was mailed Inspector I. Castle received one addressed in his nephew's handwriting.

Before a week had passed Sam Robb enjoyed the privilege of reading a circular. It dealt with loyalty to the bank. One paragraph read as follows:

"We wish to warn the managers and staff against the common tendency to ridicule bank customs and establishments. Some of our employes have gone so far as to criticize head office indiscriminately in the matter of salaries, etc. We think it only fair that instances of disaffection should be reported to us, so that we may ascertain who is and who is not loyal to the bank, and reward accordingly."

The circular did not say "punish accordingly." That would not have been diplomatic.

Robb's face grew white—not with fear. All day he was silent, although it could not be said that he was irritable. He seemed uninterested in business and quiet—merely that.

Evan found him sitting moodily in his office late that evening. The savings man had been proving up his ledger. He did not greet the manager; he was going to pass on in silence when he heard his name spoken from the armchair.

"Yes, sir." He turned toward Mr. Robb.

"Are you in a hurry?" There was no sarcasm in the tone.

Evan sat down.

"No, sir; my time isn't worth much, I guess."

The manager looked at him analytically.

"You're beginning to realize it, are you?"

Nelson explained that he meant nothing by the remark, and Robb grunted discontentedly.

"I want you to see the circular we got to-day, Evan. Here, read that and tell me what you think of it."

While the young man read, the man of forty, the bachelor banker, waited. Robb was a lonesome man. He should have had a son almost as old as Evan, but he had none—and Evan would have to answer. It was somewhat comforting to have a confidant like him.

"Looks as if Castle did write, after all," said Evan, suddenly.

The manager smiled grimly.

"You've guessed it, I think," he said. "How would you like the current ledger, Evan?"

"Fine!"

It never took Evan long to decide anything when his success was at stake. He had unlimited faith in promotions and quite a strong confidence in his own powers. The clerical quirks of banking were day by day disappearing before his persistent faculties, and he was always ready to take on new work for the sake of experience.

"Well," continued the manager, "I'm going to suggest to head office that Alf is drawing too big a salary for this branch to support. It may get me in bad, but after all is said and done I'm manager here, and deserve a little say. If they move him the staff will be raised one notch all round. Watson ought to make a capital teller, and—I like him."

Before long the Mt. Alban manager wrote about the matter, without consulting his teller. The reply he got from head office read:

Please instruct Mr. Evan Nelson to report at once to Creek Bend, Ontario. By taking on a new junior you can cut down expenses and still keep your present teller.

(Signed)

I. CASTLE

When Bill Watson saw the inspector's instructions he cursed volubly behind his ledger and exclaimed:

"That settles it; me for a move, too."

Mr. Robb called him on the carpet.

"Watson," he said, "you have a nice job in this office. I heard you talking to Nelson a while ago about a move. Now if you shift from here it won't help your salary any, and it may involve you in a bunch of work. Besides, you have a free room here."

Bill thought a while.

"I guess that's a fact," he said finally. "I won't say anything. I guess you and I can hold the fort against Mr. Alfred Castle, eh?"

The manager laughed and extended his hand.

"Bill," he said (usually he called the ledger-keeper "Watson"), "I'm in wrong already, and if you asked to leave, head office might think there was something wrong with my management."

"I get you," said Bill, unconsciously speaking as he would to a pal. "By the way, do you suppose the Big Eye knows that Alf has a girl here?"

"Sure—likely," said Robb; "I'm now convinced that that boy chirrups to his dear uncle about everything."

After musing a bit Bill observed:

"I wish I could make him blow on me. No, I don't, either—he hasn't got the physique to stand it."

Robb chuckled. They spoke of Nelson.

"He's a good scout," said Bill. "How is it they always move the decent heads away?"

"I give them up," said the manager; "the older I grow the more head office puzzles me."

Nelson rapped at the door and was invited in. "Well," grinned the manager, "our pipe-dream didn't mature, did it?"

But Evan was having one of his own, and while he did not like to leave so kind a manager as Robb, he was thinking almost entirely of himself.

"I'll probably be teller in Creek Bend, won't I?"

"Yes," said Bill, "if there's anything to be 'told.'"

The manager laughed quietly.

"Take care you don't get lazy, Evan," he said. "They won't leave you there forever. It will be a city office for yours in due course, and then you'll need to be in practice. You'll be sure to hit a bees'-nest before you quit the bank."

"If they always use me right," said Evan, "I won't ever quit."

"Well," yawned Watson, "if you're satisfied, Nelsy, I guess they are."

Nelson waited a minute before making the request he came with the intention of making.

"Mr. Robb," he asked, "could I take a day off to run home and see the folks? Creek Bend is a hundred miles away and hard to get at—so the station agent says."

"Sure," said the manager, "but I'll have to 'fix' the head office travel-slip."

"What's that?" asked Evan.

Mr. Robb showed him a slip of paper to be signed by the manager of the branch left and the branch arrived at, also by the transient clerk. This slip records the time to a minute and allows no stop-over or visits en route. Neither does it permit of delay in leaving.

Evan suddenly decided he would not bother going home. He explained to Watson later that he considered it crooked to tamper with the travel-slip and thought he would be a cad to let the manager run the chance of further incurring head office displeasure by altering it.

"By heck," said Bill, "you've got to let some of that good conscience run out if you ever expect to stay in the bank."

"Well, Bill," was the reply, "when I find that I can't be honest in the bank I'll get out of it."

Watson remembered that remark years afterwards.

Evan wrote letters home, one to his mother and one to Frankie Arling. Then he packed his trunk and bade good-bye to Mt. Alban. Within four hours after receiving notice from head office he was on the train bound for Creek Bend.

Mrs. Nelson cried over her son's letter, and went to her husband for consolation.

"Carrie," he said, "it will do the boy good."

"But why didn't they let him say good-bye to us?" she cried.

"Well," answered George Nelson, "business is business, you know."

In his store-office the father used profanity. Men swear. He voiced a wish that all banks were made of sand and situated in the neighborhood of Newfoundland.

Frankie swallowed something in her throat as she read her letter. There was one grain of comfort in it, though, prompting the utterance:

"That ends Julia!"

6

THE VILLAGE MAIDEN

Months had passed. Western Ontario was turning brown; heaps of leaves had already fallen. The village of Creek Bend was sleeping through the Indian Summer day. So was Evan Nelson—he lay sprawled on a hammock swung between two apple-trees behind the bank.

It is not to be inferred, however, that Evan was lazy, or that he had spent the summer lazily. Every morning before seven he had been out for a three-mile run, and every evening it had been football with the village team or a ride on the bicycle. He knew that physical exercise was necessary to health, and he took it as regularly as his mother used to make him take a spring tonic.

The work of the Creek Bend branch was ludicrously light. The manager was not a real one—he signed "acting." The branch had been opened for the sole purpose of keeping another bank out. Evan signed "pro-accountant." The first time he decorated a money order after that fashion a thrill made itself felt along his spine and in his hair.

Nelson's duties at first consisted of doing what little ledger work there was to do, writing settlement drafts and so forth, and attending to the mail. By degrees the manager, E. T. Dunn, initiated him into other work, until at last he did practically everything, even to the writing of returns.

As he sprawled now in the hammock between the apple-trees he gradually became conscious and his mind resumed the thread of thought sleep had broken off. He thought, with his eyes shut, about clerical work. Mentally he took a deposit from a customer, entered it in his "blotter," wrote it in the supplementary, and posted it in a ledger; it was included in the cash-book total, and from there found its way to the general ledger. So it was with every entry, credit or debit. "Returns" were merely copies of general-ledger balances, or parts thereof. Evan saw his way from beginning to end of the routine, and wondered that anything so simple as bank work could ever worry a man. He recalled the first week of his clerkship in Mt. Alban, and a grin crept over his somnolent features.

But Evan was not only musing—he was thinking. He knew the banking system was uniform throughout; and until he should be manager, he saw himself spending years working out some part of the routine now so simple to him. Mr. Dunn had worked at head office, and he told Nelson that there were clerks down there who did nothing from morning till night but add. Others there were who spent every hour of the day "checking" branch figures. What an existence! he thought; what a brainless life! Human automatons!

Thinking in these channels made Evan dissatisfied, and sometimes he offered pointed observations to the acting-manager. Dunn would smile and agree with anything that was said—but invariably settled down to his pipe and paper again, contented to let the business take care of him as it would. Dunn was one of a large class, in the bank, who are satisfied with six cigars a day, a bed each night, and seventy-five dollars a month.

The exercise Evan had accustomed himself to gave him increased vitality, and there being neither work nor social life enough in Creek Bend to satisfy this new vim he fell into the habit of reading and studying considerably. Dunn frequently expressed his surprise at seeing a bankclerk labor so, but the junior officer paid no attention, since the senior raised no objection. Evan gave his mind an excursion every day into the large world beyond him; the further he travelled the more ridiculous his present occupation seemed. But he encouraged reaction from these fits of treason and in the end criticized his own imagination more than those things, which, like the bank, are generally recognized to be tangibly great.

A book lay beneath the hammock this dreamy Autumn afternoon. It was "The Strenuous Life," by Roosevelt. One would have thought the reclining figure had grown weary of ambition and had cast the incentive from him. An Indian Summer day is not conducive to aspirations: mellow late-Autumn is more tolerant of beauty and love.

A flesh-and-blood combination of both came upon Evan unawares.

"Wow!" he shouted, rubbing the top of his head.

The girl laughed until she was ashamed of herself; then hid her face and started to run off.

"Don't go 'way, Lily," he called; "I want to say something to you."

She stopped, and eyed him suspiciously.

"What is it, Mr. Nelson?"

"Come here and I'll tell you."

She ventured near.

"Won't you stay a while?" he said, turning his eyes on hers. "I can't empty it all out in a minute, you know."

"Is it important?" asked Lily, slyly.

"Sure," he laughed; "I wouldn't waste your valuable time if it weren't."

She pouted.

"You think I have nothing to do, I suppose, Mr. Nelson!"

Evan was Mr. to her chiefly because he was a bankclerk.

"Oh no, not that. But you don't seem to be cut out for a post-office ornament. Do you ever feel dissatisfied here?"

"Why?"

"I was just wondering—I'm beginning to get sick of it myself."

She laughed.

"So am I," she said; "and it's my home, too."

She had settled down on the grass, and her eyes were on a level with the bankclerk's.

"Still you'll likely settle down here and get married at last," said Evan, soberly.

"No chance,"—haughtily. "Do you think I would have one of these dubs around here?"

"What's the matter with them?"

"Oh, they're slow. When I get married I'm going to have a smart, up-to-date fellow."

Evan had a smile ready for her when she looked at him. She colored radiantly.

"I must go," she said, rising, and skipped away, not to be stopped this time.

A few minutes later the acting-manager came out with a highly illustrated magazine.

"Say, Bo," he yawned, "things are getting pretty thick. You can't do much on that $250, you know."

Evan laughed.

"A bank fellow's not in much danger," he said.

"No," replied Dunn, "but what about the girl?"

Nelson revolved the remark in his mind a while. He decided he would not be so friendly with Lily from that time on.

"It's funny," observed Dunn, again, "how village girls fall for a bankclerk—when we are made of the very stuff their own brothers are made of. Most of us came from a farm or a village. The bank has fitted us out with a shine and a shave, also has made us more useless year after year, and when we degenerate sufficiently the girls begin to adore us. I used to correspond with ten girls in different towns, regularly."

A strange feature of banking life, and which goes to emphasize the peculiar fascination of it, is that every man knows he is degenerating and understands why, but he seldom does anything about it. He sails carelessly along with Ulysses' crew, enjoying the voyage as much as possible, and worrying not about a landing.

"Still you wouldn't be anything but a banker, would you?" asked Nelson.

"I couldn't if I would," said Dunn, lazily; "I've been at it eight years. That's all I know."

"Well, supposing you were back on my salary, do you think you would stay in the bank?"

"I suppose so," answered the other; "I was on $250 once, and I didn't quit."

Dunn's indifferent contentment had considerable influence over Nelson. It caused the junior man to severely criticize his own restlessness. One of the acting-manager's slogans was about the rolling stone and the moss. The effect of that obsolete aphorism on moss-backs is pitiful. It impressed Evan, not because of his mossiness altogether, but because of his youth, and of youth's anxiety to make good. The lad of eighteen had an example of banking in his manager, Dunn, but his eyes were not yet opened. He could see the $75 a month very plainly, but he could not comprehend the eight long years of service that had made Dunn's salary what it was—and that had made him the laggard he was. Dunn had not entirely lost ambition, any more than a hundred Dunns in every bank to-day have lost it; but eight years' specialty service makes a young man useless for anything else but his specialty, and when he does muster enough strength to sit up in the bed he has made, he sinks back on the pillow again, exhausted, because of the weight on his chest.

But Dunn's predicament was, chiefly, Dunn's lookout—and, to some extent, the lookout of tradition-bound relatives. Had he been an exceptional man his attitude toward the business would have been different, and Evan, in the beginning of his awakening, would probably have benefited by contact with him. As it was, Evan scolded his complaining brain and forced it back into bed, as a mother does her baby; in fact, it is to be feared he gave it a dose of soothing-syrup, too.

The Hometon boy actually saved a little on his five dollars per week. The manager frequently borrowed a dollar or two from him. But Evan had not yet paid back the money his father had given him—George Nelson warned him not to try.

"Keep it, my boy," he wrote, "and start an account. Try and put away a certain amount each week." This sentence was stroked out, vetoed by saner afterthought. The father doubtless realized the absurdity of asking a young man away from home earning five dollars a week to save. "Keep yourself if possible," said the letter, "on the salary you draw;

but if you run shy I am always ready to help you out." Evan thought of his tailor's bill, and decided to pay it before settling with his father.

Among the great economists at the head of the Canadian banking business there are some who seem to make a specialty of the following sermon to employes: "It matters not what you make, you can always save something." Sure! You can steer clear of a young lady on the street in case you might have to buy her an ice-cream, and you can always raise a headache on garden-party or picnic nights. The class of economists mentioned seem unable to realize that a man, young or old, is worth his salt, if he works honestly, whether he be a sewer-digger or a clerk who spends half his income on laundry.

Sometimes not only dissatisfaction but resentment took possession of Nelson. He was, in the first place, obliged to go where the bank sent him; and in the second place, to take what the bank gave him. He would receive a certain increase yearly, no matter where or what he was in the business—and the Bonehead (wherever he was) would get the same or better. Discrimination according to ability was unknown in banking—except on reports: and there it was a joke to every man in the service.

But youth is very pliant. Employers of young men are familiar with the fact. Something always came along to quiet Evan's mind before he had gone so far as to write an "indiscreet" letter to head office. What a grand thing it is to be discreet! Why was mention of this attribute, discretion, omitted from the Apostle's list? What anxiety and sorrow possession of this virtue would save us—and what enlightenment! .... Had Evan written an impulsive letter to head office he would have been ousted from the bank; he would very likely have been metaphorically kicked out. The kick would have hurt for a while, but not like the sting that must burn later on. Yet, how was he to foresee that which was coming? He might have estimated his chances by the experience of others; but boys, like young nations, do not suffer themselves to be guided in that way.

The excitement of saving money, as much as anything, now held Evan to his desk. He was putting away a dollar weekly. By Thanksgiving he would be able to take a trip home, and incidentally make his mother a present of the turkey for dinner. If the gobbler Evan plotted against could only have known how safe his neck was he would have put all the roosters in the barnyard out of business, and whetted his bill for the drake. A calamity was destined to befall the young Creek Bend teller; yet, viewed from the standpoint of its frequency in the business, this "calamity" deserved only the name of a "professional accident"—for which there is no provision made in the Rules and Regulations. It happened in this wise:

A black-whiskered man came in, accompanied by the village hotel-keeper, with a cheque to be cashed. It was "marked good" by a bank in London, Ontario. Evan paid it without showing it to the manager. Dunn saw it afterwards and let it pass for seventy dollars, the amount the customer received. The figures were a compromise between $20 and $70, but the "body" of the cheque (what a teller goes by) looked very much like Seventy. Evan thought no more about the strange-looking customer whom the hotel-keeper had identified, until the cheque came back from London, with the following memo: "This was marked for Twenty Dollars only."

The teller rushed out to the hotel and asked about the man of beard. The hotel-keeper said he only knew him as an occasional drinker; and because the hotel-keeper had not endorsed the cheque and needed no loan from the bank, he waxed impolite. Evan gathered that the shark had left town and would not be back.

Dunn, although he had not had the matter referred to him, felt sorry for Nelson and comforted him with the offer to pay half.

"I would have cashed it myself for seventy," he said.

Evan was in the depths.

"Do you think head office would let us debit it to charges?" he asked hopelessly.

The manager looked at him in dismay.

"My dear boy," he smiled, "they would almost fire you for suggesting such a thing. I tried that once and they wrote back telling me to be more careful, and insinuating that no good clerk need lose money on the cash. Never look to them for sympathy, because you won't get it."

Nelson swallowed a lump and drew a cheque on his account for all he had—$22. He thought it very decent of Dunn to make up half the shortage—and it was. The acting-manager was a good sport—too good for his own good. Evan figured that the Mt. Alban tailor would have to wait.

Mrs. Nelson was advised by letter that "seeing there are only two of us running this branch, and the manager wants to go to Toronto for the holiday, we have decided that I must stay. I'm very sorry, mother—but it won't be long till Christmas."

There was truth in the manager's wanting to go away for the holiday: Evan encouraged him in the desire, because he wanted to express appreciation of Dunn's kindness in putting up $25 of the loss.

The manager left his "combination" in an envelope in case he should miss a train back, and Evan was entrusted with several thousand dollars in cash. Dunn left at noon Saturday and would be gone until ten o'clock Monday morning.

"Don't run off with the safe," he laughed as he said good-bye.

"No, I'll only take the contents," answered Evan, cheerily.

But he felt not the least bit cheery. He thought of the last Thanksgiving spent in Hometon, of mother, sister and Frankie—and the dinner. It must be confessed that, in his memory, the dinner shared with Frankie.

If Evan had been crooked, instead of turkey-dressing and home-scenes he would have been thinking of the money within his grasp. As it was, the filthy lucre never entered his head. He did think of the double responsibility, and it made him proud; but that was the extent of his money speculations.

While he sat in the acting-manager's chair dreaming of home and wondering why he had not written Frankie a letter this week, a gentle tap came to the front door of the bank, which was always locked at noon on Saturdays. Evan peeked out to ascertain whether or not it was a customer who could be avoided. A bright eye met the bare spot in the frosted glass he was utilizing, and with a laugh he opened the door.

"Mr. Nelson," said Lily, blushing; "I beg your pardon, but could you let me have a little mucilage?"

"Sure," he said; "come in. We'll have to shut the door or some gink will be coming along for a loan."

Lily hesitated a moment, but seeing no way out finally entered. Evan went behind his desk to get the mucilage. While he was rummaging there another rap came to the door, and Lily peered out.

"It's a farmer," she whispered, running back to where Evan was.

"Don't let him know we're here then," said the clerk; "I can't open up for him."

The disappointed customer hung around, hoping, no doubt, to be humored, as he had often been. Nelson and the young girl from the post-office stood behind a high desk waiting for the intruder to leave.

"Just think," whispered Lily, "what the gossips of this town would say if they knew—"

"They won't know," said Evan, reassuringly.

"It would hurt your business, Mr. Nelson, wouldn't it?"

The sweet face was turned up to him. There was the confidence of innocence in her eyes. Fate had denied the lonely bankclerk a trip home, but it had placed a pair of baby lips within easy reach. He gazed, flushed—and kissed Lily. She trembled and the tears came into her blue eyes.

"Oh, Mr. Nelson!" she cried, crimson with excitement and pleasure.

He drew away, feeling ashamed and guilty. His embarrassment was ten-fold greater than the girl's: she was acting consistently with her childish fancies of the past few months, while Evan was betraying a girl in Hometon.

Beginning to realize the futility of waiting at the bank door, the farmer dragged himself away, muttering anathemas on high collars and patent locks.

"Here's your mucilage," said Evan, handing Lily a small bottle. "Don't get it on your clothes."

He uttered the last sentence for want of something to say.

"You must think I'm a regular baby," she replied, with a touch of scorn. When a young girl has just been kissed by a young man she wants him to understand she is a woman, full-grown.

Evan laughed and said she was anything but a baby.

That afternoon a letter arrived, by stage mail, from Frankie Arling. It was another of her school compositions.

Dear Evan,

Your letter just came, telling us you can't get off for Thanksgiving. I think it is real mean of your manager to treat you like that. I don't think the bank is fair with its clerks at all.

Now, there's a young fellow here (an awfully clever and nice chap) who counted on getting down to the city, but he was out in his books, so the manager couldn't let him off. His name is Reade: we are going to have him up to the house for tea. Father likes him, and so do all of us.

I'm going to a dance to-night; that is why I am sending this letter away in such a hurry. You don't deserve a very long one, though, do you? Hoping you spend a decent Thanksgiving, and wishing you success.

Yours sincerely,

FRANK

"Success be darned!" mumbled Evan. The smile with which he had begun the letter had died down to an emaciated grin and finally evaporated between compressed lips. "I hope Reade enjoys himself!"

He went to the telephone and rang up two longs and three shorts—the post-office. Had he reread Frankie's letter and sat down to analyze it and to think, he probably would not have telephoned; but when a fellow has lost a summer's savings and a Thanksgiving dinner all at once, it is, perhaps, natural that he should feel uncertain even of his sweet-heart, and act accordingly.

"Hello," said Evan; "is that you, Lily?"

"Yes, this is me!"

"How would you like to go for a drive? You would? All right, I'll call for you after supper."

Evan rented a livery, and Lily's folk raising no objection, the young girl went out to advertise the fact that she had a banker beau. All the town wondered.

It is easy to condemn Evan for his flirtations with Julia Watersea and Lily Allen. If he had stayed at school, matters would have been different. When the mind is wading through study it turns readily to pleasure, but does not dwell upon it. In the simple routine of the bank, in spite of the books he read, Evan found his mind drifting to excitement of some sort continually. When he brought it up, there was nothing for it to settle upon. When he left Mt. Alban he was being gradually drawn into what was called the "social life"—a life that would make him an ideal bankclerk, but nothing bigger. Now, after a few months of ease, he found himself craving the whirl again; and he must seize any small pleasure at hand.

So he seized Lily Allen around the waist and acted sentimentally.

"You mustn't," she murmured, making no effort to release herself.

"I must," said he. That was the way he felt.

When winter had come Evan had saved enough to take him home for Christmas. He was very careful with strangers, especially when they wore whiskers. He knew everybody in Creek Bend; especially did he know the Allens. After that night of the drive he and Lily had spent many an hour together. The result of it was that he let his correspondence with Frankie fall off, soothing his conscience with Reade. Occasionally he sent a picture-postal to Julia Watersea, too, and when it was answered in like manner he always felt better.

Christmas was nearing now. The snow stayed, to prepare the roads for Santa's outfit. The two stores of Creek Bend had decorated their fronts with tissue-paper and pressed raisins, and the post-office emitted holly stickers.

A village post-office is always interesting. That of Creek Bend interested Evan, not because of curious loiterers—themselves curiosities—but principally on account of its fair clerk. He admitted as much to himself. The village had him married to Lily, and he began to wonder if she really hadn't points over Frankie.

"Another of those bank letters you all look for so anxiously, Evan," she smiled, handing him an envelope from the Inspector's Department.

A few minutes later he called in the post-office again and beckoned Lily to the money-order wicket.

"I'm moved!" he whispered, excitedly.

Tears came into the young girl's eyes. Evan brushed them away that night with his handkerchief, but they would come again.

"I'll not forget you, Lily," he whispered.

And he never would forget her. In moments of introspection, in times of deepest thought, all his life through, he would remember her.

7

A Bank Holiday

Christmas had come—again. A year had gone by.

Evan Nelson was preparing to go home for a two days' visit.

"Here, Henty," he said, "put your finger on this money parcel while I tie it."

The junior at Banfield branch had a large finger, just the sort for holding down a thong, although it guided a pen badly. He was a big, red-faced, shaggy-haired fellow, born to the physical strain of a practical agriculturalist.

"Henty," said the teller, as he waxed the money parcel, "how did you ever get into the bank?"

"Why?" grinned the junior.

"Oh, I don't know. You're too strong or too something for this business. If I had your frame I'd go into the ring."

"This is ring enough for me," said Henty. "I can have a round here any time—with the cash book and savings."

The ledger keeper spoke up. (Henty's initials were A. P.)

"Say, Ape—I'll bet you lose more good sweat making out a settlement draft than you would covering a pig-pen with old tin."

"Aw, forget it," said A. P., smiling good-naturedly; "the bank has worse dubs than me. I mean than I. Take yourself for example——"

"Impossible," replied Filter, the ledger keeper.

Gordon Filter was tall, lean and pale. He was a sedentary person and loved meddling with figures. He swore continually about his salary and blasphemed against the bank, but his work was always perfect and he was always watching over it with pride. Filter was what was known as a "fusser." He worked slowly, mechanically, and without originality, but he made few mistakes. He was a good clerk—that was about the best he would ever be.

There was the strongest contrast between Henty and Filter. One was as "sloppy," clerically speaking, as the other was neat, and as healthy as the other was unhealthy. A. P. would seal the last envelope of his day's mail with a bang and rush out of the office to a game of baseball; Gordon would hover over his ledger in hope of finding an account unproved or untransferred. He always closed his book gently and allowed his hand to rest on it affectionately before consigning it to the vault. The junior drew $150 a year, and Filter $250.

Evan's salary was, by this time, $350. He had been in the bank almost two years. No man can be in the business that long without *earning* at least ten dollars a week. In office dictionaries, however, the words "earn" and "get" are a long distance apart. Nelson was teller and accountant in a branch of four. The manager was delicate and could not do very much work. Evan ran the cash, liability and general ledgers, looked after most of the loans, wrote nearly all returns, and superintended every department of the office routine. He worked three nights a week and every day from 8.30 until 6.30, eating lunch in his cage while he handed out infectious bank notes.

His was the only bank in Banfield, a village of nine hundred inhabitants. There was a good farming district around the village; a big load of stock was shipped every week, and poultry and dairy products were profitably handled. The bank did an uncommonly large business, but owing to the size of the town, head office would not allow H. H. Jones, the manager, more than three of a staff. Jones relied on the faithfulness and assiduousness of his teller-accountant, and Evan struggled through each day as best he could.

The Christmas season is always busy. Fortunately for Evan, however, the manager was feeling better as the holiday neared; he took over the cash to let the teller away. Filter was too poor to go home for turkey, and the junior was waiting in great suspense for a cheque from home. Deposits do not constitute all the money that is paid into the coffers of Canadian banks: farmers and townsmen help the bank feed, clothe and provide recreation for its employes; they send remittances regularly to bankclerk sons who must keep up an appearance in spite of starvation pay.

"Leave the twenty-third returns for me, Mr. Jones," said the teller, with holiday courage and generosity, "and let anything wait you can. I'll be back the twenty-sixth."

"All right, Nelson, we'll get along some way."

The manager's words indicated that Evan was indispensable, which was practically the case. He did the work of two men—on the salary of half a man or less. He had been working slavingly at Banfield for a year on less than a living wage, learning practically nothing that would fit him for anything but bank life. He had even missed summer furlough, because of the manager's illness. The bank thanked him by letter for the sacrifice, and promised him "an extra two weeks later on."

What had kept Nelson interested for a solid year in the village of Banfield? Chiefly work; after that a lake and girls. How many years of faithful service do branch banks owe to the attractiveness and amiability of town girls!

His work alone provided Evan with all the excitement he needed, and when reactions came there was always a young lady to be paddled out on the water. Bank work is entertaining; few clerks do not enjoy it, once they have mastered the routine. Time flies when a fellow is on the cash in a busy office; it vanishes when he is also in charge of the office as acting-accountant. Figuring out entries and chasing balances is a fascinating occupation, like vaudeville, and just as precarious a specialty.

A conscientious bankclerk cannot look on a heap of accumulated work with indifference; when he is also ambitious he rolls up his sleeves and forgets everything in the debris of vouchers and figures. Like a mole he works away, his eyes blinded (to keep out the muck); unlike the mole he never succeeds in building a nest for himself. The heap diminishes gradually before him and he thinks he sees rock-bottom, when suddenly an avalanche comes down, obliterating marks of previous effort and storing up labor for days, weeks, or months to come.

Surely, there are few occupations more all-possessing than banking. A boy is under a heavy responsibility; the thought makes him proud; pride spurs him to his best; he forgets—really forgets—to exercise. Often he is so worn out he cannot take exercise without physical suffering. Moreover, the clerical strain makes him sleepy, and, as social affairs and night work prevent early retiring, he must get his sleep in the morning; thus out-door recreation is neglected. Whether or not it should be, it is. Excessive inside work takes away the inclination to exercise, and only those who know a large number of bankclerks understand how serious are the results of this diseased lethargy.

As he sat in the station waiting for his train to Toronto, Evan tried to recall one night in the year past when he had had nothing to do. He could not remember one. When he had not been working there had always been a village function of some sort to take up his time and consume his vitality.

His head ached now, for he had labored harder than ever during the past week, to clear the way for Christmas. There would be pleasure in seeing his folk, but none in the trip—although he was fond of travel. He dreaded now the long train-ride. He yawned and felt miserable.

In the coach he was unable to sleep, and too tired to read. He had no disposition to talk; the only pastime left was to think. He wondered if Frankie still cared for him; if his parents would be impressed with his knowledge of banking, and if the bankboys of Hometon would acknowledge him a pal. Selfish as it may seem, his thoughts of Frankie were indefinite, and confused with memories of Julia and Lily.

The motion of the train gradually rocked him to sleep in his seat. He dreamt he was being moved to another branch. When he awoke the conductor was shouting "Toronto."

Evan changed cars at Union Station. This was the second time he had been through the city, but he had seen nothing of its life.

The train out Hometon way was crammed with excursionists. The weary bankclerk was obliged to stand for over fifty miles. He was more than half sick when he reached Hometon. The train was two hours late.

Mrs. Nelson and Lou were at the station to meet Our Banker. Both of them kissed him.

His mother was so happy to see him the tears gleamed in her eyes. Lou sized him up in her old way.

"Say, you look like a city chap, Evan!"

He smiled half-heartedly.

"Gee, I feel rotten," he said; "my head is splitting and I'm sick at my stomach."

"You look thin, dear," said Mrs. Nelson, examining him in detail.

"Oh, I'll be all right after a snooze," he replied, lightly, seeing that his mother felt considerable anxiety.

The 'bus was full; the Nelsons walked from the depot to their home. Evan answered the questions asked him on the way, endeavoring to appear cheerful, but took little interest in the old town. He drank a cup of his mother's tea, when they arrived home, then begged off to bed. Lou spread wet cloths on his forehead until he was asleep, and afterwards went downstairs to load his stocking.

"Mother, dear," she said, cracking a nut, "Evan looks fierce. I believe he is either worked or worried to death."

Mrs. Nelson sighed.

"This is a funny world," she observed petulantly; "it looks good from the outside, but when you come to find out it is a disappointment."

"Oh, mamma," laughed the daughter, "you sound melancholy. It isn't as bad as all that, you know. His headache will be gone in the morning. Christmas trains would put anyone out of commission."

"He looked fagged though, Louie."

"Most bankers do," observed Lou, casually.

Mrs. Nelson looked quizzically at the girl.

"Maybe I should never have encouraged him to enter a bank," she said, doubtfully.

The father came in, covered with snow.

"Hello, Santa," cried Lou.

"Did he come?" asked Nelson, returning his daughter's smile, but looking somewhat anxiously about.

"Yes," said Mrs. Nelson, "but he was tired and went to bed. Don't wake him up till morning."

"He isn't sick, is he?" asked the father.

"No, just a headache," said Lou.

By and by she went off to bed, upon which Nelson proceeded to unwrap several parcels he carried, and fill her stocking.

"It doesn't seem long," he said pensively, "since these two stockings weren't big enough to hold anything worth while."

"No, indeed, George. I often wish they were both children again."

How many times a day is that impossible wish voiced by the mothers of every nation!

Christmas morning found Lou awake early. She repeated the pranks of childhood, stealing downstairs in the dark to find her stocking. Evan slept on. His sister peeked into his room at daylight, hoping to find him conscious; but he breathed so satisfactorily she overcame the temptation to frighten him awake. Mrs. Nelson would not allow anyone to disturb him until breakfast was set, then she went herself to his room.

In his dreams he heard his mother calling him, and it seemed to be away back in irresponsible days.

"Yes," he answered unconsciously, "I'm up, mother!"

Mrs. Nelson enjoyed his dozing prevarication. It made her forget that he was no longer a sleep-loving schoolboy. She went quietly to his bedside and laid a hand on his forehead. His eyes opened.

"How are you this morning?" she asked.

"All right mother, thanks. Is it late?"

She told him breakfast was ready, and he jumped out of bed, whistling with surprise.

"I guess I'd better go," she laughed, when he seemed to forget the presence of a lady.

"Oh, that's all right," he said, cheerily. He was feeling good after a night's sleep in the bed of his boyhood.

Mr. Nelson was waiting anxiously in the kitchen—they always breakfasted there in winter—for Evan and breakfast. The former soon arrived, and the latter was then ready.

"Bon jour," said the father, without nasal and with a hard "j."

"Good morning, George," laughed Evan, using a phrase then popular in the "funny" papers.

Our Banker led the way to table.

"I'm as hungry as a cougar," he said.

Lou regarded him in consternation. "Why, Evan," she cried, "haven't you forgotten something?"

He looked at her blankly. "What?"

"I got mine before daylight," holding up her stocking.

"Oh," he grinned; "I've been away so long I forgot there ever was such a thing as Christmas."

"By the way," asked his father, "how did you spend your last?"

"Working," said Evan.

The mother sighed softly.

"You look as though that's all you ever did," continued Mr. Nelson.

"Oh, no," said Evan, promptly, "I've had some good times since that Sunday, a year and a half ago, that I spent here. I have had it sort of tough lately and maybe I'm a little run down, but things will ease off after awhile."

It is characteristic of the bankman that he lives on the hope that work will fall off. Someone is always telling him, as he is always telling himself, that things will slacken; but, somehow or other, the strings stay taut.

Evan was quite a different lad now from the schoolboy who first came home with bank idioms to tickle his mother with and dumfound his sister. As he sat at the Christmas breakfast table his countenance was subdued, almost worried. The long balance-night orgies were registered there; the fixed expression that comes from searching out differences and the strain that accompanies each day's balancing of the cash. Something more as well—debts!

All bankclerks contract debts. The careless ones do so thoughtlessly, the careful ones reluctantly—both necessarily. Evan owed about sixty dollars, tailor and other bills. A bankclerk must make a good impression on people; he must have a good appearance—head office makes that its business. The clerk's salary—that is nobody's business, not even his own. Evan did not mention the fact that he was in debt, when his father asked, good-humoredly,

"Making much money?"

"I'm living," smiled the son.

Lou thoughtlessly said something ill-advised.

"Got a new girl, brother?"

Mrs. Nelson blushed, but her Banker did not. He laughed.

"That's one thing we learn to forget," he said, brazenly.

The caresses of "sweethearts in every town" had had their effect. His sister gave him a rebuking look. He saw a question in her eyes and the shape of it resembled Frankie Arling's contour.

Some women prefer suspense to disappointment. Mrs. Arling evidently did not, for she asked, palpitatingly:

"When are you going back?"

Evan was embarrassed. He evaded the question.

"It's too early to speak of that, mother," he fenced. "Our manager is delicate and apt to break down at any time. I promised to be back—soon. I am the whole thing up at Banfield."

"Are you teller yet?" asked Lou.

"Sure," said Evan, "and then some. I'm pro-manager."

"Let's see," said his father, dropping a hot egg, "what are they paying you now?"

"Three fifty," replied Evan humbly.

It was not the diminutiveness of the figure that sounded so mean to him, but its association with the word "pro-manager." He was not ashamed of a low salary, but of a humble position. If he could convince his father that the position he held was responsible and man-worthy, he would not mind about the salary. Bankclerks are constantly fed with promotion when it is money they need, but they are so trained that elevation practically stands for increase, to them.

"I often run the office for days at a time when the manager is in bed," said Evan.

"And the cash—it's in your charge entirely, isn't it?"

"Yes," said the son, proudly.

Mr. Nelson took a deep draught of strong tea. Mrs. Nelson sat silent. Lou passed her brother a piece of fresh toast she had made for herself.

She got her brother alone after breakfast, ostensibly to show him her presents.

"Evan," she said, eyeing him as she used to years before when he had done something to puzzle her, "you don't seem very anxious about somebody."

He did not parry with a question.

"What's the use, Lou?" he said.

She thought a moment: "I guess there is no use of getting serious on seven dollars a week."

Her reasonableness comforted him and he told her so. They became as intimate as when they were children.

"You don't suppose Frank still—well, thinks she is in love with yours truly, do you, Lou?" he asked.

"Well—she doesn't act like it," replied Lou, rather indignantly. "You won't be surprised if I tell you something?"

He said he wouldn't.

".....Frankie is going with another fellow!"

Evan drew a silver case of cigarettes from his pocket, took out a "smoke" and replaced the case. Lou regarded him in amazement.

"Why, Evan!" she exclaimed.

He laughed. His mother smelt the smoke.

"My boy, I'm ashamed of you," she said, coming into the parlor.

He smiled around the cigarette, and said inarticulately:

"I don't smoke many."

"Why don't you use a pipe?" came a deep voice from the kitchen.

"I have a pipe," said Evan.

"Here, take a cigar," returned the father immediately, coming in to rarefy the atmosphere.

Promptly Evan twirled his cigarette into the grate and accepted a cigar with an adult air. Lou began laughing, but soon checked herself and endeavored to give the youthful debauchee a look of scorn. Unable to carry it out, she gazed out of the window.

"Oh, brother," she said, "come here and see."

He walked to the window. Strolling down the opposite side of the street, apparently on their way to church, were two young people—a boy and a girl. A glance told Evan who the girl was, but he did more than glance at the fellow. The two were coming nearer.

"For Heaven's sake!" said Evan, "I know that guy. Let's call them in."

Opening the front door he shouted:

"Hey, come on up and see us!"

Frankie hesitated, but her brave escort insisted and she walked shamefacedly toward Nelson's home. Evan allowed himself a few moments of rash merriment which greatly surprised his mother and sister. His strange actions were justified—if the women had only known! The chap who stepped in with Frankie was Porter Perry.

Acting on manners he had learned somewhere, the Bonehead grabbed Evan's hand before the latter had a chance to greet Frankie.

"Where on earth did you come from?" asked Evan.

"Oh, I left your bank," said Porter, importantly, "because they paid such bad salaries. Then the U—— moved me here."

Frankie distracted Evan's attention.

"How are you, Frank?" he said, feeling mean as he took her little hand and saw her blushing face.

"Just the same old way," she replied bravely; "you have changed an awful lot though——"

She did not mean anything sentimental, but that kind of an interpretation presented itself to her a moment after she had spoken and she hurriedly added: "You are thin and paler than you used to be." Her eyes alighted on the cigar smoking between his fingers. "Maybe that's the reason," she said, laughingly.

Lou drew her chum off to exhibit those trinkets again. Mr. and Mrs. Nelson were chatting in the kitchen, where the turkey sizzled.

"What post are you on, Evan?" asked Perry.

"Teller and accountant," was the casual reply.

"Gee," exclaimed the Bonehead disconsolately. He went in search of consolation.

"What do they give you?"

"Three fifty," was the still more humble reply.

Porter's face lighted up.

"I draw four fifty," he said, grandly.

"What post?" asked Evan, anxiously.

"Ledger."

This was the first time Evan had had one of the bank's chief shortcomings brought home to him—it makes little difference what a clerk's intelligence or what his position and responsibility, he will be paid according to the time he has served. He is not rewarded according to his works, but paid for length of service. The business offers no incentive to excel. Why work hard and honestly if you are going to get the dead-level wage each year anyway? Good clerks suffer because of the negligence of indifferent ones; but the former bring up the average of work—and that is all the bank cares. The staff of a bank is something to be worked en masse; the individual is an insignificant part of the works.

Perry seemed fated to be a humiliation to Evan. Bank luck had thrown the Bonehead into the spot where Evan longed to be, and had given him enough salary to live on, humbly. But more ironical still was the apparent attachment between Evan's old girl and Perry.

"If she could only have seen him balancing that savings in Mt. Alban," thought Evan, smiling. Then puffing out a mouthful of smoke, he murmured: "Bah! what do I care!"

From that moment he was jolly, to the point of humor. It was the mood of mixed feelings, prominent among which is jealousy, where one waxes jocose in spite of himself. Evan even rallied Frankie on certain personal matters. She did not take it amiss; it rather relieved the situation for her.

"Where's Bill, do you know, Evan?" asked Porter.

"No; his signature at Mt. Alban has been cancelled, but I don't know what they did with him."

"Either resigned or gone to a city," Perry supposed.

"I think we had better go, Mr. Perry," said Frankie, turning away from Lou's Christmas gifts.

"Why, what's your hurry—won't you stay for dinner?" asked Mrs. Nelson.

"Oh, no," said Frankie, "thank you. Mother has invited Mr. Perry up to our place. He wasn't able to go home."

"How was that?" asked Nelson, poking his nose in the room.

"Work," said Perry, professionally.

"Ledger!" murmured Evan, smiling inwardly. Notwithstanding, he felt more disgusted than amused—he scarcely knew at what.

"We'll see you again before we go, I hope," he said, addressing Frankie and her escort as one.

"When do you go?" she whispered to him aside, while the Bonehead was laughing at a joke he perpetrated on Lou. Frankie was beginning to weaken. Evan felt it, and it made him harden his heart. Such is man's disposition.

"Soon," he said, knowing it hurt.

She gazed into his unsmiling eyes a moment, then turned to Lou and Perry without speaking.

When she was gone, and Perry, Mrs. Nelson looked disconcertingly at her son. He mentally searched for something to hide his uneasiness and divert their minds from Frankie——

"Did you hear me say I must go soon, mother?"

"Yes, how soon, Evan?"

"To-night!"

Mrs. Nelson's dinner was luxurious, but to the whole family it tasted flat. Our Banker must leave early Christmas night. His Banfield friends had wished him "A Merry Christmas."

And he left without saying good-bye to Someone.

8

A Sport Gone to Seed

The manager at Banfield sighed in relief when Evan entered the office. An afternoon rush was on.

"Can you take this over, Nelson?" he asked, edging away from a cackling woman-customer.

Without a word the teller threw his overcoat on a stool and entered the cage with his hat on. Before the wicket farm-folk stampeded, struggling to get their noses against the iron railing and to blow their breath on the weary-looking teller. A heap of germ-laden money lay temptingly within reach of the rustics, only separated from those grimy, grasping fingernails by plate glass.

A shudder passed over Evan as he took his stand in front of the crowd. He felt something of what a martyr must feel who faces trial at the hands of a mob. It was market-day. The Banfield bank had made a practice of cashing the tickets of hucksters who came from Toronto and bought up the people's produce on a margin. These tickets had to be figured up by the teller, cashed and afterwards balanced. Many of the customers made small deposits, after blocking the way to leaf over their money with badly soiled fingers (surely they needn't have been quite so dirty!); bought money-orders, opened new accounts "in trust" for relatives, asked questions—did everything thinkable to harass the teller.

Besides the produce tickets there was the ordinary banking business of the day. Occasionally a regular customer came in to cash a cheque, and finding himself unable to get near the wicket went out in considerable of a rage, trying to slam the automatically-closing door. Evan was supposed to keep his eye open for these "regulars," but to-day his head swam and he was obliged to concentrate on the tickets to avoid mistakes. An error on his part might easily involve him in personal loss; but if he "made" anything on the cash, that went to Cash Over Account.

A loud voice was heard in the manager's office.

"I won't stand for it," said the voice. "If you can't wait on me ahead of these old women you can do without my business."

"Give me your cheque, Mr. Moore, I'll have it cashed for you," said Mr. Jones, conciliatingly.

"No, sir, if I can't——"

The manager, more than half ill, lost his temper.

"Go then and be ——!" he shouted, and left his office to the burly intruder.

Moore shouted after the manager, making sure every gossip in the office would hear:

"I'll report you! I'll report you—you're no kind of a manager, and I'll have you kicked out of here."

Storming, the big farmer strode from the bank. Henty, the husky junior, was red in the face. Evan looked at him and smiled.

"What's the matter, A. P.?"

"I was just spoiling for the fray," said Henty, comically; "another minute and I'd have thrown that yap out."

After office hours Evan discovered that the cash had not been balanced for Saturday the 24th. He had, therefore, two days' balances on his hands—hands that were weary already. It is always hard work to balance after Christmas; but when your head aches, the office air is bad, there has been an upheaval with a customer, and you have two balances to find—well, it is no fun. Added to his other troubles, there were the returns for the 23rd; they had not yet been written. Head office would be sending a memo.

Even a winter's day, in a Canadian bank, is not all gloomy, however. Nelson's boarding mistress soothed him at suppertime with a cup of her good tea. Mrs. Terry was a kind soul and a good housekeeper. She was the oasis in Banfield's dusty desert. Notwithstanding, no cup of tea on the most welcome of oases could have prepared Evan for the intelligence awaiting him at the office when he got back to work in the evening. The manager sent for him.

"Nelson," he said, "I'm going to resign. My health won't stand this business. I'm going on a farm."

The young bankclerk was dumfounded. To think of a man giving up a $1,100 position for a farm! Evan was not old enough to appreciate the value of health. He thought Jones must have had something organically wrong with him before ever entering a bank, and that now he acted on the promptings of a sour stomach.

"I'm sorry, Mr. Jones," he said quietly; "I've had great experience under you."

"Yes," returned the manager, "you're a wonder for your age, Nelson. Do you know how much you are worth to the bank?—just about what I'm getting."

Evan felt his head swim. He forgave Jones the unbalanced "blotter," and had a sudden notion that he could dig up, at that moment, any difference that ever happened.

"I'm tired," said Jones, "of being worried by unreasonable asses on the one hand and head office on the other. I'm sick of being a servant."

"How long have you been in the bank?" asked Evan, pensively.

"Twenty years, and my salary is $1,100 with free rent. I was pushed into the business when about sixteen. At that time banking was a profession that all young fellows envied. I was the proudest man alive when they accepted me. And my folk, they didn't do a thing but plume themselves on it."

The teller was silent a while.

"Things change fast in the bank, don't they?" he observed, reflectively, thinking of himself and his career.

"You bet they do," replied Jones. "Banking isn't the same business it used to be at all. Salaries haven't kept up with the times. A bunch of junior men are now employed to fill posts that experienced clerks used to occupy. The bank makes a policy of recruiting—even going to Europe, where clerks think five dollars is equal to a pound sterling—to keep down expenses. A boy like yourself can, by heavy plodding, do the work of a ten-year clerk. He may not do it so accurately, but he gets it done at last, and that is what the bank wants. He does it, too, on a wage that should frighten future battalions, no matter how brave and countrified, away from the business."

Evan felt, for the moment, that Sam Robb was speaking. He thought of the day he had accused Robb of cherishing a grudge against the business, of being "sore on his job." But here was meek little Jones repeating the sentiments of the Mt. Alban bachelor manager. It was enough to make one think. Evan did think, and he began to open his mind to a wider criticism of the business. He began to wonder if he had been cut out for a bankclerk. Why had Robb repeatedly made anti-banking suggestions to him? Had he seen incapacity for clerical work in the Mt. Alban swipe? Did Jones discern a similar inaptitude for bank service and hint things for the teller's benefit? Was there a chance that he (Evan) possessed faculties that must die in the business of his mother's choice, and that these qualifications were plainly visible to men older in life and the banking business than himself? At times Evan felt underfitted for the bank, and at other times overfitted. His spirits varied accordingly. Most of the time, however, his mental attitude "balanced," and inactivity of thought was the result. He had reached inertia of mind before his conversation that night with Jones was finished.

"Sometimes," he confessed, "I wonder where I am at."

"That describes the average bankboy," replied Jones, promptly. "He drifts along for years in just that frame of mind. When he rouses himself to thought a flood of work comes along and drowns him. Then he sleeps for another month or two. I don't believe there is a class of boys on earth who do less thinking and planning for their future than Canadian bankclerks."

"That's funny," said Evan to himself, "I had a hunch when I joined the bank that that was the case. Guess I've grown used to their ways."

Automatically his mind reverted to the work out there in the office waiting for him.

"Here I am, wasting time," he said, jokingly, "while two days' balances and a mess of other work are waiting for me. Is there anything else you want to speak about, Mr. Jones?"

The manager looked at him with eyes so unprofessional they might never have focused on anything so mean as a past-due bill, or a head office bull.

"Nelson," he said frankly, "you are the right sort of stuff to succeed. You will succeed in the bank: but take my advice and get out of it. If you stick you will some day be a city manager—but get out. How long have you been in the service?"

"Almost two years."

"Well, if you had labored in some other business two years, with the intelligence and ballast you have shown around here, you would now have had a desk somewhere and a phone at your elbow."

The teller smiled embarrassedly, and rising, asked:

"When will your resignation go?"

"Right away."

While the manager and teller were discussing the philosophy of banking, the ledger-keeper and junior were worrying a battered-looking savings. Henty was leaning on his elbows and yawning. His eyes followed endless columns of figures, while the ledger-keeper called from the ledger. Filter purposely called an amount wrong, and kept going. When he was five accounts past the "baited" balance Henty shouted:

"Hold on, call No. 981 again!"

"Well, I must hand it to you, Ape," said the ledger-keeper sarcastically. "You certainly have a remarkable pair of eyes. You travel several miles behind, like an echo or something, but you always get there. Why don't you save your memory all that extra work?"

The good-natured junior laughed.

"Don't be cross, Gordon," he teased. "To tell the truth I was thinking of Hilda Munn."

Filter looked exasperated.

"How in —— do you ever expect me to find that difference if you travel blindfolded? I'll bet a dollar we've passed over it."

Nelson came in the office.

"How much are you out?" he asked.

"Ten cents," said Filter; "this book—"

"Wait," interrupted Evan, "do you remember that deposit slip we changed after the calling about two weeks ago? Was it fixed in the ledger?"

Filter's eyes brightened. He looked up the account and found his difference. Henty regarded the teller with unsophisticated admiration, then, on the impulse, grabbed him by the muscles and commenced backing him around the office.

"Gee, you're a horse!" said Evan, wrenching himself free; "where did you get all that gristle?"

"In the back pasture," interpolated Filter, in jovial spirits now that he was balanced.

"Wrong there," said Henty. "I put on this stock of beef in the rear end of a mow one hot summer when the sow-thistles were bad."

While the boys were in good tune Nelson broke to them the news of Jones' resignation.

"The deuce!" exclaimed Filter, who rarely went higher.

"We don't need a manager," observed the junior, grinning, "when we've got a man who can remember deposit slips for two weeks."

Evan said nothing, but naturally he liked Henty for the flattering speech, the more so since Henty usually meant more than half of what he said. Praise is apt to be dangerous to one who draws Evan's salary; he felt himself growing more and more dissatisfied. Evan was awakening to a realization of his superiority as a bankclerk. He was a successful clerk, and he knew it; but he also knew, by now, that his success was due to labor rather than to special aptitude for that kind of work. He could not banish Jones' words from his mind; if he had expended the same amount of energy on some other business he would probably have achieved far greater efficiency than would ever be possible in banking. He doubted more and more that climbing steps into the bank was equal to shinning it up a beanstalk.

For a few days after Jones' conversation with him he was silent and thoughtful at his work. Instead of making poetic memos, like Service, in his cage, he made note of the work he waded through, and tried to picture himself in a private office. That was going one further than Jones' imaginary desk with the telephone at one's elbow, but the imagination is fertile territory.

It is difficult to say where Evan's speculations would have landed him—it is difficult to say, although the probability is he would have arrived where dissatisfied bank-boys usually do, Nowhere—had not W. W. Penton, the new manager, put in a sudden appearance.

It took Penton quite a while to get in the bank door, as he had with him a wife and two poodle-dogs, the latter property especially requiring much attention and considerable coaching before they would condescend to enter the office. Possibly their pampered puppy noses sniffed some of the trouble that was to come. Dogs are prophetic when there is something undesirable to be foretold.

Mr. Jones had gone out on the morning train and would not be back for a day or two. Consequently Evan, next in charge of Banfield branch, was obliged to receive the new dictator: such it was Penton's disposition to be.

He strutted through the office to the cage, where Evan was busy with a customer, and spoke half civilly:

"Are you the accountant here?"

The teller turned around, with a bunch of counted bills in his hand.

"Yes, sir," he said, "just a minute and I'll be out."

"Come out now," said Penton.

Evan finished waiting on the customer, who had been standing in front of the wicket long enough, and then obeyed the manager. The two looked at each other challengingly. Penton's expression was almost a glare. The teller stood his ground. He conceived a ready dislike for the tall figure before him. At length Penton extended his hand. It was bony and cold. Evan discarded it as quickly as possible and called over the rest of the staff for introduction.

Filter shook hands methodically, scarcely raising his eyes to meet the bulging, colorless eyes of Penton. Henty blushed, but his gaze was unwavering. The dogs barked uproariously, scampering to and fro like rats. Mrs. Penton, from the manager's office, tried to quiet them, but they seemed bent on carrying out the bluff they had started, imitating in that respect their male master.

"I've got an infernal toothache," said Penton, speaking to the junior, "would you run across to the hotel and get me some brandy? If that doesn't stop it I'll have to see a doctor."

His tone was more polite now. Henty left his work and went for the liquor. While he was away the manager and his wife took a hasty glance at their living quarters. She remained there with the terriers, but Penton soon came back for his remedy. When Evan went in he found three-fourths of the liquor gone, but the tooth was still aching. Mr. Penton was evidently in agony; he swore.

"Ask Mrs. Penton to come with me to a doctor's, will you?" he said.

Nelson rapped on a door at the end of the hall leading from the office into Penton's apartments. The dogs set up another hullabaloo. From his office the pained manager cursed them heartily. Henty was ready to bubble over with merriment, but the teller motioned him sober.

Mrs. Penton hesitated as she entered her husband's office. She could not have seen the flask, for it was not now in sight.

"Come with me to the doctor's, won't you?" he asked, with the suspicion of a whimper in his tone.

She looked behind her before answering. Evan was hovering near, to run errands or show them the way to a physician's.

"All right, Pen." She spoke timidly. Evan was sorry for her.

Penton was uneasy; he hesitated when Evan said: "If you don't mind, I'll be glad to go with you."

Mrs. Penton spoke out:

"It's awfully good of you, Mr. Nelson. Mr. Penton may have to take gas."

He did. Nor did ever a youngster take senna less gracefully. The gas alone probably would not have made a madman of him, but mixed with the liquor it did. In the earlier stages of unconsciousness Penton jumped from the table and threatened to kill the doctor. The country physician only laughed at the wild and, to Evan, appalling curses and threats of the temporary lunatic. It mattered not to that rustic doctor whether his patient carried a stiff neck or a limber one—he would do his work just the same. He happened to be a dentist, which was fortunate, for he needed dental knowledge to extract a great tooth from the patient. The further skill of a veterinary surgeon would scarcely have been superfluous, Evan thought, amid so much horse-play.

Mrs. Penton seemed very much upset, but she shed no tears. The teller wondered how she could look on at all. It was the first case of gas he had seen, and it not only awed him but filled him with repugnance. Painfully was this the case when Penton madly expectorated over an incredible distance upon the poor doctor's curtains.

Nelson had always had profound respect for whatever manager he worked under. He looked upon bank officials as something more than men. The reverence of his mother for institutions and things traditional held to him. But as he gazed on the squawking Penton, lying stretched out on a board while the village dentist-doctor dragged at a tooth, he had a sudden conception of man's equality and his likeness to the beast. Even bank-managers were poor, puling cowards in the face of pain, or under the influence of a little gas.

Having slept out his unnatural sleep Penton jumped dazedly from his board and rushed to the door. Before anyone could stop him (the doctor did not seem anxious to do so) he had reached the street. Evan ran after him, and Mrs. Penton after Evan. The long form of the new manager wobbled across the street toward the bank. Evan came up with it and steadied it. Mrs. Penton's face was burning red when they arrived under cover.

"I'm so sorry this has happened, Mr. Nelson," she said, "for your sake."

"Oh, that's all right, Mrs. Penton," he replied; "I always sympathize with anyone who is suffering."

She looked him her thanks.

"Mr. Nelson," she whispered, "did Pen have anything to drink before going to the doctor's?"

Evan hesitated before answering.

"A flask of brandy."

"That's what is the matter with him, then," she said, looking sadly toward the groaning unfortunate on the couch.

Penton was in a peculiar shade of mind. He made weird remarks at times, spoke sanely occasionally, and groaned continually. He kept his hand to his cheek and swore at the tooth and the doctor alternately. Mrs. Penton did not allow his oaths to embarrass her.

"I hope you won't mind," she apologized; "I won't ask you to remain more than a few minutes."

"I'm ready to stay as long as you wish, Mrs. Penton," he said.

"Thank you very much. It is so good of you. It's awfully nice to have a teller like you, Mr. Nelson. Mr. Penton was afraid—we were afraid we mightn't—you know, like the staff. I am so glad to find you so kind; I'm sure you will get along splendidly with Pen."

Again Evan was flattered. Here was a manager hoping he would not have to quarrel with his teller! That was, virtually, Mrs. Penton's admission.

Evan did not need this additional evidence of Penton's weakness. The toothache episode had satisfied him. He heard for days the manager's squawking, and saw before him the manager's cravenness.

Jones had come and gone: the new manager had taken over the bills and the cash. Penton's tooth was better, but he was in a bullying humor. One night he called the teller before him for review.

"Now, Mr. Nelson," he said, assuming an imperious tone, the absurdity of which amused the steady-eyed listener, "as you know, I am appointed manager here. This is my first branch, and I want to make it a success. Needless to say, I need your help, since you are my teller. I want you to see that the junior men perform their duties properly."

The flattery intended to be conveyed in "junior men" did not appeal to Evan. He sat silent, observing, never taking his eyes from the manager's.

"I want my branch to pay, and I want my town to appreciate the fact that a trained banker is running things here now. I am a friend of Mr. Jones, but I tell you he did things in an unprofessional way. I want things done according to the standard rules of banking. I am a disciplinarian, and the sooner my staff realizes that the better it will be for them."

The teller reddened with anger. Penton probably thought it was timidity. But as Nelson did not speak the other was not enlightened.

"Now," continued Penton, "I want you to be my mouthpiece to the junior men. Make them understand I am here to do things my own way. No more private banking methods—"

"Excuse me, Mr. Penton," interrupted Nelson, vibrantly, in spite of a desire to ignore with silence, "Mr. Jones had twenty years' banking experience."

Penton altered his tone.

"Don't misunderstand me, Mr. Nelson," he said, smiling a smile of defiance and diplomacy, "I am not knocking Mr. Jones. But you will soon see the results of my more professional methods. I got my training in the oldest and most aristocratic banking house in the country."

The lecture eventually came to an end. It was on a par with anything Penton was liable to say or do. Exhausted after the effort, he withdrew to his apartments behind the bank. Evan entered his box and slammed the door. Two faces flattened themselves against the sides of the cage.

"Boys," said the teller coolly, but in a tone they were not used to from him, "there's going to be —— to pay around here."

"What's wrong?" asked Filter.

"Nothing," said Evan, "but this new manager is going to get in wrong. I for one won't stand for his bluffing."

The teller went on to deliver the message given him. He scarcely fulfilled Penton's wishes in the delivery, however.

"I'm with you, Nelson," said Henty, very red in the face and ludicrously serious.

"You bet," said Filter, forgetting his ledger for the moment.

After locking up, that afternoon, Nelson went for a walk around the pond. He was sick at heart. He wondered what would happen under Penton's regime, he was certain something disastrous would. After supper he went to the post office, hoping to hear from home. He wanted to forget the bank and its worries for a while. Two letters were in the mail for him, one from Julia and the other from Lily. He dropped into the bank to read them and sat in the manager's office. A rap came to the office door.

"Come in," he cried. Mrs. Penton entered, wretched-looking.

"Oh, Mr. Nelson," she cried, softly, "I need your help."

He arose from his chair and stood gazing at her.

"He's drinking again," she said; and the tears flowed when Evan's interest was apparent.

"Where is he?"

"At the hotel," she sobbed.

Evan went out and hurried to the town bar. There he was, the tall manager, laughing insanely at the vile talk of Banfield's worst characters; drinking to the health of debauchees who pictured Heaven as an eternal beer-garden surrounded by living fountains and falls of whiskey.

9

The Seed Multiplies

Henty was accessible by telephone. He answered Evan's excited summons. Between them the boys got Penton home and in bed. It was no simple task, either. The manager was obstreperous, but at the same time he showed the white feather. Drink could not have made him so ridiculous: there must have been something ridiculous in his nature.

"Why don't you let me alone?" he whined.

"Because," said Evan, "you're disgracing the bank. If you don't come home I'll report you to head office."

They were on the street. Penton shuddered and went with them more willingly when the threat had penetrated his clogged brain.

"You won't report me, will you? You won't report me?" he repeated in a fawning manner, fearful and pitiful.

"Not if you cut this out," said the teller.

"I'll c-cut it out, old c-cock," laughed Penton raspingly, swaying to the poison in his blood, "me f-for the water wagon after this."

He raved about himself until they had him in bed, then he raved about everything.

"Do you want me to stay a while, Mrs. Penton?" asked the teller.

"No thank you, Mr. Nelson," she replied, wearily; "he will be all right now. Oh, I'm so afraid this will be talked of all over town. Do you think so?"

"Nobody saw him," said Nelson consolingly, "but a few drunks, and anything they say won't matter."

"Oh, I hope so," she said; "it would be dreadful if the town turned against us. This is our first branch, you know, and a scandal like this might ruin us."

"Don't worry, Mrs. Penton; people are kind in this town, if they *are* behind the times. They always forgive the first offence, and sometimes more. During the two weeks Mr. Penton has been here he has made lots of friends."

Mrs. Penton began to be comforted, for what the teller said was true. Penton had a way with him among people; it was a hypocritical way, of course, but the affectation of it was not clear to the kind, simple people of Banfield. His ignoble flattery passed for amiability and good-will.

"It won't occur again," said Mrs. Penton, thoughtfully; "this will be a lesson to him. I wish you would frighten him, Mr. Nelson."

Henty had to smile. The manager's wife also smiled then. It was impossible to look worried or cross in the face of what Filter called "the ape's grin." Evan, however, was the first to sober. He was thinking of the day he had entered the bank, and how he had thrilled at sight of a living manager, an appointee of head office. Now he was asked to frighten one of these potentates into subjection.

"I'll make him believe the people of the town are sore," said the teller, pensively.

As they walked to their boarding-houses up the frosty street, the two boys discussed matters.

"I feel kind of sorry for him," said Henty; "he must be a regular booze-fighter."

"Yes. I wonder did head office know it when they sent him up here?"

Henty had no idea. Being simply a junior he did not venture an opinion concerning head office. He did express himself about the unofficial Penton, however.

"I don't like him, Nelson."

"No," said Evan, "he is a mistake. I see trouble ahead for us. I can't understand why the bank sent him up here. He has evidently been used to a fast life, and there's no excitement here for him except booze."

Henty had reached his lodging. With a "good-night" and a sigh he entered the cold storage where he put in the nights.

Evan, drawing one hundred and fifty dollars a year more than the junior, went further up the hill and landed in a warmer room. He lighted a lamp and prepared to thoroughly peruse a couple of letters. They were more than a couple, they were a pair. Julia reminded him of the "perfectly lovely" times they had spent together, and Lily spoke of the "grand evenings" they had walked or driven in. The Mt. Alban girl intimated that she was without "such a friend" now, and the Creek Bend girl spoke about the scarcity of "the right kind of fellows." Both letters were a challenge for Evan to act consistently with smile or kiss bestowed in the past, and a reminder that girls do not forget so readily as bankclerks might wish.

Folding the two little love-notes together, he held them above the lamp chimney and watched them burn. He did not wear the expression of a Nero, but of an Abram offering up that which was part of himself. He was not burning sheets of paper, but leaves from his life: sheets that he declared must become ashes to him—and to them.

"Yes," he thought, "it is better to make them angry than to string them along and break their hearts at last."

He continued to reason with himself:

"In the first place, I can't tell which of them I like best; therefore I don't love either of them. In the second place, it will be years before I shall draw enough money to marry on."

There was a third place, but Evan wanted to avoid it, for in that "place" sat Frankie Arling. The Bonehead also sat there, with his arms around Frankie.

Unable to banish this picture from his imagination, Evan finally delivered himself up to thoughts of Frankie: only in that way could he depose the redoubtable Porter.

The more Evan compared Frankie with Julia Watersea and Lily Allen, and with others whom he had met, the surer he felt, of her superiority. He regretted having hurt her at his home on Christmas Day, and knew he had done it because he cared for her. Thoughts of Perry gave him a sick feeling in his vitals, but he could not convince himself that Frankie cared anything about "the porter." What had become of all the other Hometon bankclerks she had temporarily tantalized?

In his quiet room the Banfield teller mused. After two years of banking he felt himself further from Frankie Arling than he had felt the day he went away. He was within a few days of nineteen now; his views on everything had undergone a change. Yet, he knew that he was more desirous than ever of marrying Frankie. There are moments when we see our hearts before us under an X-ray more wonderful than that used in medicine. Evan was given a glimpse of his inmost self, and what he saw was startling to him. He knew he loved Frankie Arling, and that he would be happy if he married her, even at nineteen! Age probably has less to do with the proper kind of marriage than is often supposed. There are boys of seventeen who would make good husbands, whereas some men are never fit. Evan knew he could have settled down at nineteen and made a success of marriage—if he could only have afforded it.

Knowing, though, the futility of dreaming against such odds as seven dollars a week and the bank system of increases, he forced his mind off matrimony and thought of Frankie only as an unattainable object he loved. In the midst of his dreaming loomed up again visions of other girls, chiefly Julia and Lily. He felt guilty for having shown them attention. He experienced remorse, for it was possible he had (the phrase passed facetiously through his brain) "built better than he knew." The letters just burnt were not at all comforting in this connection.

Nelson had met bankboys who delighted in what they called "stringing skirts." Those fellows were despicable to him; they were scarcely worth despising. And their numbers were altogether too large. He had met others—very many—who were not in the despicable class, but who also were guilty of unfaithfulness. Why, he asked himself, were conditions in the bank conducive to such a state of affairs?

It was, experience answered, because a fellow's mind was unoccupied after hours, and for many other reasons. He was among the most attractive people, and was obliged to dress well and be amiable. If girls were attracted to him it could do business no harm—and business comes first. When a move came along a fellow was lonely for a while and longed to be back at the town he had just left. Naturally he wrote a more or less pathetic letter to the girl who had liked him best, and she, being also a little lonely, replied with a touch of tenderness. A fellow came back with another letter, stronger than the first, written in a particularly dark hour, and the girl left behind began to feel herself a party to something serious. Letters went back and forth until a fellow was invited out in the new town, or otherwise met another fair one. Then his letters dropped off. Probably he liked the girl left behind and could have fallen in love with her; but he knew he could not hold out hopes of marriage, and why spoil her chances by writing any longer than was absolutely necessary? Sometimes the girl left behind persisted in her writing. Several of them, if he had worked in a number of towns, usually did. A fellow could not be rude to them—he must let them down gradually; so he wrote regularly for a while, praying that the growing frigidity of his tone would finally discourage.

Thus it went, town after town. The bankman drifted along, taking no girl seriously, but using them all so, out of necessity. If he was an unscrupulous person he enjoyed it; if he knew what conscience meant he periodically took himself to task—but never quite solved the problem. There was no solution to it. One could not be a hermit or a boor because girls had hearts and the bank had none. He must play the game. He was taking a big chance of having his own heart cracked, and thought of danger for himself fostered recklessness toward the weaker sex.

Something, a solemn voice it seemed, whispered to Evan that a young man of iron could go through the ordeal of eight or ten years' bank service and run the gauntlet of attractive femininity without injury to a single soul; but young men are not made of iron. Evan wondered if those who wrote the Rules and Regulations had daughters, or if they remembered the letters they had received when they were clerking in little towns. Why didn't they take the whole of human nature into consideration when they laid down laws to govern employes? The fact that they had ignored the right of young men to marry at a reasonable age had wrought a thousand published wrongs and ten thousand wrongs that would never reach the press.

In his silent room the young teller rebelled against the bonds that held him and his fellows. He counted the years that must elapse before he could hope to marry. At one hundred dollars increase per year it would take him seven years more to earn $1,050. In the East the "marriage minimum" was $1,000, in the West $1,200. Like Jacob he must work seven years for his wife. And then would it be Rachel or someone else? Would Frankie wait such an age for him? Could any man expect a girl to believe in the seriousness of his intentions for eighty-four months—a year of weeks? He believed she would wait if she understood, but how could a girl understand "business" like that?

The teller's mind grew darker as he mused. He saw only gloom ahead. The drunken manager staggered into his room, in spirit, and delivered another lecture on the "aristocracy of banking." Bah!

Evan filled with rebellion as his situation stood out before him—a sudden pain in the head warned him that he was worrying. Then came a slight reaction.

"Pshaw!" he muttered, "I'm putting myself in a rotten humor. I'll feel better in the morning."

And so he did. The "light of common day" is often preferable to the illusions of night. In spite of his disturbed state of mind Evan had slept well. Penton, too, had slept, but not well. Judging from his appearance in the morning, his dreams must have been diabolical.

When the teller entered the office Penton greeted him sullenly.

"Well," he said, grouchily, "I suppose I made a nice mess of things last night. I suppose every —— gossip in town will talk about it for months."

In spite of his grouch the manager looked frightened. Anyone could see he was worried.

"Not many know of it," said Evan, indifferently.

"Do you think they will blab?" Penton was still unrepentant. His brazenness irritated the teller, who answered simply:

"Yes."

Penton looked at him angrily.

"See here," he said, imperiously, "I don't give a —— what these yokels think of me. I am manager here, and if I want to take a glass that's my business; understand?"

Evan made no reply. He walked doggedly from the manager's office to his cage and set to work. Penton stood pulling at the inflamed tip of his upper lip. His bluffing had failed. When he approached Nelson it was humbly.

"I hope you'll try to fix things up as much as possible, old man," he said.

Under the circumstances Evan would rather have been called Old Nick than "old man," but he nodded obedience to the manager's wishes and went about his business.

"I promise it won't happen again," said Penton, grovelling.

"It will soon pass off," said Evan.

He might have meant that Penton's resolution would disappear. However, his words were consolation to the nerveless manager, who, from that time on, was quite servile. He ingratiated himself with the teller at every opportunity. His mock humility was loathsome to Evan and made him fear indefinitely. He worried over it. But he could not decide what to do or how to treat Penton.

Business was rushing. The work in the box had gradually increased, and other work had piled up since the new manager's arrival. Jones, though sick half the time and half sick the rest of the time, had done more than Penton would do. Penton, despite his criticism on the former manager's system, made no real effort to establish anything better. He often pointed out "how we used to do it in the M—— Bank," and sometimes Evan agreed with him but he never took off his coat and dug out the submerged junior or ledger-keeper as Jones had done, He seemed to be engaged forever in a mental calculation. Frequently he did not hear questions addressed to him. What little work he undertook was haggled at in spasms and usually left for the accountant to finish.

All the boys were loaded down with routine. They never thought of leaving the office until six o'clock, and night-work was now the rule. Evan began to have headaches.

The people of Banfield kindly let Penton's first offence pass, as it had been prophesied they would. Everyone knew about it, of course—what village of nine hundred population ever lost sight entirely of such a piece of news?

Mrs. Penton was delighted to know that she and her husband had not been disgraced. Penton pretended, now the danger was past, that he would not have cared.

"It's a funny thing," he said, with an adjective, "if a man can't take a social drink without insulting the town."

This remark was addressed to the whole staff. At times Penton was absurdly pompous and uncommunicative before the boys; at other times he entered into a mysterious intimacy with them, a relationship distasteful to them. They preferred his professional tactics to those others.

～❦

"By heck," said Henty one afternoon, after one of Penton's good-fellow demonstrations, "I naturally hate that devil!"

Nelson laughed immoderately, in the way one laughs who has been under a strain too long. Filter, even, thought the remark funny.

"I understand," he said, "that Penton has bought all his furniture on credit from Hunter's."

"Who told you?" asked Evan, interestedly.

"Jack Hunter," replied the ledger-keeper.

Nelson consulted his thoughts. He was conscious of an addition to the vague fear he already cherished.

The end of the month (January) kept the Banfield staff so busy they had little time to discuss the one great theme—Penton. He kept to his office pretty well and seemed to read the newspaper for hours every day. He did work a little on the loan return, after Evan had balanced the liability ledger, but left the totals to his teller. For one thing, however, Penton deserved credit: he was the most industrious signer of names that ever escaped jail for forgery. He even initialed items on the general ledger balance-sheet, where initials were ridiculous, to give the impression that he had checked the work.

For the first week in February the boys worked every night. Henty's face kept its color, but Nelson began to look like Filter. The ledger-keeper plodded so slowly and fondled his ledger so tenderly, his pasty face did no worse than remain pasty. There was new vim for him in every new account opened. He knew the names of every man, woman and child in his ledger. He might be moved away any time, and all his special knowledge would become useless to him—Filter knew that—but he did not live in his ledger from a sense of duty: he just loved clerically killing time. He was too lazy or too unoriginal to think, so he kept his mind occupied with insignificant things, and made an ideal clerk.

It was afternoon, toward the end of a certain week in February. Henty had been down to a grain elevator at the station with a draft. It usually took him a long time to deliver a draft in that direction, because Hilda Munn lived out there; but this day he came back rapidly and rushed excitedly up to the teller's box.

"Nelson!" he whispered ominously, tapping the cage door.

Evan turned around and smiled at the expression of A. P.'s face.

"What's the matter, Henty?"

Filter had foregone the temptation to make an entry, and stood listening and watching.

"It's Penton. He's drunk again. He took the 3.30 train south."

"Was he alone?"

"Yes."

Immediately Evan went and found Mrs. Penton. She was nursing the white poodles. They nearly went mad when a stranger entered the domain of their mistress.

"Mrs. Penton," said the teller, "do you know where Mr. Penton is?"

She paled at once. Evan could see that she lived in dread of her husband's habit, and was on the watch for outbreaks.

"Has anything happened, Mr. Nelson?" she asked, painfully.

"Yes. He's gone on the southbound."

"To Toronto!" she cried. "Was he intoxicated?"

"Yes."

The teller gazed on her in pity. After she had stared at him a while her eyes saw sympathy and understanding, and she cried. He assured her the work at the office would not be neglected, and promised to forge Penton's name to the daily cash-statement so as to keep the matter a secret from head office. She clutched his shoulders and sobbed against them. His heart ached for her, and he promised to help Penton all he could.

"Oh, Mr. Nelson," she stammered, wiping her cheeks, "if only Pen were like—like you!"

Then she wept again. The spell over, she inquired about the trains and found she could get to Toronto in the evening.

"I know where to find him," she said. "We lived in Toronto a year. Mr. Nelson, you can't imagine how I have suffered through it all. When I married Pen I knew he took an occasional glass, but I didn't dream that he was a drunkard."

"Is it as bad as that, Mrs. Penton?"

"It is as bad as it can be." She spoke excitedly. "I have known him to spend fifty dollars in one night, when he was only making nine hundred dollars a year. (We got married by special influence.) It just seems as though something draws him toward a debauch every little while. I'm afraid this small town will be our ruination."

Evan tried to make her load lighter and, in a degree, succeeded. There is no burden so heavy that true sympathy will not budge it a little. Mrs. Penton coaxed him to have tea with her; preparing it, she said, would occupy her mind. She couldn't bear to stay alone. The teller pretended to have pleasure in accepting her invitation. There was a certain amount of novelty in eating alone at a table with a strange young woman. Still, the circumstances were not very romantic.

Neither were the circumstances surrounding Penton's return. He contrived to get away from his wife in Toronto and board a train for Banfield. He arrived several hours ahead of her, and advertised himself all over town as something to be pitied. This was two days after his drunken flight. When Mrs. Penton came on the scene the manager was standing helplessly before the staff, crying like a bruised youngster. Evan sat up all night with him, studying the pathos and humor of delirium tremens. The drink demon is a tragic devil, but he has fits of fun.

For days the manager could not sign his name. The teller did it for him, feeling as he did so that he was supporting a rotten structure that must soon fall. He did not picture himself among the debris, however.

10

Trouble Comes

By quarrelling with his wife and kicking the pups Penton managed to entertain himself, apart from the keg, for over a month. Then he went and did it again. He took some money to a place called Burnside to cash cattle tickets for a drover who did business at the Banfield branch. When he got back he was in a boisterous state of intoxication.

"Hello, old kid!" he said to Henty, whom he met at the door of the bank.

Henty backed up and went in the office again, to consult with the teller.

"This is getting monotonous," said Nelson. "What would you do about it, A. P.?"

"Report the son-of-a-gun," said Henty, florid of countenance.

"Sure," said Filter; "he'll be holding us up some of these days at the point of a gun."

Evan thought over Filter's remark, for he had been tempted to entertain similar notions himself. What might not happen if Penton got in a drunken craze? The teller worried more and more as he speculated on the possible outcome of events.

Mrs. Penton got the manager to bed and then came out to the office.

"Mr. Nelson," she whispered through the cage, "could I speak to you?"

Evan went into the manager's office with her.

"I know you are going to tell head office about it this time," she said, despairingly. "It isn't right for me to ask any further consideration from you. The business here will be ruined."

"I won't say anything," replied Nelson, "until some of the customers begin to kick. I have an idea they will not do any reporting without warning us, though."

The manager's wife sighed.

"It would be a relief, I sometimes think," she said, "to get back to the city. Pen was busy there and it kept, his mind occupied. I see there is no hope for him here. The trouble is head office might drop him from the service altogether. Of course, his relatives in Berlin are big depositors—"

"That might help some," said Evan, treasonably. Then, "Don't give up, Mrs. Penton. We may be able to scare him good for another month or so."

She made an effort to smile, but it was a tired one.

"You are my only hope, Mr. Nelson," she said, forcing back her tears. "I'm going to tell you something more."

He wondered what was coming next.

"Pen," she continued, "is in debt, I'm afraid. How could he help it when he spends so much on liquor? His salary here is only nine hundred dollars and rent, you know."

That seemed a great deal to Evan, who got board for $3.25 per week.

"Do you mean he owes money in town?"

"Yes."

The teller recalled what Filter had said Jack Hunter told him. If the manager owed Hunter money, he probably was in debt elsewhere, too.

"Well, Mrs. Penton," answered Evan, "I don't know what to say. I wish I had the money myself to lend. Do you know what I get?"

She blushed.

"It is only your advice I ask, Mr. Nelson," she replied, sadly. "As to your salary, I think they ought to pay you more than Pen."

Evan's chest went out an inch or two, but he found himself still unequal to the task of advising her. Things would have to take their course, as they always do.

Now, in the course of things, there came a very busy day. The manager had been sober for a fortnight; he sat in his office pulling at that long upper lip of his, and consuming inwardly with the fierce desire that drunkards know. Perhaps no one sympathized with him sufficiently. Who, after all, knows anything about hell but those who have been there?

Before the teller's box thronged women and men from all the country roundabout, smelling strongly of poultry. It was such a cold day that the bank was chilly and windows could not be raised. The aroma that arose before the wickets was indescribably potent. Evan felt his head swim and his stomach sicken. But work was behind him, pushing him along; he knew he must get through somehow. Filter was not able to handle the cash, especially on a market-day, and Evan would not have trusted Penton in the cage, under the circumstances. If anything happened the teller was responsible for the cash: he would be taking a chance on Penton—and a fellow can't afford to be a sport on seven dollars a week.

When a man fills a position where he is practically indispensable, so far as the work, not the position, is concerned, his job is his master. Many a bankboy, on the verge of collapse, is unable to leave for a single day his unhealthy environment. Some, like Evan, are tied down by circumstances; the majority of them are bound by their own foolish tenacity. All of them realize, sooner or later, that their labor was in vain. When their health is gone, like Jones', and their efforts stored up in bank buildings, those modern Egyptian obelisks, who knows or rewards them? If they find themselves, after years of service, unfitted both mentally and physically for anything but clerical work, and yet unable to longer endure the strain of it, what are they going to do? The man who sells his vitality is a fool, but he who gives it away is worse than a fool. The trouble with us fools is that we don't believe it about ourselves. Evan was sceptical of the harm bank toil was working upon his constitution. He would not allow himself to think his health was failing rapidly—or even slowly.

Silver was always in great demand on market days. In the midst of his rush, this very busy day, Evan discovered that he had not brought from the safe enough quarters to carry him through. A murmur arose from the stampeders when he left his box and walked to the vault. The murmur became a grumble when he fumbled the vault combination without opening the door.

"Filter," he called, impatiently, "open this hanged vault, will you? I can hardly see the numbers."

Calmly the ledger-keeper turned the combination, clicking it open unhesitatingly. He turned and winked at Henty.

Evan brought out a bag and deposited it on a small table in the cage, there for the accommodation of odorous money parcels and noon lunches. On opening the silver he found there were five packages of quarters, one hundred dollars each. He took one package out, tied up the bag, and set it under the table out of the way.

His cash was two dollars short that day. Too weary to look for his "difference" in the mess of work he had gone through, he put it up. But it worried him. He could not afford even so small a loss, for he was in debt as it was. His father had sent him a remittance, but he had sent it back, saying: "If I can't keep myself by this time, I'd better give it up as a bad job." He was too game, when writing home, to put blame for failure on the bank, so he took it himself. But he would not take money.

Locking-up time came late that market day, for the hucksters' list was enormous. The teller had paid out five hundred dollars in small bills and silver. He yawned as he packed away the filthy money in his tin box, and yawned as he carried it into the vault.

Henty and Filter were preparing to go up to supper.

"Wait, fellows," said Evan, "I'll go with you."

Penton sat in his office as the boys passed out. He had not initialed the teller's book, but had watched him lock the cash in the safe.

"I suppose you'll be back to-night," said the manager, not looking at any of the boys in particular.

"No," said Evan, "I won't. My head aches already."

But he did come back an hour later, and his head ached worse than ever, for he was worrying about the bag of silver he had forgotten to take from under the cage-table and lock up in the safe.

There it was, tied up, and how and where he had left it. With a sigh of relief he picked it up and locked it in the vault. Only Evan and Filter had the vault combination. Penton said he preferred not to have it, as he did not want to accommodate farmers after hours; it had never been done in the M—— Bank, where he had received his training.

It is customary for a manager to check the teller's cash once in a while. He is supposed to do it irregularly so as to keep the teller in constant suspense. Market day at Banfield was Tuesday. Wednesday afternoon Penton came round to count Nelson's cash. In the morning, first thing, the bag of silver had been locked in the safe, inside the vault.

There were two compartments in the safe; in one of them the "treasury" (a sort of local rest fund) and certain documents were kept; in the other, the cash box and bags of specie.

Penton first checked the bills and silver in the teller's drawer and tin box, then got the treasury notes and found them right.

"How much gold have you on hand?" he asked the teller.

Evan told him.

"I guess it's all right, but I'll count it, anyway."

He did, and found it correct.

"Bring me the silver, will you?" he said; "I might as well check everything while I am at it."

Evan brought several bags from the safe, and stood by while Penton opened them. When they came to the bag of quarters that had been left under the table for an hour the previous day, they made a discovery. At least Evan did. He found a package of one hundred dollars missing.

"What!" exclaimed Penton.

"Yes, there were five yesterday when I opened the bag, and I just took one out. There are only three here now."

The teller felt his head throb. Penton grinned sceptically.

"My dear man," he said, "you're mixed. The money was only left out for an hour, you say. No one was in here but myself."

Evan felt a chill. He was just as sure Penton had stolen one of those hundred dollar packages as he was that one had been stolen.

"Check your blotter," went on the manager, with a strange accent and a fearful glow in his colorless eye; "you couldn't possibly have paid out an extra hundred in silver. Good G——! man, you're crazy."

Mechanically the teller went over the additions in his blotter. That was always the first thing to do in a cash difference that looked like a mistake in addition. The blotter was found correct. Next came the vouchers. Penton worked assiduously on them with the teller. His mind somewhat clarified by checking, Evan began to think. Penton had said it was impossible to pay out one hundred dollars too much over the counter in silver—as it was. If he could trace the silver back to when the cash had been checked before, the difference could easily be located in the silver. He offered the suggestion. The manager made a gesture of impatience.

"I tell you," he said, "there must be a mistake somewhere; either in your work, or else you paid out one hundred dollars too much in bills and—you've been counting the silver wrong for days or weeks, that's it!"

Nelson knew he had not. Fortunately for him the manager had checked the cash a week before, and initialed it as correct. While Penton followed with his eyes, Evan ran over his cash-statement book, showing the decrease in silver each day to be about twenty-five dollars. Market days always took about one hundred and twenty-five dollars. But there was a falling off between Monday and Tuesday this week of two hundred and twenty-eight dollars.

Penton stared glassily a moment, as the boys had often seen him do. Then his cunning came to the rescue, as it always did.

"That bag you have been counting as five hundred dollars has only contained four packages. The loss is away back somewhere, and this is a coincidence. There has been a double error."

Evan knew differently, but felt that he could not say anything plausible. He was silent. Penton waited a moment before remarking:

"It'll come pretty hard on you, old man, with your salary."

So diabolically triumphant was Penton's tone that it filled Nelson with a horror.

"I'll quit the bank before I'll put it up," he said, gutturally.

"That would make things look suspicious," replied Penton.

So it would! Evan had not thought of that. Penton seemed to have figured the situation out fully; directly he said:

"Well, let's sit down and write head office the particulars. They may let you off, seeing you are getting only three hundred and fifty dollars."

Realizing his powerlessness, Evan obeyed. For the first time in his Banfield management Penton took command. He was self-possessed; acted like one who was right at home. Probably he was, in that kind of a game.

Nelson wrote unsteadily in longhand to his manager's dictation, and was strengthened in the conviction that Penton had stolen that parcel of silver. Usually the manager composed hesitatingly, especially when addressing head office, but now he was glib, and seemed familiar with his subject. He even appeared to be in suppressed good humor over the matter.

"Don't look so grim, old man," he said, oilily, "they'll not make you put it up. Why, that would be absurd, on your allowance."

An idea struck Evan. Penton, if he had taken the money, probably hoped his teller's low salary would influence head office toward leniency. The amount was not so very large; it was, indeed, just about the proper amount to take. One hundred dollars was such a common loss in banking, it would not look suspicious. Anything more would have aroused inquiry, while anything less would scarcely have been worth stealing. The thing had been well executed; taking one package from the bag and tying it up again, then innocently desiring to check the cash next day, all showed thought; and it occurred to Nelson that Penton's head was just the shape for such thought. He had not been dragging at his upper lip in vain: he had extracted a piece of strategy, which had originated in the cerebrum. There was a peculiar sympathy between Penton's lips and his brain, anyway: what the former craved satisfied the latter.

Women are accused of having a monopoly on intuition, but men have a corner on "hunches." From the moment his eyes rested on three parcels of silver where there had been four, Evan had a hunch that Penton was the thief. The trickery of it was so in accord with the expression of Penton's eye!

"But who has taken it?" said the manager, when the head office letter was finished.

"Either you or I," said Evan; "no one else has been here."

Penton grinned. It mattered not what he did, appearances would remain as they were—and that was not against the manager any more than against the teller.

"Go home and get a sleep, old man," said Penton; "we may be able to think the thing out to-morrow."

The tone of the manager's "old man" rang in Nelson's ears all evening. He rebelled against Penton's insinuating manner; like the touch of his hand it was coldly, clammily smooth.

In his room the teller sat worrying. Mrs. Terry called up to him that he had a visitor. Evan asked her to send him up. It was Henty.

"Here's a letter for you," said the junior; "I didn't see you at the post office and thought you would be glad to get this. The mail was just closing when I left."

"Thanks," said Evan. "Wait till I read it; I want to tell you something."

Henty chewed the end of a fat five-cent cigar while Evan read the letter, which was from his mother. It read:

Dear Evan,

We always enjoy getting your letters. They don't tell us much about yourself, to be sure, except that you are well. That is the main thing. Be sure and keep on your heavy underwear until the end of April, and don't wash your hair too often. I do hope that boarding-house of yours is good to you. I'm making a fruit cake which we will express to you in a day or two. If you could take care of a barrel of apples we'd be glad to send one.

Just think, you have been away from home over two years now. Dear me, it seems like ten. Lou is still the tantalizer she always was. Father keeps busy and well as usual. We all look forward to having you back at summer holidays. When do you expect to arrive? Be sure and let us know ahead. Frankie Arling was in the other day, and asked about you.

Hoping to hear from you soon.

MOTHER

Nelson sighed and handed the letter over to Henty. A. P. blushed as he read it. His red corpuscles had a habit of rushing to the surface, like a shoal of small sea-fish, at the slightest disturbance of their element.

"I guess a fellow never forgets home," he said, thoughtfully.

"No, I guess not," replied Evan. "Every morning when I wake I feel as if I am somewhere on a visit."

"By gosh," said Henty, "so do I—except that Mrs. Wilson doesn't use me much like a welcome visitor. I always have to break the ice to get into my water pitcher."

Nelson did not smile. In fact, he had not heard: he was thinking of the disappointment coming to his mother if he should have to make good the one hundred dollars loss and miss his holidays.

"There's trouble down at the office, Henty," he said, slowly.

The genial junior raised his eyes in wonder.

"Drunk again?"

"No," said Evan, "worse than that. Someone has stolen a hundred dollars."

"The dickens!"

Nelson related him the story. A. P. drank it in with the expression of a child listening to Andersen's fairy tales. And he asked just as practical questions as a child asks.

"Do you suspect anybody?"

Evan smiled: he was growing tired of tragedy.

"I sort of suspect Filter," he answered.

Henty was serious.

"You don't like to say, do you?"

"No," said Evan.

The junior was silent a moment, after which he observed, bashfully:

"A certain party certainly needs the coin."

Evan sighed, and Henty looked at him quickly.

"You're lucky it wasn't a thousand, don't you think so?"

The teller had not thought of that. He was surprised both at the idea and the junior.

"You're right, Henty," he said, with interest, "I'm taking an awful chance. I believe in my heart Penton is a crook."

"Surest thing in the world!"

Evan thought a while.

"I'm going to write head office," he said finally, "and ask them for a move—but I can't peach on Penton's doings."

An answer to the manager's letter came from head office, but the teller did not receive a reply to his own. The one addressed to Penton said that manager and teller would have to put up $50 each, on account of the loss, to be paid in monthly instalments. It was a shrewd compromise, and characteristic of head office.

Penton swore volubly and pretended to be sorely aggravated.

"Well," he said, "*you* got off easy, anyway."

Filter was professionally indignant when he heard of the affair, but a man came in who couldn't write his name, and asked to open a savings account. He so interested Gordon that Gordon forgot all else and settled in between the covers of his ledger like a pressed moth. He came out of his shell (to change the simile) toward the close of the day's work and went into a minute examination of certain deposit slips that had gone through the day of the shortage, but his interest was purely clerical, and his sympathy amounted to: "Did you ever see such rotten writers as these Banfield storekeepers?"

Henty looked up from a sponge, which, he said, he was training to lick stamps and envelopes, but did not speak. Words would have added nothing to the humor of his expression.

For two weeks after the affair of the silver, Penton surpassed himself in signing his name. Also he took a social turn, and began once more to hypnotize the good people of Banfield. He had a faculty for ingratiating himself with people who were not great students of human nature. The town mayor was a particularly easy victim of his.

"Hello, Mr. Muir," Penton would say as the mayor entered the office, "I'm glad to see you looking so well. How's Mrs. Muir? I understand you are doing big things on the dam." (Here Henty would emphatically repeat the word from his desk in the rear of the office.) The mayor would grin and begin divulging municipal secrets. Penton always made a point of talking loudly with Muir and laughing yet more vociferously at his jokes.

There were women in Banfield, too, who were not impervious to Penton's flattery. He had a way of looking into their eyes and speaking softly that charmed them.

Nelson knew that Penton could have managed the branch well if he had gone to work; Penton was, evidently, familiar with the great circus man's aphorism about humbugging people, and could have given them all they wanted of it—to the bank's profit. It was, no doubt, owing to this hypocritical asset and the appreciation of it by head office officials, that Penton was managing a branch.

There is a certain stock-company actor in the States who periodically goes on a spree, comes back and weeps to his audience, and is forgiven. That is virtually what Penton was doing. He had hit upon the scheme as by inspiration, and it worked well. He asked a young dentist and wife down to his apartments behind the bank and fêted them on the best in town. Above all, he flattered them, and he made Mrs. Penton help him do it. She was, in fact, blind to the greater part of his badness, and was so anxious to help him into the favor of Banfield's best customers that she was willing to do a little wrong in his behalf. The surprise he perpetrated on her and the town, his new policy of ingratiation, gave her hope and made her rather proud of his versatility. She was very agreeable indeed to the dentist and his wife.

In a little town like Banfield good tidings spread just as rapidly as bad, among the better souls. News of the Pentons' hospitality and geniality went abroad until many of the ladies of Banfield desired to see more of Mrs. Penton, and, incidentally, her husband. Using the dentist's wife as a medium, they secured introductions to Mrs. Penton. Soon pink-teas began to be stylish.

It was about a fortnight after the affair of the silver. Mrs. Penton was giving a euchre party (whist was unknown in Banfield, and bridge was considered a sin) for the big dogs and ladies of Banfield. Her husband was the biggest dog of the bunch; he had gone so far as to deck himself in a dress-suit, and his stiff collar was almost the shape of a cuff.

The staff, of course, was invited, and had to go. Evan would gladly have stayed away, but he was afraid of hurting Mrs. Penton's feelings. She gave him a special invitation. He loathed the thought of drinking Penton's cocoa and eating his food. He well knew that the manager had counted on getting business—and forgiveness—for every mouthful of his miserable provender. Also, he was quite sure that the cocoa was either unpaid for or had been bought out of a mysterious silver package.

The teller played cards, for a while, at the same table as Penton, and saw him smirk down upon his guests as no one, surely, but W. W. Penton ever smirked. Evan felt that he would suffocate unless he got away from that table. He wished he could stand on a chair and reveal the character of the manager as he knew it—but a smile from Mrs. Penton reached him, and he filled with pity for her. He knew that a revelation of Penton's real character would sound as strange to her as to any person there. She knew her husband had "faults," but what does that common word signify to a woman in love? The atmosphere became too stifling for Evan. He felt his head throb and threaten to ache. He excused himself, to take air.

He went out through the office and threw open the front door of the bank. It was a clear April night; the air was cool and fresh.

There were only two living creatures visible on the front street. One was a dog, the other a man carrying a small valise and wearing a well-barbered beard. He was walking toward the bank.

The stranger ascended the steps where Evan stood and spoke in a tenor voice:

"Are you Mr. Nelson?"

"Yes, sir."

"I'm Inspector Castle."

11

JOYS OF BANKING

The Banfield teller shivered an instant, but, on sudden thought, braced himself and began to say:

"You came in answer to my—"

"I came to inspect the branch," said Castle, quickly, looking Evan in the eye as he pushed past him into the office.

The teller's hopes fell. He thought the inspector was going to take him aside and ask him all the particulars of his loss. He would have had to tell them—and he wanted to. It flashed across his mind that had Castle come in answer to his (Evan's) letter, it would have been sooner. Why had the inspector allowed two weeks to elapse?

"Where is Mr. Penton?" asked Mr. Castle, when a light had been turned on in the office.

"He's giving a party to-night, sir," said Nelson.

"Is that so? Well, we won't interrupt it. You might just ask him to come out for a moment and open up. Where is the rest of the staff?"

"They are in there, too."

"Good; we can set right to work."

Evan took Penton aside and whispered the news. The manager paled slightly and his colorless eyes looked queer; but a flush suddenly overspread his face, and he said:

"Couldn't have come at a better time. We're entertaining the best customers in town."

He greeted Castle with an affectation of great friendliness. It was well done. Penton surely was an artist at deception.

The inspector spoke blandly to him, and politely refused to interrupt Mrs. Penton's party.

"Just you open up for us, Mr. Penton," he said, "and go back to your—customers! The staff and myself will get the work started."

Evan was watching not the inspector but the manager. Penton's eyes moved uneasily in their sockets, and he protested:

"Oh, no, they won't miss me. I'll jump right in with you."

Castle was delving in his bag.

"Well," he said, "I suppose you know them best; but I don't want to interfere with—business."

Penton laughed, relieved, at the remark, and hurried into his apartments to excuse himself. The party folk were awed by mention of the inspector, and their interest gave Penton an idea: he would introduce Castle to them. The inspector thought the suggestion a good one. Penton whispered him hints about the men whom he would present, so that Mr. Castle might know how to dispense his pretty words. Evan listened to those whisperings until they were silent in the hall that led to Penton's house, and an uncomfortable feeling crept over him. The manager was currying Castle's favor.

Henty and Filter came out to the office before Penton and the inspector.

"What do you know about that!" cried Henty, crimson.

The teller smiled faintly. Filter's pallid face was glowing in anticipation of coming balances. It was ten o'clock.

To Evan, who knew what a bank inspection meant, this one was particularly unwelcome. Inspections always are, to experienced clerks, who have no regard for the novelty of the thing; they mean from one to three weeks' work, day and night without let-up. But the blinding work is not the worst of it; the suspense is what unnerves and worries. A fellow never knows what moment he is going to get a figurative knock-out from the head offic e official. The inspector, if he happens to have indigestion or domestic trouble, can be appallingly disagreeable.

Henty had never been through the ordeal of an inspection, but he had heard about it. He stood now staring at the teller, comically.

"Gee," he said, "and old Peterson has had one of my drafts out for three days. A sight, too."

Filter was in a dream about the ledger. Evan was thinking. He did not like Inspector Castle; he felt that he could not expect much of him. Still, he determined he would tell his story. Evan had no very definite conception, at the time, of what that story would be; and when Castle and Penton went over to the hotel for a drink, before setting to work, he wondered whether it would be advisable to speak about the silver at all.

Penton stayed close to the inspector, as though unwilling to leave him alone with the teller. Evan saw it plainly, but what could he do? It was not for him to thrust himself on I. Castle, or tell him whom he should or should not ignore. Ignored! that was it! The $350-man was beneath the notice of an inspector. It occurred to Evan now why head office had not answered his letter. What right had he to write head office? He could not, in this connection, forget the look Castle had given him at the bank door, with the words: "I came to inspect the branch."

The manager's efforts to please and assist the inspector were both pitiful and burlesque, to those who knew his daily habits. He wedged himself into the cage with Castle, handing him parcels of money to count, and playing the caddy to perfection. He lifted a bag of silver, and as he did so his bulging eyes rested waveringly on the teller, who was watching. At the same moment Evan heard his name spoken softly from the hall. Mrs. Penton was calling him.

"Mr. Nelson," she whispered, when they stood out of hearing in the shadow of the hall, "I want to ask you something."

Her patient face bore a frightened look, her eyes and voice were beseeching.

"What is it, Mrs. Penton?" he asked, kindly.

"It's about Pen," she said. "You'll try to help out, won't you?"

He wondered if she knew about the missing money. Had Penton told her?

"You mean about—about drink?"

"Yes," she answered, vaguely; "there's nothing—else—is—there?"

No, she did not know about the silver. Why had Penton not told her? It seemed to Evan that she should have known about the loss, especially since her husband was putting up half of it. But he knew she would never suspect Penton of stealing, and therefore any reference to the shortage would be incomprehensible to her. If she thought the teller suspected her husband she would be heartbroken. Evan's thoughts flew. After all, he had no proof that the manager had taken the silver, and before he voiced his suspicion to Mrs. Penton, or head office either, he must have proof.

She stood gazing at him, waiting for his promise. She looked so girlish and dependent he forgot danger and only remembered that a woman's happiness was at stake. It gave him a heroic impulse.

"I'll do all I can, Mrs. Penton," he said, quietly. "Things seem to have started off smoothly, and I think everything will be all right."

The young woman was in a party dress and a party humor. She took Evan's hands in her own and pressed them. "You are a dear," she whispered, and fluttered back to her guests.

Evan hated Penton at that moment more, perhaps, than he ever had—though not so much as he would hate him. The young wife's faith resolved the teller, however, to watch the manager instead of telling head office about his drunkenness. It was hardly likely Penton would get another chance to rob the cash; he was a coward and would be afraid to try again.

It surprised the teller to know that Mr. Castle would take a drink, particularly with Penton. Was it a trick of the inspector's? If it was, he would approach the teller before going back to Toronto. Evan would let it rest at that. He would not take the initiative, both on account of Castle's peculiar actions and Mrs. Penton's pleading.

At 2 a.m. Henty swore. It was a pretty early orgy, but A. P. probably felt justified, at that.

"When are they going to ring off?" he asked Nelson.

"I'm going now," said Evan; "my head is splitting."

Penton heard.

"Why didn't you say so before, old man," he said, softly; "we don't want our teller to go out of business."

Henty winked at Evan from behind the manager's back, and when Penton had eagerly answered a summons from the inspector, whispered:

"What's his game, I wonder?"

"If you stick around, A. P., you may find out."

"By Jove," said Henty, "I will stick—till the cock crows!"

Nelson climbed the hill to his lodging. He lay in bed an hour before sleep came, and then dreams bothered him. They were nightmares; a confusion of figures, money and old associations. He dreamt that he was an inspector and that Penton had taken him out for a drink, talking, the while, about swollen deposits, curtailed loans and expanding prospects. There was an unknown and unfortunate clerk mixed up in this dream; a queer, vague fe llow.

Next morning A. P. left his lodging for work much earlier than usual. He called on the teller, whom, for some reason, he desired to escort to the office. Evan was eating breakfast.

"Just up?" asked the junior.

"Yes," interposed Mrs. Terry, "and he should be in his bed. See how tired he looks, Mr. Henty."

Evan laughed.

"Mother would be jealous," he said, "if she knew how well Mrs. Terry treated me."

The kind woman smiled, pleased.

"I can't make much headway," she said, coughing, "for what I try to do the bank goes and undoes."

"That's true enough," interjected the teller.

"And now this inspection affair is on," continued Mrs. Terry, "I'm afraid they'll lay him up."

Henty blushed tremendously, but looked steadily at Mrs. Terry, as he said:

"I sure envy your boarder."

Nelson glanced up from a dish of cherries.

"Maybe Mrs. Terry would let us room together here," he smiled.

Henty's eager expression was enough.

"He's welcome," replied Mrs. Terry, and added: "then when they have done for my present boarder I'll still have someone."

To the junior's delight he was thus invited to share Evan's room, and Mrs. Terry's cooking. He kept stammering out his thanks until Nelson was through eating.

"Let's walk around the block before going to the office," said A. P. when they were outside; "I want to tell you what happened last night."

Evan lit a cigarette, probably to fortify his nerves against an anticipated shock.

"You weren't gone long," said Henty, "when the manager went over to Filter and talked a while in whispers. Then he came to me and began shooting off about my good work and a lot of other rot, gradually leading up to what was on his mind, and sort of preparing me for the third degree. 'Henty,' he said at last, springing it, 'I suppose you know we had a loss around here? Now I want to ask you something confidentially. You don't think Nelson would take it, do you?' I looked at him and told him he'd better roll over—not exactly in those words. 'I don't think he would either,' said Penton.

"When he and the inspector had their heads together inside the vault I asked Filter what the manager had been saying to him. It was exactly what he had said to me. 'What's the matter with them?' said Filter; that's all. Some day Filter'll wake up and get enthusiastic about something; I think it'll be in the next world, though."

Evan laughed. It was such a fine spring morning he could not have forebodings. He was not worried by what Henty had told him.

"He's just trying to smooth things over, A. P.," said the teller.

"Do you think so?"

"Sure."

The junior sighed, like one who tells an ostensibly funny story without effect. The teller threw away his cigarette half-smoked.

"I don't feel much like work this morning, A. P.," he said. "I'd rather go out into the woods and tap a tree for sap."

"It's a little late for that, I'm afraid."

"Do you know anything about sugar-making, Henty?"

"You bet; I made sap-troughs all one winter and emptied two hundred of them every day in the spring. You'll have to come down home with me sometime."

"Thanks," replied the teller, "I'd like to. Will you return the visit?"

"Just try me."

When they reached the bank Penton was already there, but the inspector was not yet around.

"Well, how are you this morning, Nelson?" asked Penton, in a business-like tone. Henty walked on through to his corner of the office. He never stayed in the neighborhood of W. W. Penton any longer than was absolutely necessary.

"All right, thank you," answered the teller, turning to go to work.

Penton framed up a stage mien and spoke in a dramatic or tragic whisper. Evan had no difficulty in seeing through the make-up.

"You don't suppose either Henty or Filter would be capable of taking that money you lost, do you?"

The teller laughed sarcastically. He was angry, and had it on the tip of his tongue to say: "You're crazy!" but he thought it better to hold his temper.

"Has the inspector been asking you about it?" he said.

"Well—yes," replied Penton; "he said I'd better ask all of you your opinions, just as a matter of form. Not that he suspects anybody; he thinks it probable that someone climbed in the window, between five and six o'clock that day, and got it."

"Impossible," said Evan; "besides, they would have taken it all."

Penton's unpleasant eyes grew still more unpleasant.

"Good G—, man," he said, "the money's gone, and we've got to account for it in some way!"

"We have accounted for it, by putting it up," answered the teller. "What good can our speculations do head office?—they're not losing anything anyway."

Without further palaver he went to his cage. He tried to focus on the work before him, but his head swam. He saw pictures of himself and Penton in a fight; himself equipped with new grips far superior to the toe-hold in point of pain. He tried to figure out Penton's object in asking the questions just asked. "We've got to account for it," afforded a clue. That was it: Penton wanted the staff to substantiate any ridiculous explanation he should see fit to give the inspector. He interviewed them so that he might be able to put words in their mouths, when reporting to Castle. Evan realized that should he be asked any questions by the inspector, he must tell more than would be good for Penton.

The day's rush started in the regular market-day fashion. To begin with, several dames brought in an amalgamation of barnyard soil and spring ice in their boots and stood over the hot-air grates to thaw. That simple act put the clerks in a market-day mood and gave the office a market-day "atmosphere." Then things went spinningly. The bank and the staff became a machine and the parts thereof, as if incited to action by the combustion of certain gas-mixtures in the place. Especially the teller's head took on the character of a metallic organism: he could almost hear the wheels buzzing. Occasionally a cog somewhere grated, as, for instance, when a drover brought in a cheque for $500 and had to wait in line behind the wife of a neighbor whom he hated, until she got $1.79 for her produce ticket, and had deposited $1 to the credit of Janet Jorgens in trust for little Harry Jorgens.

It was three o'clock before Evan had a chance to eat lunch. It lay on the little table in his box, dry and sour. He looked at it with enmity, and, snatching a few bites of this and that, which he washed down with cold water, threw the remainder in a waste-basket, and went back to the dirty money.

Penton was all aglow. He perambulated up and down the office shouting through the wicket at people to whom he had never spoken before. He would run to the ledger, find out the name of a poor innocent farmer whose whiskers told of a possible buried treasure somewhere, and bawl out that name, to the owner's consternation.

"You've got a busy office here, Penton," said the inspector, just before the door was closed.

"Yes, Mr. Castle. Of course we have no opposition right in the town. But I mean to hold it, even though another bank opens up. I hear the N—— Bank is coming in."

"Yes," said Castle. "By the way," he remarked, addressing the teller's back, "wasn't it a market day on which you lost the silver, Mr. Nelson?"

Evan turned around; the two men were leaning against a desk behind the cage.

"Yes, sir," was the simple reply.

The inspector nodded, then walked into the manager's office. Penton followed him—but that was nothing unusual. The boys returned to their work.

"First shot!" shouted Filter, who had been working on the current ledger balance off and on all day.

Henty stopped licking an envelope, and allowing it to stick to his tongue, whispered hoarsely:

"Loud pedal, Gordon; the inspector's in town."

Filter colored. It must have been quite a relief to his placidly pale face; but his eye caught an unextended balance, and he forgot the offence immediately.

It was six o'clock before Evan had his cash balanced. A money parcel had come in from Toronto, another had to be sent out, and the cash-book had not been able to compare totals until after five.

The inspector and the manager went over to the hotel just before supper, and afterwards to the Penton apartments, where Mrs. Penton had a spread laid for I. Castle.

Three times during inspection Mr. Castle accepted the same invitation. Evan wondered if Mrs. Penton had woven her charms about the inspector; he thought it quite likely. She would do it for her husband's sake. Castle, by the way, was a bachelor. One day he held up a bunch of collateral before a head office clerk who was clamoring for permission to get married and said:

"Look at that; if I had married I would not have this bunch of security."

Evan had given up hoping that Castle would favor him with a private interview; in another day the official would be gone, to repeat his tortures on some other unsuspecting branch.

"What do you think of it, Gordon?" asked Henty.

"Of what?"

"It, i-t."

"You mean the inspection?"

"Your foot's asleep—sure; did you think I was talking about the World's Series?"

"I don't mind the extra work," said Filter; "you see, that's the difference between a good man and a bum one."

"Ugh!" said Henty, slapping his own cheek, "Right on the transmitter!" He turned toward the teller and suggested a walk around the Banfield pond, called a lake.

"It will do you good, Evan," he said.

A few nights' companionship had made the teller and junior chums; had accomplished more in that respect than months of office association had done. Henty sometimes called Nelson "Even." He said he thought the nickname was a good one; in the first place it meant a poetic summer evening; and in the second place it looked like the masculine gender for Eve. The night Henty enlarged on the probable derivation of his friend's name, Nelson laughed Mrs. Terry awake. It was the time of night when anything sounds funny to the one who cannot fall asleep.

Evan liked the big rough-and-ready junior. He looked like a farm-hand, and acted like a young steer; but he was amiable, and had brains, too. Above all, he was wholesome.

"I'll be with you in a minute, A. P.," said the teller.

They walked along the lakeside. Spring had really come. Crows were flying around aimlessly, early robins piped from a willow where the "pussy-tails" were budding, and a blackbird with glossy neck chirruped unmusically on a stump.

"Don't you ever get the fever to go back on the farm, A. P.?" said Evan.

"This time of year I do. Dad would like me to do the prodigal. Sometimes I feel like going, too."

"Why don't you go?"

Henty licked his lips—a childish habit of his—and asked innocently:

"Straight, Evan, do you think I'll ever make a banker?"

"I don't know; they say a poor clerk often makes a good manager."

"At that rate," laughed Henty, "I ought to make a peach. Filter says I'm on a par with those market-women when it comes to clerking."

Evan smiled, and picking up a stone threw it out into the lake. Something in his action interested the junior.

"Darn it," he said, "I don't know why I ever left home. I could have gone through all the colleges in the country if I had wanted to."

"Oh, well," said Nelson, carelessly, "a fellow gets certain experience in the bank that college men know nothing about. They get the baby taken out of them. They have to live in lonesome burgs and make up with uninteresting strangers. I suppose it all helps make a man of them."

"Give us a cig," said Henty; then—"Don't forget the girls, either. They're a great education."

Nelson was silent: he had graduated from that sort of thing.

"A fellow shouldn't string them, though, Austin," he said, thoughtfully.

To give valuable advice on matters of love one must have experience, but to get experience one must suffer and make others suffer; consequently, love-advice is undesirable from both experienced and inexperienced. In the first instance it makes the adviser inconsistent, and in the second case it is valueless.

"I've made up my mind I'll never trick the dear creatures," said A. P.

"You will if you stay in the bank."

"How's that?"

"Well, for instance, when you leave here, what will become of Miss Munn? You can't marry her till you draw at least one thousand dollars a year. Very soon now head office will be moving you; you'll gradually forget Hilda; you'll have to."

The big junior blushed, licked his lips, and sighed, but made no reply. For the rest of the walk he seemed sunk in reverie.

Inspection over, Penton walked up and down town where all might see. When he appeared in the main office his manner was overbearing. He placed heavier emphasis than ever on his "my's," and flattered the mayor to the point of idiocy, and cursed his current account with a vim foreign to his old self.

Then gradually he settled into his chair again. There came a lull in office work, and in general business, for the farmers were seeding. Penton began to drag at his upper lip. The film over his eyes thickened, and his brooding deepened.

A silent messenger came from Toronto:

Instruct Mr. E. Nelson to report at our King Street office, Toronto, at once.

(Signed)

I. CASTLE

The teller was engrossed in work when Penton handed him the letter. He read it dazedly, a moment, then his face glowed with excitement.

"I won't be able to swipe any more silver," he said, facetiously.

The manager did not reply to the levity; he stared out of the window and Evan could see his cold hands shiver.

"I'll be sorry to lose you, Nelson," he said, humbly, and walked into his house.

Some time later Mrs. Penton came out to bid the teller good-bye. She had been crying; that was the poor woman's chief occupation.

"Are they really moving you away?" she asked.

"Yes, Mrs. Penton, my train goes in a couple of hours."

She held out her hand, and turned away before he had released it. He watched her slight form disappear in the dark hall, and stood gazing into the gloom that enwrapped her.

"Say, Ape," said Filter, "will you take me in your room at Terry's?"

"You can have it all," said Henty, holding up a sheet of paper; "here's my resignation."

12

SOME WHEEL-COGS COME TOGETHER

I t was the rule in Evan's bank that the branch to which a clerk was moved should stand the expense of transportation. Evan was, therefore, obliged to borrow ten dollars from the Banfield branch to buy a railway ticket. There was no account, though, to which the voucher could be charged, so the manager agreed to hold a cheque in the cash for a week; that would give the transient clerk time to find a lodging in the city and to put through his expense voucher on the Toronto office.

"Are you really serious about quitting, Henty?" asked Evan, as they stood on the little depot platform. Filter was back at the office, transferring leaves from the ledger to a file.

"You bet," said Henty; "I don't believe I ever would have stuck here if you hadn't come along. That night you hit this dump I was down-and-out, but you came across with a line of talk that cheered me up. Honest, Nelson, you're one of the decentest lads I ever met."

Evan's laughter echoed from the woods west of the station. A few Banfield folk scattered around waiting for the daily excitement of seeing a train, looked at him askance, as if to say: "What do you bankers care about a town? We see little of you when you're here; and you go away with a laugh!"

"But," said Evan, "it will be a month before you can get off."

"That's nothing; I can stand it for four weeks, when I know that I'm leaving."

"You speak as though the job really weighed on you."

"It does; I didn't realize it till now."

Up the track the train whistled.

"Well—good-bye, A. P. I think you're wise to quit."

"Thanks. Good-bye, old sport."

The color came in a flood to the big junior's face. There might just as well have been a tear in his eye, under the circumstances. He watched the train hurry away, eager to make up for the minute lost in Banfield; then turned down the board walk toward the bank, with a sigh.

The hotel Evan found his way to, on arriving in the city, was on King Street West. After checking in his baggage he wandered in some direction, and, to his surprise, found himself gazing rube-fashion into the very office to which he was assigned. Half the desks were lighted, and clerks still worked on them, although it was past ten o'clock. Evan sighed, like a sleeper who is tired out, and walked further on. The first cross-street he came to was brilliantly lighted; its life and gaiety had an effect upon him. He thought there were a great many people going about. He dropped into a picture-show for over half an hour, and when he came out the theatre crowds were pouring into the street. Then he thought the city must be a delightful place to live in. What a bunch of pretty faces!

About eleven o'clock he worked his way back toward the hotel. He watched for the bank and found it still full of spectral activity. It occurred to him that city life must be made up of pleasure and work, without any rest. He was to find that largely the case.

Wondering what post he would be asked to fill in the main city branch of his bank, the Banfield teller fell asleep. There is, however, a somnolence unworthy of the name of sleep. Such was Evan's unconsciousness. It may have been that he had a more sensitive temperament than most bankboys, but, at any rate, it is a fact that whenever anything out of the ordinary occurred in his life of routine he was cursed with sleeplessness. Dreams had a liking for him, the kind of dreams that incline to acrobatic feats and magic transformations. He dreamt, this night as he tossed about, that he and Henty were driving a herd of cattle up King Street, trying to steer them toward the bank, where it was desirable to corral them, when suddenly the kine raised up on their hind legs and became human beings, many of them with charming faces.

As a result of his hallucinations he was burdened with yawning next morning. After a light breakfast he set out for the bank, arriving there at half past eight. Several of the clerks were working. He rapped on the door, and the janitor, who was dusting, let him in.

"I'm a new man here," he said.

"Another victim, eh?"

Evan smiled. Apparently the place had a reputation.

"What's your name?" asked the bank's man.

"Nelson."

"Hey," called the janitor, "come here, Bill. Here's a new pal."

The individual named "Bill" slouched up the office.

"Well, for heaven's sake!" cried Evan. "I thought you were dead."

Bill Watson shook his old desk-mate's hand heartily, and wove undictionaried words into his speech.

"Where have you been, Evan?"

"Why, don't you know? I've been teller and accountant at Banfield."

Watson smiled.

"One of those three-entry-a-day places?"

"No, sir; I worked nights more than half the time."

Bill grunted.

"This business is getting to be a son-of-a-gun, Evan. Even in country towns the boys are being nailed down to it. The bank keeps cutting down its staff, or otherwise losing them, and crowding more and more work on the boys who stick."

Evan was silent for a while. Bill's familiar voice carried him back to Mt. Alban, and he could see the office as it looked the day he began banking. He could, moreover, see the faces of Julia Watersea and Hazel Morton.

"Have you heard from the old town lately, Bill?"

"No, not for a year. I left there soon after you did. They sent me to Montreal, then here. I got a few letters from Hazel when she was there."

"Is she gone from the Mount?"

"Yes, d—— the bank and poverty!"

Watson's eyes fired and he spoke passionately. For the moment Evan's presence had brought back Mt. Alban days too vividly. The color gradually died from Bill's face.

"I'm a jackdaw, Nelsy," he said, trying to smile. "Do you remember how I used to carry on up there? I had a rotten time in Mt. Alban, but it was the best time I ever had. I wish to the good Lord I could do something besides banking. But my salary is now $750, and I'm twenty-three; I couldn't draw the same money at anything else, and stand any chance of promotion. No mercantile house, for instance, wants a man of twenty-three. What's a fellow to do?"

Unable to answer the question, Evan gazed out of the window at throngs of men and girls on their way to business.

"Just look at that mob," said Bill; "lots of them are working on about one-half what they're worth, and they've been years getting in where they are. Take the young men you see, they've been specializing for years, some of them, and draw about fifteen dollars a week now—just what I do. Their chances are away ahead of mine, as a rule, because some day they'll be salesmen or managers or something—and they're in very little danger of being fired. Do you think for a minute I could step out of here into their boots and get fifteen dollars. No, sir."

"Why stick to clerical work then?" asked Evan, repeating a question that had often been ineffectively put to him.

"What else can I do?"

Evan opened his mouth to advise, but closed it again in thought; and the longer he thought the more thoughtful he became. Bill was right, what could he do? He might dig drains, but where would that lead him? Downward, certainly. Still, there must be positions in so large a city as Toronto, for men who could fill them. He expressed himself to that effect.

"The trouble is to find them," said Bill. "When a fellow works from eight in the morning until ten or eleven at night, and usually on Sunday, what chance has he to look around? I'm never out of here till six o'clock, at the earliest. You can't run across a job through the night, you know. We don't even get out for lunch."

"You don't!"

"No; we eat those ten-cent stomach-aches handed around in carts. Occasionally we get a cockroach, to relieve the monotony; but not often. Usually it's just common flies. Sometimes I have such pains in my interior I have to double up on a stool and pray for relief."

Evan smiled wanly. Bill was a reckless talker, but he generally managed to say something sensible every two or three sentences.

"How about stenography, Bill?"

"That's all right for a fellow of eighteen or nineteen, Evan, who can afford to start in at ten dollars a week. But when a fellow of twenty-three applies for a job like that they think there is something wrong with him, and some kid of seventeen, fresh from business college, steps in ahead of him.... By the way, why don't *you* quit?"

Evan looked toward the street again.

"I haven't had time to think about it lately. I thought, when they moved me here, that something would turn up in the city. That's one reason why I was so glad to come."

"Well, don't fool yourself," said Watson. "Your work in Banfield will look like kindergarten when you're here a week. And don't have any idle dreams about studying shorthand and typewriting at night; you'll kill yourself if you try it. It isn't possible where fellows work like they have to in a city bank. I imagine they'll shove you on the cash book, where I am now. If they do, good night!"

"Is it written like the town cash book?" asked Evan, turning his attention, from habit, to the work before him.

It is singular how soon a bankboy learns to give work or the discussion of work precedence of everything else. He will go out on the verandah at a party, with some of his confreres, and discuss banking until he forgets the prettiest girl at the dance. He loves to flirt with his work at a distance; at close range it fascinates but does not charm.

Watson laughed briefly.

"The general idea is the same," he said; "but there are a hundred extras. It's the details of the city cash book, and of all other city routine, that get your goat. It's not so much the quality of the work as the quantity that eats you up. Believe me, kid, you're never done."

Realization only comes with contact. Watson led the new man back to the cash-book desk, and proceeded to give him an outline of the work. Evan's vision swayed. At first he was unable to formulate an intelligent question. When he began asking Bill said, apologetically:

"Sorry, kid, I'm not balanced yet. You'll have to take another lesson again. Maybe they won't put you on this post after all. No use of wasting good energy till you have to."

Therewith Bill grappled with his big red-backed book, and looked neither to the right hand nor to the left.

Toward nine o'clock the boys began coming into the office in instalments. As they passed Nelson, who was leaning against a desk, some of them nodded, recognizing a comrade, but most of them passed by with merely a glance. Men were coming and going every week.

Evan had speculated on the sensation he would make as he—a real, live pro-accountant—walked into the city office. Where was the sensation now? Within himself. He experienced an involuntary chill; the machinery of which he constituted a cog was beginning to grind. He should not have been so susceptible to those petty influences that impregnate a new environment; but he was below normal health by reason of work and worry endured at Banfield, and inclined to look on the dark side. Instead of going to work in a city bank he should have taken a trip to the country and engaged with a farmer to plant onions or shingle a barn.

At the front of the office there were two desks. Evan asked one of the juniors, of which there were three, who occupied these desks.

"The accountant and assistant-accountant," was the answer.

Branch men were familiar with the signature of the Toronto accountant, for he always signed the letters; but not with his assistant.

"What's the assistant-accountant's name?" asked Evan.

"Castle," said one of the boys; "Mr. Alfred Castle."

Toronto was destined to be a nest of surprises for the Banfield clerk; he might as well begin getting used to them.

"Do I report to the manager?" he asked Watson.

"No," said Bill, "the manager won't know you till you're here a month or so. You report to Alfy."

"You didn't tell me *he* was here," said Evan.

"Didn't I? Well, it wasn't very important anyway. I forgot you ever knew Castle. I'd like to forget him myself. Without kidding, Nelson, he is the best imitation of a sissy I ever saw. He has a pull, though, and it almost makes him brave, sometimes. I don't say anything to him any more—he'd have me fired, and I need the little fifteen dollars per week, minus guarantee premiums."

Bill had wasted a minute, so he cut off short and delved into the cash book once more, muttering curses on the third teller, who was out in the additions of his teller's cash book.

Castle entered the bank about 9.15. He wore a light tweed suit, a light felt hat, tan gloves, tan shoes, and a black necktie stuck with a pearl pin. The juniors, who had been indulging in an early row over the condition of the copying rags, sobered down when Castle's narrow form glided through the inner door.

Evan, who had been watching for him, went toward him easily, and held out his hand.

"Well, Nelson," said Castle, without offering to shake hands, "you'll go on the cash book."

Evan lingered a moment, expecting to be asked a personal question, even if it were a careless one; but Alfred dived into his mail and did not pause as he added: "Watson will break you in."

"And if ever I get the chance," thought Evan, "I'll break you in."

With that and other hostile reflections he turned and walked to the rear of the office.

"Bill," he said, "I'm to go on your job. What do you suppose they'll do with you?"

Watson looked at him comically.

"Never worry about the other fellow," he said; "not here. It's each man for himself in a city office and God help the hindermost. Don't forget that, Evan, or you'll be imposed on right and left. Now, come here and get a bird's-eye view of your new friend. You'll find him a nasty brute to handle; he rears, bites, bucks and balks. The time you think he is going to take you over the river he turns tail, and you hit a balance about 1 a.m. You not only have to balance your friend the cash book, you've got four tellers to balance, and they have everything beat for bulls. Our old friend 'the porter' wasn't in it for a minute with these mutts here."

"Are you ready?" shouted a resonant voice.

"Yes," said Bill. "Mr. Key, meet Mr. Nelson, from Banfield. Now, Nelsy, beat it to the basement till we get through calling. You'll need a cigarette to fix you up for the day's work."

"Yes," said Key, "take all the constitutionals you can get;" then in a loud voice: "Credit clearing house—come on, come on!"

Away they went, while Evan stood by in hope of learning something. He lost the trend of things looking at Key's white hair and faded face. He wondered how many years the little man had been a bankclerk. Besides Key there was another clerk with grey hair.

"Who's that?" Nelson asked the oldest and most talkative junior.

"Mr. Willis. He was a manager once, but head office didn't like his policy, so they cut his salary down from $2,400 to $1,400 and sent him here to this sweat-shop to finish it out."

"To finish what out?"

"Why, his career. Some career, eh?"

Evan suddenly remembered that he was a country accountant, and it was poor policy to abet a junior in heterodoxy.

"He must have done something wrong, didn't he?"

The junior, a sharp youngster, looked extremely indignant now.

"No chance," he said; "Willis is one of the decentest heads around this dump. He made no bulls: it was a pure question of policy. Ask anybody. The collection man over there" (pointing to a red-haired fellow of about thirty) "used to work with him. I brought Johns in the bills before three o'clock last fourth of the month and he opened his heart to me. Johns is my pal around here, although he never sees me outside the office."

"You seem to like him pretty well," said Evan, smiling.

"I do. I let the other kids have Castle's work; when that guy travels east I always go west."

Seeing how nihilistic and iconoclastic the young chap was, Evan deemed it unwise to longer remain in his society; he wandered across to the "C" desk. There, two men were ruling up large books in preparation for the morning's clearing. They were standing with their faces to the light and working with indelible pencils. That job always affected their eyes, Evan was told, after a few weeks or months.

The clearing came in. The paying teller shouted for the fourth teller. The latter was in the basement—but not for long. Two "C" men had him by the collar and were bringing him up the cellar steps in jumps.

"We're sick of late clearings," said Marks, the "husky guy with the small ankles," as he was called.

"Any more of this monkey-doodle business," rejoined Cantel, "and we'll distribute you around the coal basement."

"Aw, shut up," growled the fourth teller; "you'd think your clearing amounted to something."

Ten minutes later the two current-account ledger-keepers were howling for "more stuff." They looked like a couple of hungry wolves, and kept up their yowling as persistently as those wild rovers.

"See here," bawled Marks, "you guys got to wait till we get it. What in —— do you think we are—jugglers or magicians? It's rather hard to balance it, you know, Brower, till we get it out of the envelopes. Get me?"

"No, but I will get you," retorted Brower, "if you don't grease that adding machine."

Cantel grinned, and kicked his desk-mate, Marks.

"Say, Ankles," he said, "we'll get him in the basement at noon and I'll suggest gloves, eh?"

He with the tapering figure made no reply; he was chasing nine cents up and down a long adding-machine strip.

"They must have a brilliant bunch over at the S——," he said, grinding his teeth; "I never knew one of their slips to balance."

Key had done so much checking in his day he looked upon the calling of the cash book as a morning recreation. The rest of the day he had little time to talk, so he got a large number of stray sentences into the totals that made up the cash book.

"Debit nine eighty-five drafts issued," he called—"tell Banfield to come over here—get it?—credit head office branch account six hundred even—how long has he been here?—I called that once—exchange on money orders fifteen cents—Well, Mr.—er—No! I said fifteen. What's the matter with you, Watson, were you drunk again last night?"

And so on. Key suggested to Nelson that he wander around the office during the forenoon and get a general idea of the way things were done. "You'll find it a new business altogether from country banking," he said, not very much to the new man's encouragement.

Following Key's advice Evan endeavored to learn a few generalities. About the only thing he learned, however, was that every man had a post that kept him busy every minute, and did not want to be interrupted. One grouchy chap looked at the Banfield man and said:

"Say, Nibs, the bank doesn't pay us to instruct greenhorns; it only pays us to get through this dope you see here, and half pay at that."

Evan was offended; one of Henty's blushes came to his cheeks.

"I don't think anything you could teach a fellow would be worth much anyway," he replied; and the teller next door stopped in the middle of a heavy deposit of putrid money to laugh and remark:

"Strike one for Banfield."

It seemed to Evan that he was going through

juniorship days again. Nobody appeared to have any respect for him. Still, as far as that was concerned, nobody had any respect for anybody. He consoled himself with this observation.

What was called "noon hour" came anywhere between noon and three o'clock. The tellers bolted their portion of food with monied hands, stopping between bites to serve a customer. The ledger-keepers ate with their backs to the wicket, turning around nervously every time anyone rustled a slip of paper or made sounds like a pass-book on the ledge. The "C" men and one or two others were privileged to eat in the basement, but when one was balanced another wasn't, and as a balance aided digestion and the man ahead had not the time to wait for the one behind, they usually ate alone. Sometimes, by particularly good management, several of the boys got together for five minutes below and scuffled; but the fun was short-lived.

Evan ate his hand-out on an old lounge in the furnace-room. It was for all the world like a prison cell. Outside, the city was bright and wonderful; in the dark, chill office and gloomier cellar there was but one factor, one idea—Work.

The Banfield teller felt singularly alone in that basement, eating a cheese sandwich. The boys were so engrossed in their own affairs they had no time for welcoming new men. Aside from the two ledger-keepers and the two "C" men, the boys were almost strangers to each other. The Banfield man would have to learn, like the others, to affiliate with a book. He wondered, as he sat in the basement alone, how long it would take him. He speculated on the hit Filter would make in that soulless, endless city-office swirl.

The morning had been confusing to the new man, but the afternoon was chaotic. He stood beside Watson, trying to get the multitudinous cash-book entries through his head, until he was played out. He yawned repeatedly and his head pained ominously. Two and a half years of office work were telling on him, although he scarcely realized to what extent, and but for a very fortunate circumstance—which seemed to Evan an extremely unfortunate one—he would have experienced a nervous breakdown before long. But more about that circumstance later.

The bank door closed at three o'clock. Many people have an idea that work inside a bank ceases at that hour. That is one of the many delusions cherished respecting the business, one of the harmless delusions. After three o'clock, especially in a city office, the real strain begins. Tellers must balance their cash, and, on salaries varying from $600 to $1,200 (often less than the former, but not so often more than the latter) make good any loss sustained through the day. Every balance is a nervous shock and drains away its share of the clerk's vitality; if the chance of personal loss is hidden away in his balance, the strain is that much the worse.

In the din that followed closing, Evan thought his head would burst. The boys lighted their pipes and cigarettes, threw off their coats, and commenced the scramble. Curses and complaints came from every quarter. The place was a madhouse.

Even up in the accountant's department there was loud talking. Evan was up there looking for the draft register when he heard the accountant say:

"It's got to be stopped. If you think we're going to stand for this sort of thing you're badly mistaken."

The man to whom V. W. Charon was speaking trembled slightly, not from fear of the accountant but under the influence of alcohol. He lifted his weary, glassy eyes to reply, but his lips moved inaudibly and he stared at Evan.

"This has happened twice in the last month," continued Charon, sharply.

"Three times," corrected Castle.

The broad-shouldered figure paid no attention to anyone but Evan. He staggered past the accountants and held out his hand to the new man.

"Sorry to—s-see you here," he stammered.

Evan grasped the hand of his old manager, Sam Robb.

13

The Machinery Grinds

Castle turned his head and sneered, just as he used to do in Mt. Alban.

"You must come up and s-see me," said Robb.

"I will," replied Evan.

Watson came along for the draft register, winked at Robb, and returned to his desk, followed by Nelson.

"Is Mr. Robb one of the clerks here, Bill?"

"Yes—liability ledger. I had it on my mind to-day to tell you, but you were not around when I remembered what it was that bothered me. Sam's been here several months. They took his job away from him because of letters Alfy wrote."

Nelson could hardly believe it.

"The calf," he muttered. "What does Robb think about it?"

"Oh, he doesn't say much. He works like a nigger, all but about two days a month—when he goes on a tear. Been hitting the can a lot lately."

"I don't wonder," said Evan; "what has he to live for?"

He had something, though, as every man has—his self-respect. But one sometimes loses that when others do not attribute it to him.

Evan had never felt more incompetent than when Watson asked him to take out a balance. He could just as easily have "taken out" a degree at the Toronto University. While he fretted his still pounding head, Bill rode the round-up of registers, supplementaries and totals. Long drawn out exclamations reverberated in whatever corner of the office he happened to be searching.

"Teller's book," he shouted behind the paying teller; "come on, Sid."

The poor teller was short in his cash. Bundles were piled almost to the top of the cage; he snatched them up one by one and ran through them. He had a sore hand, too; it had been poisoned by infectious money. Two weeks later, when the teller had returned from sick-leave, head office refused to pay his doctor's bill, insinuating that the poison might be something else!

"Get out of here, you wolf," yelled the teller; "you're more —— bother than ——"

"I'm sorry for you, old kid," interrupted Watson, laughing; "give us your book, I'll add it up and maybe find your difference."

Sid Levison hesitated, picked his book up quietly, and faced Watson with:

"You're a yard wide, Bill. I wish we had more of you around here. I got in $50,000 in parcels this afternoon and Charon wouldn't send any relief. Gee, but I'm tired, and my hand pains infernally."

He yawned so widely his glasses fell off. Relieved of them, his face looked peaked and his eyes inflamed and weary.

"Meet Mr. Nelson from Banfield, Mr. Levison."

"How are you?" said the teller, offering his hand; "used to work there myself, years ago."

Then he turned to his money.

"How long has he been in the bank?" Evan asked Watson.

"About ten or twelve years, I think."

"He should be a manager by now."

"Sure," said Bill, "I could handle an easy chair myself for that matter. There are at least ten clerks in this office who could manage a branch, but everybody can't have one, you know. Managerships are sugar-plums to be handed out carefully by head office."

"I see," said the new man. "But," he added, "the banks claim they are very hard up for managers."

"That's because the job isn't up to much when you do get it; a good many fellows get out when they find what they're up against. A lot of this talk about the great opportunities of banking originates in head office and is peddled around the country for a purpose. The bank has the greatest advertising system in the country and the least expensive. It carries the biggest bluff on earth. The bank's on a par with political flag-wavers when it comes to handing the people the bunco."

About five o'clock Mr. Willis, the old general-ledger clerk and ex-manager, edged over toward the cash book, with his hat on and a pipe in his mouth.

"Well, Watson," he said, lighting a match, "how's your successor coming along?" The match was burning down, but Willis held it tantalizingly away from the pipe while he added: "Why don't you introduce him?"

While the match threatened to burn the old clerk's fingers he slowly greeted Evan, and puffing a last flickering flame into his bowl, in a way that showed how closely he had, during years of smoking, studied the science of combustion, asked:

"How do you think you are going to like city work, Mr. Nelson?"

"It doesn't look very good to me," said Evan. "I'm off color to-day; my head is bursting."

"Why don't you go home?"

"Yes, go on," said Bill; "I didn't know you were all in. You certainly don't look any too frisky."

"I may be on the job alone to-morrow, though," replied Nelson, "and just yet I don't know the first thing about it."

Neither Willis nor Watson advised him against the wisdom of learning things when he had a chance, so he stayed. No doubt they knew how it felt to be up against a new post in the middle of a day, with everyone too busy to lend a hand, or even a suggestion. The perspiration that has been lost under those circumstances would make quite a stream.

Bill had a bad balance. He worked till ten o'clock, taking half an hour off to eat supper. Evan stuck to it, too. When he got to his hotel he had nervous indigestion and a violent headache. He took quinine and went to bed, more or less disgusted with life. When the drug began to work and the pain of his head was soothed, a peaceful lethargy crept over him, and he wished that he might lie in such repose forever. He dreaded thought of the days to come, for he had had a glimpse of sedentary slavery.

"Oh, pshaw!" he murmured, and ebbed out into Dreamland.

The next morning he awakened late, and did not wait for breakfast. He was the last man to work.

"We begin operations here at nine, Nelson," said Castle, as the new man walked past him.

Evan stopped and looked back, but said nothing. He was not in a humor to explain his semi-sickness to one like Alfred Castle.

"We were waiting for you," said Key; "jump in, old man."

Although he had little idea where he should jump, Evan plunged, like a reckless diver, and fought his way through the previous day's work as best he could. Bill took advantage of a strip of smooth sailing to steal away and have a smoke in the basement. Soon Key found Evan hesitating over the work, and hollered impatiently:

"Hang that man Watson, where is he?"

Stimulated by the slang Evan made a great effort to qualify. Key noticed his earnestness, and softened.

"I beg pardon, old chap," he said, "you'll be all right in a few days."

Thereafter they were good friends. Whenever Evan wanted to know anything he went to the little grey-haired discount clerk and had it explained.

The day after his off-day Robb was on duty, working away silently and morosely. During the slight hill that marked the noon-hour he walked back to the cash-book desk to see Evan. His coming was welcome, for the third teller had just dumped twenty-odd sterling draft requisitions into the cash-book dish.

"Heavens!" said Robb, "they certainly load you down with work, Nelson. Have you eaten lunch yet?"

"No, I forgot to buy one when the kid was in." He didn't say he had also missed breakfast.

"Send out and get something," said Robb; "I'll make out these drafts for you. This isn't work for the cash book, anyway. I don't see why in —— they want to kill a man."

Robb's face was grey. He ground his teeth as he ripped the first draft from the pad. As he worked he talked to Evan, who was swallowing dry slices of bread with mustard and stray ligaments of gristle sandwiched between.

"Nelson," he said, "how would you like to come up and room with me?"

Evan's eyes opened with interest.

"Fine," he replied, "if it wouldn't cost too much."

"How much salary do you draw?"

"Three fifty."

Robb turned and gazed at his young friend.

"By G—!" he cried, "that's a crime. I hope when I die that they send me where I can see the torment of bank officials!"

The elder man's face was paler. The alcohol was not yet entirely out of his system. He trembled slightly after delivering so vehement a remark. Evan knew then—or thought he knew—how deeply Robb hated the bank.

"What would board cost me up there, Mr. Robb?" he asked.

The ex-manager thought for a moment.

"I pay seven dollars," he said, "but I can get you in for a month on about four, I think. By that time you will have found another place."

"That will suit me," said Evan; "I'll still have three dollars a week to live on."

Robb's lip curled, and he made a blot over an "i" instead of a dot; but he offered no comment.

"Come up for supper to-night," he invited, "and I'll show you the room. You might as well move right in, and make a couple of days' hotel expenses out of the bank."

Hurrying through the ordeal called "lunch," in order to let Robb back to his liability, Evan took the Sterling book and figured out exchange.

"Where did you learn that?" asked Robb, watching him do the first draft.

"Watson showed me last night," replied Evan; "we never issued them in the country."

"And they're giving you seven dollars a week. Do you know what this post is worth, Evan? Fifteen hundred dollars a year!"

The figure dazed Evan. He could not conceive of his being worth such a fabulous amount to any corporation.

"It's just as difficult as my job," continued Robb. "There's no difference between one post and another—except in the amount of work done, of energy wasted. It's all a matter of getting into a rut and plugging along there, like a plowman. A fellow needs certain qualifications like accuracy, speed, and a rhinoceros' constitution; but what is there to it, from the standpoint of prospects? Nothing—except work. I began in this very office twenty-five years ago. In two years I was almost as capable of handling the liability as I am now. All I needed was a little practice. I'm just where I started. I've been going round in a circle. That's banking! Do you think for a holy minute that if I was young again I'd give myself another twenty-five-year sentence? Great Heaven! what wouldn't I give to be back at your age? You may flatter yourself with the notion that you're going to have something nice handed to you some day. Well, you'll get it handed to you, all right, but not in a silver salver. You'll get it where the chicken got the a-x-e; you'll get it with the bank guillotine. You're now doing thirty dollars worth of work each week at a salary of seven dollars. What guarantee have you that the bank will ever change its policy toward you? If they tie a can on you to-day, it will be a tin pail to-morrow and a milk-can the next day. Haven't they done it to me, to Willis, to Key, to Levison and a hundred others? My boy, they don't give a fig for you."

So saying, Sam Robb humped his big shoulders and slouched up to his desk, there to bury his head in a gigantic ledger for the balance of the day.

Evan was troubled. He still believed that Robb was exaggerating; had not the ex-manager brought upon himself most of his failure? Evan had heard that pet charge made against disgruntled clerks, and it came to his mind automatically. Still, he had evidence of Robb's faithfulness both at Mt. Alban and here in the city branch, and—he was troubled.

To Evan's surprise, mail from the north brought the cheque Penton had promised to hold in the cash for a week. Not having checked out of his hotel yet, he had not submitted an expense account to Toronto office, and consequently had no funds.

The accountant brought the cheque to Nelson.

"Don't you know that floating cheques is against the rules?" he said, menacingly.

"Yes, sir, but Mr. Penton promised to hold it for me. Besides—"

"That makes no difference," returned Charon, impatiently, "this sort of thing has got to stop."

Evan tried to get a word in, but the accountant, declaring he had no time for parleying, turned away with: "We'll hold it over till to-morrow."

Had Penton tried to get the ex-teller "in bad" by sending the cheque so soon? It would, thought Nelson, be perfectly in harmony with the Banfield manager's knavery. Probably Henty had quit, suddenly; and, angered, Penton had sought revenge on Henty's old associate. However, there was no harm done, thought Evan; and he dismissed the matter from his mind—the cash book was load enough.

The cash book was, in fact, more than enough of a load, at first. On the second day of Evan's city experience, about six o'clock, Robb came around and asked him how he was progressing.

"I'm all balled up," was the answer.

Robb grinned.

"Never mind," he said, "come on up to the house and I'll help you out after supper. Never work—especially on a cash book—when you need nourishment."

Unwillingly postponing work, Evan followed his old manager. He said he knew Robb's boarding-house would suit him, so he went over to the hotel and ordered his luggage sent up. Robb went with him; and, finding a mistake of one dollar in the hotel bill, called the clerk down without blinking. Evan thought he would like to be able to do that. He was going to learn the art away out in Saskatchewan.

Robb's lodging suited his young friend perfectly. It was quite central, just a nice walk from the bank. After dinner the two of them sat in the living-room, smoking.

"This is going to feel like home to me," said Evan. "I don't see how they can put up board like this for four dollars."

"Well, it will only last a month," replied Robb, and whispered: "Don't tell anybody you're getting it so cheap; that's a secret between us and Mrs. Greig."

"All right," Nelson promised.

Mrs. Greig played on the piano, at Robb's request, after the other boarders had dispersed. She was a young widow, good-looking and clever. Robb seemed to like her.

Before long Evan showed signs of restlessness.

"I'll go on down, Mr. Robb," he said, "you can come later, if you wish."

Robb consented. Mrs. Greig's music seemed more suited to a man of forty-two than to one of nineteen, anyway. But the elder clerk was not long in putting in an appearance at the bank. He found the cash-book man in a state of siege. Evan was, in fact, hemmed in on all sides by warlike figures, obstinate and invincible.

Several clerks were working at "night jobs." They looked sideways at Robb and Nelson working with their heads together over at the cash-book desk.

"Sam's taken a notion to Banfield, I guess," said Marks, who was still out in the morning's clearing.

"You boneheaded mutt!" cried Cantel, glaring at his desk-mate.

"What's the matter with you—did you ever see an ex-manager come back to help the cash-book before? Next time we have to tick off we'll press him into our service."

"Get wise," returned Cantel, "or I'll press your mitts into service. Do you see that?"

He held up a cheque, which at first glance looked like $3.74. Its resemblance to that amount had caused all the trouble: the cheque was for $37.40.

"Every cent of our difference!" exclaimed Marks. "By heck, let's all go out and celebrate."

Accepting his suggestion as an invitation, the other "C" man, a junior, and a "supplementary" man banged their books shut and accompanied Marks to the nearest hotel. "Celebrating" is a favorite pastime of bankboys. Every balance found, every inspection finished, almost anything accomplished, requires a celebration. It is easy to get in the swim, and then one makes a fish of himself.

Sam Robb, the ex-manager, was almost as much at sea over the cash-book as Nelson was; but he had been a clerk longer than the young man, and he plodded ahead methodically, without that nervous anxiety that gets young clerks "up in the air." Robb's frequent remarks rendered the strain less intense to Evan; he worked with greater freedom and assurance than he would have done alone. Between them they struck a balance within a reasonable time, and locking up the vault went out to the street.

The lights of Yonge Street, the city environment, the pleasant April air, all revived Evan's spirits. For a while he forgot that he was a bankclerk living in danger of concussion of the brain.

"Let's take in a picture show," he suggested, with interest.

Robb smiled, and agreed. They entered a picture house called "The Rand," in the middle of a film (who ever entered at any other time?). It was one of a popular series of crooked clerk pictures then going the rounds; one of those in which some fellow robs the till and somebody else gets the blame: a woman comes on the screen, snatches her heart out of the villain's hands, and throws herself on the hero's neck.

"I wonder if those things ever really happen," said Evan, when they were on the street again.

"Sure," said Robb. "There isn't anything that can't happen—to a clerk."

Evan laughed. He was now chumming with his old manager; why not be more familiar and confiding?

"You don't think much of a clerical job, do you?" he ventured.

Robb regarded him seriously and with a certain amount of satisfaction.

"No, Evan," he replied, "I do not. I've seen too much of this dependent life. That's what a clerk's life is—dependent. He never knows the day or the hour when the axe will fall. Besides being in constant suspense, he is in danger of actually losing his job, any day. Now, life is too short to spend in dread of losing a position. If I were a young man again I would build on a solid foundation. As it is all I know is the bank. It would keep me guessing, after all these years of banking, to make my present salary anywhere else; and yet I'm not sure, at that, that I will always remain in the business."

They were walking up University Avenue.

"I'm awfully glad to get staying with you," said Evan, suddenly. "I believe I would have had a renewal of homesickness down in that hotel."

"It's a pleasure for me to have you, old man," returned Robb. "That homesickness you speak of is bad, while it lasts. It doesn't last long, though. When you come to my time of life and realize that you have had a different kind of lonesomeness for years and years, you'll begin to think ordinary homesickness wasn't in it."

The ice was broken: Evan asked a question he had long wanted to ask:

"Why didn't you ever marry, Mr. Robb?"

The old bankclerk showed neither annoyance nor surprise. One does not mind being asked a frank personal question out of friendship.

"It was like this," said Robb, unhesitatingly, "I couldn't afford it until I was thirty. I mean to say, the bank wouldn't let me afford it till then. The girl was from my home town, down in Quebec. We wrote to each other for two or three years, but I got discouraged and quit. I figured that it wasn't fair to spoil her chances; it isn't right for a man to do it. There were lots of men as good as I that she could care for, and what right had I to ask her to wait until she was on the shelf? It happened she married a bank man after all, but he was one of those guys with a pull; he drew two hundred dollar increases and that sort of thing. Well, when a fellow gives up in the love-game he usually begins to booze or do something just as danged foolish. Although I might have known she could not wait for me, still it hurt to have her marry somebody else—especially a bank man—and it took me years to get over it. And," he seemed to breathe the memory of it away in a sigh, "you'll find scores and scores of men in the bank in my fix exactly."[1]

Robb's reference to drink reminded Evan that he had not told him about Penton and the Banfield trouble. Why not tell him? As they sat before a grate fire he related the tale of the silver, of Penton's strange actions, and of the inspection.

"Take it from me," said Robb, when the story was finished, "you're a dead one in the bank's eyes from now on. To-morrow the increases come out. Just watch yourself get

---

1. The writer of this book took statistics in Toronto among eight of the leading banks in the summer of 1912, and found that out of 450 clerks 13.1 per cent. were over thirty, and 13.0 per cent. were married. Among those 450 bankclerks at least, a man had to be thirty before he could afford marriage.

a lemon. Penton has blackballed you to Castle. Why couldn't it have been Inspector Ward?—he's a good head. I'll bet they give you a measly fifty to-morrow, Evan."

"In that case I'd be justified in quitting the bank, wouldn't I?"

Robb snorted.

"If you don't quit, increase or no increase, you're crazy. If I get you a job somewhere else in town, will you leave the bank?"

"Perhaps," said Evan; "but I'm low in energy now, you know, and I doubt if I would make much of a hit with a strange man on a new line of work."

"If you're feeling like that you'd better go on a farm for the summer and get your feet on solid earth."

The following morning Nelson put in his expense account covering cost of moving from Banfield to Toronto. He did not charge the bank with three days at a hotel, as he might have done. They might be unfair to him, but at least he would be honest with them. Robb saw the debit slip among the charges vouchers lying in the cash-book dish. He walked over to the cash-book man.

"You're hopeless, Evan," he said. "You deserve to be fired."

"What's the matter?" asked Key, who was always nosing around in his good-natured way, trying to find things out and dig clerks out.

Robb told him about the expense voucher.

"God bless the bank," said Key; "it seems to have a faculty for picking honest boys. I wish a few professional crooks or gunmen would slip one over on them occasionally."

Evan smiled and began to say something, when Castle came sailing along and cried, in his high voice:

"It's pretty near time, Nelson, that you knew how to draw a sterling draft. I don't want to have to cross one of these again."

One draft out of fourteen had escaped being red-inked. It was that gigantic omission that brought Castle back from the front of the office. He loved to show authority.

Robb and Key looked at one another, the assistant accountant gone, then burst out laughing simultaneously. Evan joined them.

"There you are," said Robb, turning to the cash-book man; "that's the kind of things the bank soaks you for. They've got a pick against you, Nelson. I have a hunch you and I'll be left out on the increases."

The ex-manager's hunch was not quite strong enough. Evan received an increase of $50, bringing his salary up to $400 per year, less guarantee premiums. Robb was cut down from $1,400 to $1,250, "until he manifested a willingness to accept what head office considered to his interests."

Robb had refused, for personal reasons, to accept an appointment to a place of ostracism, and that, along with the ill-will of the accountant and assistant-accountant of Toronto, was sufficient, in the eyes of head office, to justify the cutting down of his salary $150. It had been reduced $750 when he was first sent to Toronto—after more than twenty years' faithful service.

Sam Robb, that night at dinner, looked like a man who had been through a severe illness. He ate little.

"They want me to resign, Evan," he said gutturally, "or they wouldn't have chopped me again. A nice way of squeezing a fellow out, eh?"

"What are you going to do about it?" asked Evan.

"Get drunk," said Robb.

He did, too.

14

POKER AND PREACHING

A night or two after "Sam's souse," as the staff called it, four of the boys came back to the office and found Evan working, as usual, on the cash-book.

"Still at it?" asked Levison, the paying teller.

"Just struck a balance," replied Nelson.

"Good," said the teller, "we want another man to take a hand in poker. Come up when you're through."

"I don't know how to play," said Evan.

"You'll soon learn."

"I don't think I want to learn."

Sid grinned and Brower, the ledgerman, called:

"Aw, Nelsy, be a sport; we need some of this outside money."

The boys laughed in chorus and trooped through the office in the direction of the back stairway. There were rooms for juniors above the bank, and one of these was the party's destination.

"We'll look for you, kid," whispered Marks in passing the cash-book desk.

Nelson did not reply. He did not like to refuse the boys; besides, he was curious to know just how they acted in a game of poker, and he wanted a little cheap diversion. When his cash-book was ruled up for the following day he locked the vault, and saying to himself that he would just have a look-in for sociability's sake, went upstairs.

The four players were seated at a round table on which were five heaps of matches, one in the centre of the table and one at the elbow of each man. Evan sneaked in quietly and had learned something about poker before he was noticed. Several mysteries, including that attaching to the name "pot," had been solved in his mind before Levison felt the presence of an intruder and turned around with:

"Hello, Nelsy, come right in. Did you bring a little of that outside money?"

Evan smiled.

"I don't even know how to spell money," he said.

"All the more reason why you should take a hand," chimed in Brower. "I was broke the night before last, and now I've got three dollars and seventy-five cents, and am specializing in velvet."

"What's velvet?" asked Evan.

"This here," said three of the boys together, indicating reserve heaps of matches.

"And how much does each match stand for?" continued Nelson.

"We're playing penny," answered Levison, "with a nickel limit. That means fairly small losses for each man and a pretty good clean-up for the winner, with five playing."

"Have you been only two nights making three dollars and six bits?" Evan asked Brower.

"Yes," was the reply, "that's more than I can make in two days in the bank."

"Of course," observed Marks, "when you get a bean for a day's work you make it out of the bank, but this night-pay comes out of us. A slight difference, to use the words of a—"

"Come on," interrupted Brower, "ante and get the game a-going again."

"Sure," said Levison, turning away from the cash-book man.

Evan was coaxed no further, but stayed behind the boys and watched their plays. By and by he asked the teller about certain cards.

"Just a minute and I'll show you," said Sid. "Raise you five—pay me—ace high!"

"By Jupiter," grumbled Marks, "my heap looks like the Farmers Bank clearing."

"See," smiled the teller, while the others enjoyed Marks' ill-luck rather than his joke, "I made enough that time to retrieve half an hour's losses."

Evan looked across at the C man.

"How about Marks, though?" he asked, half-seriously.

"Don't worry about muh," cried Marks, "I see a 'straight' coming this time."

The C man laughed so hard and colored so quickly on seeing his hand that the other boys gaped at him and played carefully. He finally bluffed them out with a pair.

In the laughter and uproar that followed, Evan was studious. He had seen through the play, of course; but the excitement rather than the humor of it appealed to him. Here, he said within himself, was entertainment, company and economy combined. None of the boys were losing much, could lose much, and the pleasure they took out of it was surprising. Still, Evan was not fond of the idea of taking the smallest sum from his companions. He knew how hard they worked for it.

"Well, what about it?" asked the teller, suddenly, looking up at Nelson.

"I'm afraid I'd clean up on you fellows if I started," said Evan. "I think I'd be tempted to hand back my winnings at the end of each game."

Marks laughed and the others smiled.

"Don't consider us," said Brower, "if you want to play and pay for the fun you get, go to it; that's all we're in it for—just the sport."

"But it's gambling," protested Evan.

"So is going to the Island," observed Levison. "Maybe you'll have a good time and maybe you won't, but you pay your money just the same."

The sophisticated argument amused Evan, and helped him believe the boys were in their moderate little game only for amusement, cheap amusement. They could not afford to take girls out often or even go out alone, so they had invented an economic substitute for out-door pleasure. They were trying to take him in with them in their penny-saving pursuit and he wondered if their company were not worth the mental effort it cost him to surrender certain ideas about playing cards for money. In this state of mind he watched the game proceed.

For half an hour longer he stood behind their chairs, studying hands and trying to figure out the percentage of chance against each man. At the end of the time he was surprised to see all their reserves just about even, as they had been at first. Levison saw him intent upon the game.

"You see, Nelsy," he said, expectorating the stub of a cigar, "it's fair to every man. Occasionally somebody has a run of luck, like Brower had last night, and it's worth losing a little to see that happen; but usually we end up pretty much as we started."

"Except me," said Marks; "I just borrowed these chips from Cantel."

Until now Cantel had been silent, bent on earning the price of two theatre tickets for the coming Saturday night; but Marks' words roused him.

"Don't believe it," he said. "In the first place I never have chips to lend, and in the second place I wouldn't take a chance on this guy. I don't mind holding two deuces, but two I.O.U.'s of Marks' are too many for my job."

"Shut up and decorate," growled Brower, who, Evan immediately discovered, was the unhappy possessor of the four, five, six and seven of diamonds and the eight of clubs.

Marks tried a bluff and Levison called it.

"You're too industrious," cried the other C man "this bunch relinquishes its Angora only once a night."

Evan laughed, and felt his fingers itch for a draw. Instead of asking for a hand, though, he took a letter from his pocket and wrote on the back of it something for memorization. Then he told the boys he had not yet eaten supper, and they excused him with good-natured remarks. After indulging in a sandwich, a small bowl of rice-custard, and two slices of brown bread, he went up to the boarding-house. As Robb was not in, he was obliged to entertain himself. He hit on the form of entertainment uppermost in his mind—cards. He took the memorandum he had written above the bank, and dealing out a poker hand to four imaginary players and himself, proceeded to create flushes and other combinations. He was unfair in his playing, however, as he looked at each man's hand and selected cards from it instead of the pack. In this way he managed to deal himself a royal flush three times in fifty minutes. The exercise was tiring, though, and he leaned back in his chair. In that restful attitude a lethargy came upon him, and he day-dreamed about poker.

It was a game of science and chance, but were not all other games also dependent upon science and chance—even to a game of ball? There was something in what Levison had said: in going to the Island one did buy the *chance* of having a good time. And as to the selfishness of the game, did not the boys want him to join them? If they were going to lose by having him with them it was not likely they would invite him. As far as his own possible losses were concerned, Evan had seen enough to feel sure he would break about even. Thus he would have all the fun for nothing, and would be one among the other fellows. Being without the money to participate much in a city's recreation, he welcomed the opportunity of getting something for nothing, which it seemed he would do in an odd game of poker at one penny ante.

The strain of daily work was severe; one could not think of spending the evenings with a book—that was too much like more work. What one needed was something with many laughs, a few cigarettes, and the company of other bankclerks. But where did bankclerks, on salaries varying from $300 to $800, congregate? At clubs? In the drawing-rooms of society? Under the white lights of theatre facades? No—in a shabby, lonely room somewhere, where a nickel looked like two bits. That was where one must go to be among them, and to be one among them he must buy, with his spare pennies, the chances of pleasure they bought.

Evan's dreaming was bringing him near the dividing-line between sense and nonsense. But what, O Employer of Labor, determined the trend of his dreams? If he had been able to take an occasional trip up to Hometon, only three hours' journey, would he have lain awake nights devising means of filling up the dreary evenings? If he had even been able to take a friend out to the theatre occasionally, those cool spring nights, without borrowing the money, would penny poker have so interested him? But you will not listen, Mr. Employer. You say: "If we raise him $200 instead of $100, *he will only spend it anyway!*" If your Maker had given you one hand instead of two, because of the possibility of your doing more harm with two than one, would you not doubt His wisdom, to say nothing of justice or mercy? What if the bankclerk does spend all he makes—who made *you* his guardian? You are his employer, not his father or mother. If he can earn $1,000 a year after three years' service (and in the *Star Weekly*, Toronto, summer of 1912, a Canadian Bank official declared that a bankclerk was no good unless he could) what right have you to give him only $500 or $600?

Evan dreamed of amusing himself, until sleep came; sleep, almost the only inexpensive and valuable amusement some people get. Next morning he awakened in a sporting frame of mind, and went to work somewhat buoyant for having strangled an awkward scruple.

"Are you going to play again to-night?" he asked the paying-teller.

"Sure," said Levison, "but we've got five already. Bill Watson is coming. I don't think the fellows care for a six-handed game."

Evan did not notice the smile on Sid's face. He went back to his cash-book with the intention of coaxing his way into the evening's game. By and by Brower came along from the accountant's desk.

"Say, Nelsy," he whispered over the cash-book, "Marks got a sure tip from the races through his uncle to-day, and we're all going in on it. It's all right, believe me. He gave us one at the last races and we all made a five to one clean-up. This is a ten to one, sure. If you've got a dollar to throw away give it to Marks."

"I haven't got any to throw away," replied Nelson, annoyed that on top of his recent surrender to poker someone should try to coax him into playing the races.

"Oh, very well," laughed the ledgerman, "no harm done."

Evan made a sudden resolution that he not only would not bet with them that day but that he would pass up the poker game that night: it would show them that he had a mind of his own, even though he did want to be sociable. However, late in the afternoon he began to wonder what he would do in the evening. He almost wished the cash book would not balance before nine or ten o'clock.

Nevertheless, and strange to relate, about six o'clock the big red-backed book did balance. No one was around to hear Evan exclaim: "A first shot!"

He was washing his hands at the tap when a key turned in the front door and Cantel came running in.

"Hurrah! Hurrah!" he shouted, "we're all rich."

Evan asked him if he had gone crazy.

"No," replied Cantel, "but Levison has. He bet ten dollars and cleaned up a hundred. The rest of us made from ten to thirty. Here, Nelsy, here's your ten bucks."

The cash-book man laughed ironically.

"You certainly have gone nutty," he said, wiping his hands on the towel. "I didn't bet anything."

"Listen here," said Cantel, "this is the dollar I owed you. Brower told me you wouldn't bet, and we were so danged sure of cleaning up that I decided to place your bet myself. I made twenty on my own account."

Evan was struck with the sporting generosity of his fellow clerk, but could only decline the money.

"That's going too far, Cant," he said.

Cantel began to swear and continued swearing until several other clerks had clattered down through the office, whooping and laughing. Watson was almost fizzing with gin and lemon. Levison, too, walked with a slant. They gathered around Nelson, telling him what a good cash-book man he was and what a fool for not getting in on some of their "outside money."

"I'll tell you what I'll do," said Evan at last, "I'll take the dollar out that Cantel owes me and stake you the other nine on a poker game, providing you do not ask me to play."

"You f-foolish f-fellow," stammered Watson.

"Wh-what's s'matter?" asked Sid, thickly, "weren't you asking s'morning about a game?"

"I want to see how it's done once more before playing," parried Evan, who was in reality beginning to hanker after the game. It would, he figured, be almost as much fun looking on as playing—one night longer, anyway.

Upstairs in the little room five reserves and a pot stood before Nelson's eyes. The boys had been playing half an hour. Levison, drunk and reckless because of the day's winnings, bluffed out three jacks with a pair of kings and laughed until he nearly choked. Watson, too, played recklessly, but was singularly lucky. After three successful plays Bill exclaimed:

"Let's raise the limit; I'm sick of this monotony."

"I'm game," laughed Levison.

"Naw!" cried Cantel, who had been losing.

"Come on, be a sport," said Brower and Marks in different phrasing.

"Not for mine," replied Cantel; "I quit the game. Maybe Nelsy will sit in a few hands."

"Sure he will," said Marks, "there's class to him. He's a sport or he never would have thrown away nine bucks on millionaires like us. Come on, Nelson, get in the game."

"Yes, come on," coaxed Levison, in syllables impossible to write, "and if you lose too much we'll give you back something from the pot. It's only for fun—we want your company."

Without taking into consideration the raising of the limit, for the reason that he knew he would not need to bet, and figuring that he could play merely for the fun of it a while at penny losses, Evan gave in at length.

"Well, I'll try it," he said, ashamed of his stubbornness, "just for sport."

As luck would have it he raked in a few pots right on the start; then came odd losses and another succession of gains. His success seemed to please rather than tease the other boys, and, to repay them for their consideration, Evan decided it was up to him to make a few bets. He played rather recklessly after a couple of good winnings, saying to himself that the game was going to be short-lived; and his recklessness brought him luck.

How the time flew! Evan looked at his watch and could not believe his eyes—it was ten minutes to ten. He mentioned the fact to the boys.

"By Jove!" exclaimed Watson, "I must go down and have a swig before the bars close. Come on, Sid."

In a few minutes the two tipplers returned with what Bill declared to be a "full house"—three bottles of beer and two flasks of whiskey. Evan was sorry to see the stuff brought in and told them so.

"Now don't be too hard on us, Nelsy," pleaded Watson, in a drunkenly comical tone, "we won't ask you to drink."

"No, shir-ee," said Sid, "Nelz all right. Good sport."

Flattered in spite of himself, his blood warming up, Evan played on, and tolerated the drinks. Toward the close of the game he proceeded carefully, however, not that he intended to keep the money he had gained and use it for clothes or board, but that he might hold it over for other nights and prolong this newly-found form of amusement! He swore to himself, and told the boys, that when the money he had gained was spent he would not play any more, because he was beginning to see that some of the fellows might lose more than their salaries could afford. This was a special night, and they didn't notice it much, but as a precedent, and so forth, excuses and arguments *ad infinitum*.

Evan might have been able to stop after losing the sum he had gained, and he might not. Some bankboys had turned away from the exciting pastimes of the majority, to find what pleasure they could in walking the streets and patronizing the picture shows, but whether Evan would have been able to do it or not is not for this story to decide. He was not destined to remain in the bank, to suffer through the years its impositions; he was not going to be saddled with the responsibility of choosing between hopeless monotony and a life of blind recklessness. That miserable lot was for others, whom Nelson would some day assist in throwing off the yoke.

Sid Levison, now thirty years of age and drawing $1,100 a year, had made resolutions like Evan's, believing himself to be stronger than circumstances. He had started off in the bank with just as high ideals as Nelson's, and with a sweetheart just as true as Frankie; but years of disappointment had crushed both his hopes and his ideals, until now he lived for the petty and illusive pleasures of the moment; drink, gambling, and other demoralizing "recreations."

Sid Levison, and other bankclerks like him, were abandoned to a life of waste because they had never been given a fair chance. Had they been honestly paid for service in the early years of their banking life they might have spent, at first, all of their salary and done considerable mischief to themselves and others, but when they came out of their youthful nightmare the future would not have been blank and lustreless—as it often is to Sid Levisons, as matters stand. They open their eyes for a moment to the impossibilities of their situation, and close them again with a sigh or an oath, hating the light of common day, so cold and blinding in comparison with the witching glow of midnight flame.

Bill Watson and those other young poker-players were following in the way of their paying-teller, innocently, naturally. Every day they are following in that way, and the bank is perfectly willing that they should. Does not a man become dependent upon the bank in proportion as he loses his own self-dependence, and in proportion as a man is dependent upon his employer is he not subject to the whims of that employer?

The public often wonders about bankclerks, and about other office-men, too, in fact. Why don't they settle down at a reasonable age and do their part toward building up a nation? Young men in their teens are expected to be silly, but when a man of thirty is still a waster he becomes an enigma.

"What's the matter?" people ask; "where lies the origin of the trouble?"

"In human nature," the capitalist answers. That is the answer that pleases and excuses him. But is it true and sufficient?

Those whom fortune has favored may, until the day of doom, invent sophisms to veil their selfishness, but they cannot get rid of the obligations resting upon them—without discharging them.

When those obligations are ignored injustice is wrought, and oftimes the result is crime.

15

Fired

The month with Robb was nearly up, and Evan was beginning to look for another lodging. He had a suspicion that his old friend was putting himself out by entertaining another at four dollars a week. He knew it would be useless to mention the matter to Robb; he decided that the only thing for him to do was to vacate, then watch his chance to serve the ex-manager a good turn some day. He really believed Robb was paying Mrs. Greig extra on account of the accommodation.

As they sat, now, talking over trivialities, Evan told his friend that he had found a new boarding-house, which, of course, he had not. The ex-manager drew a breath deep enough to be a sigh.

"I guess it's better, Evan," he said, thoughtfully; "but I hate to see you go. Not only because I will miss your company, but I would like to knock the bank-bug out of your head. That was one reason why I wanted you here in the first place. I haven't been lucky in turning you up a job anywhere else just yet, but I'm going to get one for you, and going to hold you to your promise."

"If you can show me," answered Nelson, "where I'll be better off, it's me for the new job."

The small increase had not affected Evan seriously.

"I've been showing you all along that you couldn't be worse off than you are, haven't I?" said Robb.

Evan was not sure; he had had no business experience outside of the bank; naturally the only job he had ever had looked good to him.

The day after the increases Sam Robb had been off duty again; but the accountant had said nothing, considering, perhaps, that the Mt. Alban ex-manager had been "called" substantially enough in the reduction of his salary.

Robb had been quiet since his latest rebuke, and since the drunk following it had not been absent from duty a single day. All the same, he had been drinking steadily, quietly. Nelson often felt like doing something about it; he had no idea what. Always when the impulse came to him he closed his half-opened lips, leaned back in his chair, and kept his troubled thoughts to himself.

May was past her prime. The "Island" was becoming more popular every night, and the Sunday crowds at Scarboro grew rapidly. Robb and Evan walked down University Avenue to the bank.

"Well, we'll have a rest to-morrow," said Robb. "I'm getting to be an old man, and as long as I remember we've celebrated the 24th."

"I guess we always will remember Queen Victoria," replied Evan, "but I'm going to work tomorrow. Jack has to transfer his ledger, and I promised to help him."

Robb looked daggers at a robin.

"There you are," he said, in a soft, ominous tone; "that's the bank. They give a fellow a post that keeps him going night and day, Sundays and holidays, knowing that if he gets up against it absolutely, some other mark will chip in and help him out. They get the greatest possible labor out of the least possible staff at the lowest possible figure."

Evan smiled, and repeated another bank chestnut handed down from time immemorial among the staff as a valuable exotic intended to satisfy the ambitions of those who had them:

"That's supposed to be good business, isn't it—economy?"

"Economy be hanged!" said Robb, "and good business be ——! Good business, my dear boy, is giving reasonable value. Whether you are a farmer, a merchant, an employe or an employer, good business consists in delivering the goods, or paying cost of delivery, as the case may be. One of the most valuable articles on earth is Labor, and when a man buys it a decent price should be paid. The Bible is a wise old book; doesn't it say that 'the laborer is worthy of his hire'?"

Robb spat against the curbing and went on.

"Do you know why banks build so many fine structures throughout the country, and how it is they can afford to purchase the best locations in all the cities?"

"I have often wondered," said Evan, meekly.

"I'll tell you: it's because of dividends that can't be declared. The banks' profits are so high they couldn't begin to share them in dividends; the public wouldn't stand for it. So they buy property, build buildings, and pile up capital. At the same time they are starving their clerks."

"But," said Evan, feeling obliged to stand up for the institution that gave him employment, whether that employment was respectably paid for or not, "isn't it up to the clerk? If he is willing to work for a certain salary the bank isn't going to throw money at him."

Robb, to Evan's surprise, laughed heartily, then sneered.

"My dear Boob," he said, "they've got you by the whiskers all right..... Now look here: the bank hangs a great big bluff from beginning to end. It tells juniors they *will be* well paid after a while—as soon as they are experienced. But it doesn't fulfil that promise. When the junior becomes a senior he is told that he *would have* succeeded if he had done certain things. Isn't that what they told me?"

They were at the bank. The day before a holiday is no time for distracting thoughts. Evan went in and concentrated on his work, and Robb on his. The conversation they had had must come up for future consideration. That is the way with bankclerk "consideration": it is always future.

Four weeks had made Evan fairly familiar with the ways of a city office. On the cash book he had a good opportunity to see the workings of the entire system, for the cash book is a concentration of all business; it is an itemized general ledger. Evan was rushed from morning till night, and worked many a night. Yet he did not find that in the routine which satisfied his intellect. He knew himself to be a machine; not a creative machine—there is no such thing—but a reconstructive instrument. He was a meat-grinder, a fanning-mill, after that a phonograph—nothing more. Yet, from sheer physical and superficially mental activity he was, in a measure, satisfied with his lot. He derived satisfaction from a comparison of his working ability with that of other clerks. He should have compared himself with a star in the sky instead of a knot-hole in the fence. There is a ridiculous, childish satisfaction in measuring one's self by an inferior, or even a peer. It is an ignoble source of content. But, aside from flattering himself into a species of content, in that way, Evan sated his natural ambitions in continuous work. The laborer is reconciled to his place because he really gets something done, though it be to another's benefit almost entirely: Evan knew he could not work so hard without accomplishing something. He did accomplish something—for the bank.

Evan Nelson was wearing himself out, body and brain, for much less than a living wage. The experience he got was no longer of value to him; every day's work was a repetition of the previous day's work. He had no time for study or advancement of any sort. For what then was he working?—the salary. Evan did not realize it, but, he worked night and day for that seven or eight dollars per week. It was all he got, therefore it alone must have been his reward. And year after year in the bank, it would be the same way. If the business did not keep faith with him, if it did not reward him according to his works, in 1907, would it do so in 1908 or 1912? No; it would keep up its policy of delusion and perpetuate for ever and ever its vain promises. Then, some day, it could, with impunity, turn on him and b reak him.

"Good morning, Nelson," said Key, coming to call; "what time did you get balanced last night?"

"I had a first shot," replied Nelson.

"Hooray!" cried Key.

"At ten o'clock," added Evan, grinning. "I couldn't get things rounded up for a trial till then."

"Oh," said Key, rubbing his chin. "They ought to give you some return work…. How are you feeling these days?"

"Just average," answered Evan; "I had to cut out the cigarettes. I never smoked more than three or four a day at the most, but I find that I have fewer headaches when I leave them alone."

"Fewer headaches," repeated Key, in his peculiar way.

Evan smiled, and dived into the calling, drawing the time-worn battered old Key in with him. After a while the little man said:

"I suppose you count those headaches part of the game."

"Yes," and another chestnut rolled to the floor, "every business has its drawbacks."

"And every horse has its hold-backs," said Key, wondering whether it would sound like a joke or a child-speech. When it seemed to be lost on Evan, he corrected: "I meant 'every jackass.'"

"I see," returned the cash-bookman, "you think I'm a jackass for letting the bank hold me back."

"Yep!"

"So does Mr. Robb."

Key rested his blue pencil on an amount and looked across at Evan.

"You think we're soreheads, don't you, Nelson? Maybe we are. But let me ask you something. Supposing you had worked twenty years in the bank, and then they gave you, with great show, a little branch down in New Brunswick; supposing you went there and found that the bank had practically no business because it wouldn't oblige the community, and you started to lend money on good security, believing that a bank should be an asset to, not a leech on, the country. Supposing you suddenly had the branch taken away from you, because you tried to make it, and were making it, a benefit to the community—and were sent back to a sweat-shop on reduced pay: then supposing a bright young fellow came into the branch with the dreams you used to dream yourself, when a boy—tell me, wouldn't you try to make him understand what a fool he was?"

For answer Evan asked a question:

"Is that what they did to you?"

"Yes, and that's what they've done to dozens of managers. Every other bank has done the same thing to some of its old stand-bys."

"Well," said Evan, "don't they do the same thing in other lines of business, in corporations and so on?"

"I hope not," replied Key, tearing a voucher with his pencil; "but even if they do that doesn't excuse the banks. I suppose all trusts pull off arbitrary stunts, but the bank trust is the only one I happen to have personal experience in."

"A fellow simply has to trust to luck, I suppose," replied Evan. "Some fellows seem to get along well enough in the bank."

Key grunted.

"There are two kinds that eventually get the best that the bank has—that's little enough: First, the willies with a pull, and second, the sissies who siss. The fellow with originality and get-up is choked off, sooner or later. He usually manages to offend head office early in his career, and the rest of his bank life is—like mine! There are occasional lucky ones, as you say; but personally I'm not very strong for charms and stars. A fellow who has nothing stronger than luck to bank on may make a good race-track tout or fortune heeler, but not a business man. Don't work for any corporation or at any job where you're, so far as the position itself is concerned, dispensable; unless you are necessary to your employer, whether he be a magnate or an acre of land, jump the job."

Castle was passing.

"Key," he said, in his falsetto-femina voice, "you're too slow at that calling. The clearing men need Nelson on a machine from now on. You'll have to do less talking and faster work."

The grey-haired clerk reddened, but said nothing, aloud. What he said under his breath was sulphur-tipped.

It seemed to Key that every time the boys took a minute off to discuss personal affairs or the world outside the bank, a jealous bank demon showed its teeth.

The sentiments of Robb and Key made quite an impression on Nelson, but he argued that where there was so much said against the bank there must be a good deal to be said in its favor. He might have used the same argument with reference to a national evil, for instance.

"Hey, Nelson!" called Marks of the C's, "are you nearly through there? We're in an awful mess here with the C—— Bank. Their clearing is balled every day."

"All right," replied the cash-book man, leaving a few odds and ends of his own work, "is it the Queen Street branch again?"

"Yes," said Cantel; "I think it's too near the Asylum grounds."

The savings man turned around and chuckled. "Mutt and Jeff get quite humorous at times," he said, pointing to tall Marks and short Cantel.

The paying-teller laughed, so did Willis and the cash-book man. There are moments of fun in a city bank, but they are brief and reactive. The boys never get acquainted to any extent. They rarely help each other out, either, for they all have their hands full, and every bit of extra work they do reacts on their own post at night, early mornings, or Sundays. Sometimes there is a utility man, but he either dies young or prays for a move to the Maritime Provinces, where he can recuperate in a summer resort.

"That's enough from you, Johnson," said Marks; "crawl into that pipe of a savings and close the cover, or we'll make you smell the leather down cellar."

"You call the savings a 'pipe,' do you? Say, Marks, you'd have seven kinds of delirium tremens if you smoked this pipe."

Cantel tore off a slip and looked up.

"Ninety cents out," he said. "Marks is familiar with seventy times seven snakes already, Johnsy. He's getting to the crocodile stage. Last night at the Gai—"

"Shut up, Cant," whispered Marks, frowning; "it isn't time for the great trump to sound, just yet."

"Who mentioned trumps?" inquired Jack Brower, one of the current ledgermen, who had come around to drum up "stuff."

The boys laughed in chorus.

"Hey, less noise out there," called Levison, already experiencing a "kick" from the laugh of a minute before.

Marks was about to waken Brower to a proper understanding when Charon popped around the paying-cage.

"Look here," he said sharply, "this noise has got to stop. What are you doing here, Brower? Can't they keep you in C's? What's the matter with the clearing anyway? ..... Nelson, I'm going to put this in your charge, and I want you to see that the ledgers have their stuff by ten-thirty at latest."

Thus another responsibility was loaded on the creaking shoulders of the cash-book man; but nothing was said of added remuneration. Every week or month, as a man increases his speed or loses his power of resisting imposition, he is screwed more and more tightly to the "wall," which, in banking, means a desk.

"Do you know what you are?" said Johnson to Evan, when the accountant had gone. "You're a darn idiot. Why don't you kick?"

"Aw, shut up," Marks butted in, "how's a fellow going to get out of it? Why, Johnsy, you'd have a hemorrhage if you ever let yourself dream of talking back to the accountant."

Mr. Charon might stop the noise, but he could never put an end to the conversation of the clearing men. They rattled on, like their adding machines, jabbing back and forth and getting off speeches that are never heard in vaudeville, but still turning out the figures at a rapid rate. They worked mechanically, and their minds had to find diversion. That it was not valuable diversion was due to the environment. In the first place the work was monotonous, and the mind naturally sought a channel of entertainment, rather than of thought; in the second place, one got accustomed to the line of talk popular with the boys and unless he mixed with them he was out of the swim and in a cold, silent current of his own.

Sometimes the diversion Evan permitted himself took the form of Frankie Arling. It was not often, now, that he thought of her seriously—that is, as his wife. Seven years was too long a time to look ahead. He could not, after a good many months in the world of business, realize Frankie as he had done in those old school-days; but he could still think of her, in an ideal way.

Would Frankie be proud of him if she could see him handling that mysterious jumble of figures called the "cash book?" He wondered how the "city" way, which he believed himself to be acquiring, would appeal to the sweet country girl. He smiled as he thought of summer vacation—not such a great while off—when he should go back to Hometon and—and what? He did not know. He couldn't carry back tales of success, for his salary was only four hundred dollars a year. He couldn't go back well dressed, because he was fifty dollars in debt to the bank, and owed a tailor's bill in Banfield.... Invariably thoughts of the girl he knew he loved brought him misery and despondency. Thoughts of home brought him little less. He might have known, from that, that either he or the bank was a failure; but a fellow of nineteen looks through a smoked glass. To say that Evan did not think is scarcely the fact. He did think, but spasmodically. The mind is a dual thing: the superficial mind can be employed on an adding machine and leave the thinking function free to operate in any direction; but before that is possible the superficial mind must be familiar with the object that engages it. It is not an easy matter to figure sterling exchange, for instance, and at the same time think about irrelevant things; but it is easy to run an adding machine, or even to add, and think simultaneously. On the cash book Evan found himself engaged in all kinds of work; on some of it he had to concentrate (although no "brain power" was necessary), while on some of it he worked mechanically. Whenever a period of serious dissatisfaction, brought on by something Robb or Key had said, troubled him, it was of short duration: something always broke into his mind and scattered the argument framing there. By the time he was free to resume the argument foreign thoughts had intervened, and his brain was in a muddle. Before the muddle could be dissipated by a cold point of common sense, something else had come along. And so things went. So the days and weeks went.

When Evan got a night off, sick and tired of struggling with figures and fancies, he indulged in some of the exciting amusements of the city, which were new and attractive to him, and in "quiet little games." He was slipping into a rut, and probably he would have stayed there for months or even years, like hundreds of other young Canadian bankboys, had not the poverty of his existence driven him to the temporary form of relief known among bankclerks as "kiting."

"Bankclerks are always hard up." This is one of the public's chestnuts. It is not a horse-chestnut, however; this one is digestible. It is a fact. The reason is, chiefly—poor pay. It is absolutely necessary for a fellow to either get money from home (even after three years' service) or to borrow and fly kites. Kite-flying is the last resort. It is simply a matter of cashing a cheque on your own bank through some other bank whose clerks are known to you, or through some outlying branch of your own bank, and keeping that cheque out (keeping the kite flying) until pay-day comes and you can deposit to meet it. There is nothing dishonest in the transaction: customers float cheques all the time. The bank cannot lose through the kiting of clerks; only tellers who cash the kite can lose, and they know the "flyer" before taking a chance.

Sometimes a floated cheque floats home sooner than expected, and then there is some sudden high-financing to be done.

It was the custom in Evan's bank for the accountant to look after all clearing items on which exchange had been added by other banks. When the clearing men on the machines registered a bill with exchange they laid it aside for the accountant to see. The clearing of that 23rd of May was very heavy, and everybody was rushed.

"Here are your exchange amounts," said Marks, turning his bunch over to Cantel.

"Do you want them now, Nelson?" asked Cantel, "or shall I rush them up to the accountant and give them to you later?"

"Take them up," said Evan, puzzling over a badly-figured cheque, "and wait for them. He's been holding them back lately, and the ledger-keepers are developing claws."

When Cantel came back he had the exchange items, but he seemed thoughtful, and looked askance at Evan.

"Nelson," he whispered, "come here; I've got something coming…. Whose cheque do you suppose Charon kept back for further investigation?"

"Not mine from Creek Bend, was it?"

"You're on."

The cash-book man's face reddened.

"I didn't expect it in for three or four days yet," he said. "Dunn never would do a trick like that on me; he must have misunderstood."

Cantel laughed.

"I wouldn't take it so hard," he said; "everybody's doing it."

"I know," replied Evan, "but when I first came here Pen——"

"Forget it," said Cantel, turning to his work, "they need guys like you and me around here too much to kick over a kite."

So the "C" man thought. Every junior man seems to think that he is necessary to the bank. The older he grows the smaller he becomes in his own estimation, because in the bank's estimation. The bank understands the advantages of "depreciation" in stocks—and employes.

Before Evan could find a clerk who was willing or able to lend him enough to cover the cheque for eight dollars he had issued to pay board and buy a pair of shoes, Charon had set eyes on him from a distance and was beckoning to him.

The accountant had little glittering eyes. They shone out of his smooth, round face like boot-buttons from a lump of dough. He fixed them on the cash-book man.

"Mr. Nelson," he said politely, "I'm sorry to tell you that head office has just telephoned down and asked for your resignation."

"My resignation!"

"Yes."

"But Mr. Charon, you're not going——"

"It's not my doing at all," said Charon, interrupting; "anything you have to say had better be told to the manager."

Evan had never been introduced to the manager, but he walked into the big private office and started saying he scarcely knew what.

"Oh, are you Mr.—er—, the young man whom head office has asked to resign?"

"Yes, sir."

"I'm sorry I cannot do anything for you."

"But won't you tell me why I'm fired?"

The cash-book man gazed fiercely into the manager's eyes. A thought for his personal safety probably decided the pompous old gentleman to compromise a little.

"It's on account of that cheque you issued—and—and—"

"And what?"

"And that Banfield affair!"

The truth dawned on Evan. He stood for a moment oblivious of his surroundings, thinking of his father and mother and friends. He was suspected. It was worse than Robb had said: he was not only under disfavor, but under suspicion. Head office had only waited for a pretext to fire him.

"But I didn't take that money——" he began.

"Those are my instructions," replied the manager, turning to his work.

Evan felt sick. He tried to make the accountant talk, but all Charon would say was:

"You'll have to grin and bear it."

"Well, can I see the inspector?" asked Evan, in desperation.

"I wouldn't advise you to; it will do no good."

Turning away, the cash-book man entered a telephone booth and called up Castle.

"This is Mr. Nelson," he said, "of Banfield. Can I see you, sir?"

"No," snapped Castle; "I'm very busy."

"But I want to tell——"

The receiver clicked. Evan was aware of an answering sound somewhere within himself, as though the ties that bound him to honesty and good-faith had suddenly snapped.

16

Blackballed

During the progress of the drama in which Nelson played so conspicuous a part and which he regarded as a tragedy, Sam Robb was at the Receiver-General's exchanging money for the paying-teller. He had not returned before Evan was gone from the office for good.

"What am I to do, Mr. Charon?" Nelson asked the accountant, after Inspector Castle's insult.

"Grin and bear it," repeated the accountant, thinking, no doubt, that he had hit upon a very happy phrase.

Evan felt that it would take all his moral valor to "bear it" without the "grinning." He fulfilled that latter half of Charon's command—it seemed like a command rather than a suggestion, to the bank-trained clerk—three or four years later.

"But what about the fifty dollars I owe the bank?" he asked.

"I suppose you'll have to put it up," said Charon, studying the expression of the face before him.

"But there is three months' salary coming to me, according to the Rules and Regulations," replied Evan.

The accountant did not have to scratch his head; apparently he was prepared to act deliberately.

"Well," he said, "since they haven't said anything about the silver you had better say nothing. We are paying you two weeks in advance; let it go at that."

For a moment Evan figured. There is no crisis where a bankclerk can't figure. Three months' salary would be $90. That was coming to him. But he owed the bank $50, and they had paid him $15 more than was due, leaving only $25 due him. It would not pay to fight them for so small an amount. In fact, he did not know how to fight; besides, the vim was knocked out of him and he only wanted to get away from that wretched office. A strong revulsion possessed him; he turned away from the accountant without answering, and his eyes wandered about the dark, bad-smelling office. He suddenly discovered that he hated every desk, every book, and the brazen-faced fixtures.

But coming to his own desk he found the work piling up, and mechanically he lifted a pen to straighten things up a bit before leaving. A good bankman, under any circumstances whatever, cannot endure to see things in a mess. Evan had scarcely taken up his pen to make an entry in the "bank book" when Alfred Castle glided toward him and said in a high-pitched, authoritative tone:

"Never mind that, Nelson; you're through here and we want you to quit."

The fired clerk was too badly wounded, for the moment, to be angry. Later, he wondered why Fate should have been so spiteful as to send Castle, above all others, on that humiliating errand. He suddenly remembered the way Alfred had greeted him on his arrival in Toronto, and came to the conclusion that from the first he had been under suspicion with that respectable nephew of the "Big Eye's."

Evan went down to the basement for his hat, not quite expecting to find it there; in truth, he would not have been much surprised to find the basement itself gone. Certainly, the foundation had disappeared from under a structure mightier and stronger, as he viewed it, than piles of stone and mortar. He had frequently criticized the office slavery of the bank, but he had never lost faith in the institution's magnitude and imperishability. It was the solidity of it that he had banked on and clung to, in spite of blinding work; but now the golden god had crumbled, like the smitten image of Daniel's dream—so far as Evan was concerned. The idol still stood for idolaters, of course, like that other image in the Prophet's time; but to the enlightened, the awakened, it had perished. And, to carry the analogy further, Evan, like Daniel, saw before he understood. He must have his vision interpreted for him. Time would accomplish that. Just now he gazed and wondered.

Clearly he saw a ruin, but as yet it was inseparable debris, and the sight of it put his head in a muddle.... While he washed his hands in the basement he stared at the wall, and looking away from that his eyes met those of Bill Watson.

"Hello," said Bill, hurriedly, "what are you fooling away your time down here for at this hour of the day? You must have the c. b. down finer than ever I got it, Nelsy. By gum, you've travelled some since you came here; I was on the job six months——"

Watson paused suddenly.

"What's the matter?" he asked.

Evan saw that Bill was uninformed. Such is the rush of a city office that one man does not know what happens to another, until the pipes are lit and "chewing the fat" commences.

In a few words Nelson told his old desk-mate what had happened. Bill was speechless. He did not even swear. He stood looking at Evan, but his eyes seemed too wide-open to see anything. While he was trying to frame words the voice of Charon sounded at the head of the basement stairs.

"Watson, Watson!" A customer was probably waiting to deposit.

Urgent as was the accountant's voice, Bill delayed long enough to shake hands and say:

"Come up and see me at the boarding-house; I want to tell you something."

Evan half promised—but never went. The next time he saw Bill they were far away from Toronto and banking.

As the cash-book man walked through the office with his hat in his hand, Marks, the C man, shouted:

"Hey, the banks are balanced!"

Evidently the accountant had kept the matter quiet. The boys who happened to see Nelson pass out of the front door probably thought he was taken with one of his violent headaches, and had gone for a druggist's dose. He had done that several times during his cash-book experience. Once he had been taken with an acute indigestion pain and a doctor was called in. The doctor advised him to take a taxi home. A few days later the bankclerk was presented with a bill for $3.50—half a week's salary. The indigestion, needless to say, had been caused by eating a cold lunch under the nervous excitement of waiting work. Another time he had been searching in the vault for a package of old vouchers and a book had fallen on him, breaking both lenses of his glasses: cost $4.50—more than half a week's pay. Those things were all "in a day's work," Willis used to say. So were board and bed. The fact of the matter is, Nelson was given nothing and had nothing outside of a day's work; a day's work was what he lived for. And there are hundreds of Nelsons in the banks now.

As Evan passed Charon, the accountant did not raise his head; nor did Castle lift his. Evan did not care; they were nothing to him now. Neither was the bank anything to him. He cursed it; in oaths he had never expected to use he cursed it.

With the very taste of profanity on his lips, Nelson stood absently gazing into a liquor store. The shiny bottles fascinated him. He wondered if the stuff in them was all that it seemed to men to be; would it drown care and disappointment? Above all, would it bring unconsciousness?

He had seen Robb lying drunk, and the sight had interested him. Robb's sprees were not bestial like Penton's; they were dead, harmless. That was the sort of thing Evan, in his melancholy state of mind, would like. He had tasted liquor and it rather tickled his palate; why not carry a bottle up to the boarding-house and go in soak for the afternoon? He knew it was wrong, but he wanted to do something desperate; also, he wanted to make sure of falling asleep and forgetting everything. He thought of his mother and sister, and of Frankie, as he looked into the liquor store. That was just the trouble, he thought too much about them. What would they think of his dismissal? It would break the mother's heart and the girls could never understand. Evan was in a torture of worry. He wanted to cry, as he would have done ten years before, but that was out of the question—he was twenty; so he repeated an oath that made him shiver and feel penitent, then went deliberately into the wine shop. He bought two flasks of cognac, and slipping one into each hip-pocket turned up Queen Street to University Avenue.

Mrs. Greig was in the kitchen when Nelson reached the boarding-house. He went quietly up the stairs to his room, which had been done up and would not see the maid again that day, and shut himself in. Unscrewing the top of one flask, he put the neck to his mouth and swallowed two gulps. The room was warm, but he did not think to open the window. He sat back in a wicker chair and concentrated his mind on the liquor. How much would it take to make him drunk? how long would it take? He looked for immediate results from the first two mouthfuls, and finding none drank again. Feeling a slight nausea the second time he waited several minutes, and a tingling sensation succeeded the nausea. Then he gulped some more, and the flask was half gone. He settled back in his chair and his eyes grew heavy. Afraid the effect might work off he drank again, after which the room swam so that he had difficulty in catching the bed. His mind was acutely alert to everything for quite a while, although his limbs were incredibly heavy. But by and by he seemed to see his soul retire behind a black drape—and came oblivion.

It was after-hours in the bank. The boys worked away as though nothing had happened. It had been whispered that Nelson was fired, but each clerk had something in his own experience which he considered just as sensational as that. Far from philosophizing on the treatment accorded Nelson, some of the boys made his misfortunes serve to emphasize the reckless awfulness of their own careers, the uncertainty of which was a source of pride and self-congratulation. There are bank-fools who take delight in the very unsubstantiality of their occupation; instead of treating their avocation with the seriousness one's life-work deserves, they look upon it as a game or a joke. These fellows are greatly in the minority, of course; but usually a city office harbors several of the type. Two or three of them had their heads together around the cash-book desk, where Marks was now reigning monarch.

"Shut up, will you," bawled the ex-C man, flushed with the worry of a new post; "it's a wonder they wouldn't fire —— things like you instead of a good man."

Marks was speaking to boys of longer service in the bank than himself; but it is an unwritten law that the cash-book man is supreme in his own circle—and the gabblers mentioned were standing on one of the radii. They glanced at his red face, his burly figure and small ankles, and gradually moved away.

In the furnace-room three old clerks were solemnly conversing, like the ghosts of departed bank-victims once incarcerated there.

"It's the old story, Sam," said Key, referring to something Robb had been saying about the Banfield affair; "Penton has gone there so recently the bank couldn't transfer him without rousing suspicion in the minds of Banfield customers; so they made Nelson the goat."

"They couldn't do it in Banfield, though," suggested Willis, "because everybody there must know the boy is honest. They moved him to the city to get him out of the way, and then waited a chance to fire him on a trumped-up charge."

Robb turned his head and expectorated on the concrete floor.

"Boys," he said, "it's too dirty to talk about. It's like them, by ——, it's like them! They know that Penton is the thief and crook, but they are afraid of losing business if they move him away. Evans tells me another bank had a man up there and thought of opening. Old Castle knows that, and he's afraid of giving a bad impression by shifting managers. But he wants to make Penton believe that head office trusts him, and in order to do that he fires the poor innocent kid. In cases like this, to justify its bluff about seeing and knowing everything that goes on, the bank *must* have a suspicion, the wrong *must* be atoned for. If it will not answer to convict the guilty one look for a goat. It doesn't matter a hang to the bank whether a fellow's reputation is ruined or not. Bah! I'm sick of it."

Willis smiled around the stem of his pipe.

"I wonder," he said, "what they'll do with Penton. They certainly must suspect him. They at least must know he's a booze fighter."

"Oh, don't worry," replied Key, "they're watching him. It doesn't suit their present purpose to fire him, therefore they keep him on; but they know perfectly well he won't try any more of his monkey work for a while. They'll soak him some time, when the psychological moment comes. I used to know the son-of-a-gun; he's a yellow dog, and he'll be good now for a while out of pure cowardice. As for drinking, he's not the only bank manager who souses regularly. They'll stand for him a while, until it will look reasonable to move him."

Robb grunted.

"They know Penton wouldn't take a chance on anything big in the way of a personal loan from the cash, and they'd rather have a teller lose fifty now and then than to lose business."

In that strain the three old clerks talked about the Business they had once—and their relatives still—worshipped.

Quite early Sam Robb arrived at the boarding-house. He met Mrs. Greig on the verandah and looked for signs of news in her eyes. But she merely wished him good-evening.

"Has Nelson been home yet?" he asked, forgetting to speak about the beautiful May weather.

"No, I don't think so," said Mrs. Greig.

"I suppose he went over to the Island," thought Robb; "although that wouldn't seem like Evan. I'll bet this thing has bust him all up."

Absent-mindedly Robb turned the knob of his room door and walked in. He uttered a whispered exclamation.

On the bed, in his clothes, lay the ex-cash-book man, dead to the world, as he wanted to be. An uncorked flask almost empty stood on the dresser, and beside it an unopened flask.

For a moment the humor of the situation struck Robb, and he laughed silently in a chair. But by degrees his face sobered, and he gazed pensively out of the window, a shade of sadness reflected in his countenance. At length he rose and taking the flasks from the dresser emptied their contents in a basin. Then he took off the sleeper's shoes and undressed him by degrees. Evan groaned during the exercise but did not waken. He slept through, indeed, until the following morning.

Very early he crawled out of bed and doused himself in the bath-tub. He was sick at his stomach and his head felt like a hogshead; unaccustomed to liquor as he was, the cognac had taken violent effect. He staggered, although perfectly "sober," and wondered if he would ever get his shoes laced. His room-mate in the bed opposite him heard the rummaging.

"Good night, Evan," he said sleepily, as though just turning in.

For a moment Evan was confused and actually thought it must be evening, but a smothered chuckle from beneath the sheets of the other bed notified him that it was really the morning after.

"What time is it?" he asked; "my watch has stopped."

Robb made an effort to keep sober, more than Evan had done the previous day, and told the time. He dressed with his back to the young man, indulging the while in inward bursts of merriment. The soberness of Evan's countenance made it all the more difficult for his friend to contain himself.

Evan did not suspect that Robb was enjoying a one-sided entertainment, until a mirror betrayed the fact; then he, himself, laughed. The louder he laughed, the louder he wanted to laugh. The old clerk joined him frankly, and when they had done, cried—

"Isn't this a ridiculous world?"

Evan agreed that it was. Gradually he lost his sense of humor, however, for after-intoxication is a series of reactions, and a headache reminded him that alcohol was said to be hard on the nerves.

"Where are you going?" Sam asked him, as Evan took his straw hat from a hook.

"Out in the air," he said; "I feel rotten."

"Get some good strong coffee, Evan; that will fix you up sooner than anything. Fresh air is too natural a remedy to cure an unnatural thing like a drunk, especially a fellow's first drunk."

Again the elder man laughed, and this time he begged his young friend's pardon.

"You mustn't be sore on me for having such a good time at your expense," he said; "but really I never saw anything quite so funny in my life. You the temperate and sober-minded cash-book man.... By the way, you must stick around here until you land a job."

Nelson began to say that he was under too great obligation already, and felt that it would hardly be square; but Robb interrupted him with a couple of powerful expletives, and they agreed to another week's companionship.

After coffee Evan thought he would like to walk down University Avenue with Robb, and did so for a few blocks; but the lightness of his head counselled a shady and steady bench. He fell by the wayside.

"Just rest up to-day, old man," advised Sam, "and don't worry. It's very dangerous to stew when you're already pickled."

Evan smiled half-heartedly and promised to spend the day at Island Park.

"I'm glad you're not coming all the way," said Robb, without much humor in his face.

"Why?"

"I wouldn't want your destination to be the bank, for fear it might sometime get to be your destiny—like mine."

"Are you glad they fired me?"

"Not exactly, Evan; but I'm glad you're out."

"What do you think of the way they did it?"

Robb glowered at a passing limousine.

"Don't ask me," he said fiercely. "From now on my daily prayer is for a chance to get back at them. I hope it will come. All my life in the business, Evan, I've seen instances, like this, of the bank's mercilessness. I'm sick and tired of it. It's you who are lucky, my lad, and I who am unlucky."

"Still," said Evan, "it's an awful thing to feel that you're suspected of being a thief."

Robb's eyes flamed.

"They don't think it," he said sharply; "the rascals know you are innocent! It is not their opinion that hurts, Evan, but their influence—I hope—" He did not finish it. "I wonder," he continued, "if these fellows know what it is to hear their hearts beat? They claim to be big men; they make a great display of affection among their own folk, but when it comes to showing humane consideration for someone, they can't do it. They only invest friendship or justice where it will, like the money they invest, bring big returns. The clerk is only one of the many who don't count with them. What does he matter to them?—they wear him out and pay him out for gain."

The ex-manager spoke with emphasis and his lips puckered as after a bitter expectoration.

"I hope," said Evan, "that some day you'll get a chance to quit."

"That sounds good, coming from you," replied Robb. "I only live on that hope myself. Sometimes it seems forlorn enough, though.... By Jove! it's after nine; I must beat it. I'll see you at dinner to-night, eh?"

"All right."

Evan watched the old clerk down the avenue, and he remembered the first time he had seen that gait. It was in Mt. Alban on a May day, too. The juvenile bankman had pictured himself walking down the main street of some town inside a manager's clothes and shoes—just like Mr. Robb.

But thinking made Evan's head thump. He decided it would be a good idea to catch a McCaul car and connect with the ferry for Island Park. He boarded the car, together with one or two women and a little girl carrying a lunch indigestible anywhere but on Centre Island.

The beauty and quietude of Toronto's rest resort and the sparkling freshness of the surrounding water, revived Evan a little; but a stronger liquid than H_2O was around his brain somewhere, and the Island became uncomfortable. In spite of the pleasant environment he found himself unable to take his mind off the bank and what it had done to him. Early in the afternoon, he suddenly imagined that he could endure no longer to sit and worry, so he took the ferry back to the city and went to the office of the *Star*.

After inserting an advertisement for a position as bookkeeper—saying nothing about recommendations—he waited around the Star office with a crowd of other work-seekers until the afternoon edition emanated from the large mouth of a small newsboy. He felt more like crawling away in some alley and dying than hunting a job, but he was anxious to obliterate the bank from his mind; and besides, he wanted to have another situation before writing home that he had quit the bank.

Evan did not have the faintest intention of telling his people he had been fired. They would not understand it, he knew. How could they understand such medieval work? This was not a day of inquisitions or guillotines! But when he was established in a better position than the one he had left, it would be easy to explain that he had resigned. He knew that his father was not much in favor of banking anyway.

The first ad that attracted the ex-clerk belonged to an abattoir company near the lake-front. He wasted no time in getting to their office.

"Where have you been working?" asked the manager.

"In the S—— Bank," replied Evan.

"Why did you leave?"

"My salary was too small."

"Well, I believe you will be all right. Just drop in to-morrow morning at nine o'clock, Mr. Nelson, and I think I can put you to work."

The salary was to be eight dollars a week with good opportunities for advancement. The slaughter-house smelt quite pleasant to Evan as he passed it on his way to the car. He felt joyful at heart, and hopeful for the future.

But, oh, that head, how it ached! What sense was there in drinking to drown sorrow when a fellow suffered so the day after? His stomach was sick, and he couldn't endure the sight of a wine-shop. After all, he thought, the liquor was not a drowner of sorrow, but a procrastinator; and, as in the case of postponed debts, interest was added.

Robb was in their room when Evan arrived at Mrs. Greig's boarding-house.

"Well," said the old bankclerk, "how do you feel now?"

"No more booze for me," replied Evan, smiling.

Robb answered with a smile. "I'm glad you're not worrying anyway, old chap. Things will be all right before long."

"The reason I'm not worrying," said Evan, "is because I've got another job. I go on in the morning."

He explained about the abattoir company's offer.

"Well, you're the limit! What salary?"

"Eight a week. They asked me where I'd been working, and why I left."

Robb asked quickly:

"What did you say?"

"I told them the bank, and said I left because of insufficient salary."

The elder man was thoughtful. "I guess that's about all you could say," he replied.

If Evan had not felt so fagged he would probably have written home that he had a new position: as it was, he went to bed early, and arose next morning feeling like a human being. He walked down the avenue with his room-mate, who wished him good luck at Queen Street.

It was before nine when he reached the office of the abattoir company. The manager came in punctually, and gave the young applicant a cold nod.

"Mr. Nelson," he said, "I'm sorry we cannot give you that position. I telephoned the manager of the bank you worked for and he referred me to head office, who said they could not recommend you."

Thunderstruck, dumb-smitten, unable to say a word in his defence against the lies of head office, Evan turned away. He walked north to King Street, more miserable than he had ever been in his life. He wondered, behind his misery, why the bank would not recommend him; were they intent on making a criminal of him?

The day passed slowly. Evan waited for his old friend at the boarding-house, and nursed a growing headache.

"I was afraid of it," said Robb. "Bank officials justify themselves and the bank no matter what happens. Besides being determined to carry out any bluff they have started they will never admit that they pay a man too little salary. If he quits because of starvation pay they say he was no good as a clerk. The bank must maintain at all costs what it calls its dignity. Dignity be—"

Instead of swearing the old bankclerk sighed. He had often said he was tired; now he thoroughly looked it.

Evan sighed too, but chiefly on account of the pain in his head. He went to bed both sick and discouraged, but in an hour he was too sick to think of discouragement. Mrs. Greig had a doctor in, and the ex-bankclerk was given a hypodermic injection. It drove away his pains and sent him sailing into a pleasant land.

Sam Robb did not rest so blissfully.

17

A Bankclerk's Girl

After three days' sickness Evan realized, and the doctor emphasized it, that he had been near to nervous collapse.

"The country and outside work for you now, young man," said the physician; "leave offices to men with broad shoulders, like Mr. Robb's."

"Yes," observed Robb, present at the consultation, "let them kill the man who wants to die. I think you're right, doctor; Nelson needs a dose of farming. I have it, Evan! .... I know a fine fellow on a fruit and vegetable farm near Hamilton. He'll be tickled to death to have you, as long as you want to stay; and you'll save money, too."

"A good idea," added the physician, to whose profession money usually looks good.

In a day or two Evan was ready to go in search of health. A telegram from Robb to the Hamilton man brought a phone response that fixed a salary of thirty dollars a month with board. It looked like a fortune to the ex-bankclerk, and he was eager to begin work.

"Before I go, Mr. Robb," he said, somewhat backwardly, "I want to ask you to do something for me."

"Name it," said Sam.

"I don't want my folks to know I'm out of the bank. If they knew I was farming for my health they'd be offended because I didn't go to Hometon. But I can't bear the thoughts of going back home down-and-out—-you know how it is."

Sam nodded. "I understand how you feel about it."

"Well, I'm going to forward the weekly letter I write to mother and let you re-mail it from Toronto, addressed on the typewriter. I'll only be a month getting in shape, and then I'll have an office job somewhere."

An "office job" embodied Evan's conception of success, as it did that of his relatives, and many another golden-calf worshipper. He had yet to be weaned.

"I'll do it, my lad," replied Robb, cheerfully; "now then, off with you. And don't forget to write. If, after a month or so, I run across anything in town that I think would appeal to you, I'll wire. Japers lives right in the suburbs of Hamilton, and has a telephone."

The "T. H. & B." carried westward a considerably happier mortal than had been in Evan Nelson's shoes for many a day.

Japers' farm showed up to advantage on a fine May morning. So did his daughter, Lizzie. She was plump, pretty, and peasant-like. Her efforts to sneak cream and sugar into the new "hand's" tea a second and third time were evidence of her normal good nature, if nothing more.

The first day out the ex-bankclerk did not do much. He was busy admiring the symmetry of gardens and orchards, though not of daughters. In his part of the country those who took any interest in fruit raising allowed the trees to grow up, out, and into each other without molestation, believing in the ever-lasting benevolence of Providence and the frailty of pests; with the result that fruit became wormier and scarcer every year. But in the "Fruit Belt" conditions were different; everywhere was order and care; the budding blossoms made the well-ordered fruit patches fairy groves for beauty. The first day of his sojourn Evan opened his nostrils, closed his eyes, forgot the bank, and thanked God some doctors knew their business.

His employer would have had him rest a second day, and particularly would Miss Japers have done so, but Evan wanted to show that he was a worker, and also had an eye on the coming dollar per day. So he walked manfully up the rhubarb patch and set to work. Occasionally a muscle slipped and he jerked a whole root out of the ground; but this error was remedied immediately by clawing a little dirt around the root and leaving it—to die. Evan, of course, was innocent of harm done: he saw no reason why rhubarb should not grow in loose dirt as well as tight.

In his sleep, the second night, he wandered in a field of burdocks, plucking the largest stalks for Burdock Blood Bitters. He stopped to chat with a buxom girl possessed of an innocent, rustic manner, and thought she laughed at his white, feminine hands. Next day, as a coincidence with his dream, Lizzie Japers did remark about the ex-clerk's hands, but the stains on them and not their whiteness elicited her observations—and decided her to telephone to the grocer's for a box of snap.

When his back got used to bending Evan began to enjoy gardening. He felt like a bird that had flown out of a cellar into a garden. Lake Ontario sent a breeze up to him, to carry his mind away on its wings. Peach blossoms were turning more pink; sight of them and the smell of them made the world irresistibly charming. Was it really he who had wallowed in janitor's dust and vault damps with a monster called "Cash Book?" Was not that but a figment of those vague nightmares he had had as a child, when he fell asleep with his clothes on?

Anyway, it did not exist now; and the superb happiness of that realization made the days fly—and days brought dollars. Of course, money did not matter so much now that he had no landlady to pacify; he would have been satisfied with fifty cents a day and board. Such meals as he got!—onions, radishes, lettuce, cream, butter made from real cream, eggs still bearing traces of the hen, and everything to build without poisoning.

During the first week a letter came from Hometon. It had been addressed in care of Mrs. Greig, Toronto, and forwarded by Robb. It was from Evan's mother. She complained of not having received much news lately, and hoped nothing was wrong. Above all things she hoped her son was not working too hard. The son smiled as he read; if his mother could only see him sitting in a lettuce patch, dairied and sleeves up, what would she think? What would Lou and Frankie think?

The letter Evan answered with was diplomatic. It went, in part, like this: "I am feeling better than I have felt for two years. The work I am doing is not hard on me; I like it mighty well. My health was bad for a while after landing in the city, but now it is changing for the better every day. My appetite is past the decent stage. And what do you know about this?—I'm saving money at last!" There were no committals in the letter.

The second Saturday of Nelson's engagement with Jim Japers, the old gentleman came around and said: "About time you was ringin' off, Mr. Nelson." (He always addressed his new man respectfully: could an ordinary mortal come out of a bank?) "It's Saturday, you know. Me and wife always goes into town a-Saturday, and sometimes the kid. We count it a day off, and now that's what we wants you to do."

A countryman always enjoys getting to anything pleasant in a roundabout manner. Evan felt the good news coming and warmed up to a full appreciation of it. Saturday afternoon in the bank had always been a time for cleaning up loose ends of work.

"Thank you, Mr. Japers," he said, warmly; "I believe a show *would* do me good. I didn't have time to see many in Toronto."

"That's right, my boy, enjoy yourself. They say them Toronto shows isn't as good as we get here. What do you think, now?"

"I don't imagine they are," replied Evan, quickly; and then, in one of those absurd rushes after an idea to make plausible a consciously absurd utterance, "I suppose it sort of—they sort of—"

"Yes, you're right," rejoined Japers, fully believing that he and Nelson between them could outwit most theatrical critics. The gardener and his assistant blathered away until Miss Japers was obliged to float her ribbons out of the front door in a dazzling hint that the family party was ready.

The Japers did not wait for Evan to dress; Lizzie was constrained to do so, but her mother looked so uncomfortably fussed up that the girl had compassion, and left the romantic excitement of a bankclerk's presence for the less alluring sensation of Hamilton's main street.

An hour or so later Evan sauntered up town. He did not feel exactly lonesome, there by himself in the Saturday crowds, but rather out of his environment. It seemed strange to him to have no immediate task on hand, to have nothing to balance or look up. His mind felt almost vacant, for want of something to burden it; but the vacant feeling was, oh, such a relief! Only the weary clerk can understand this thing; he knows so well what it means to carry a burden with him on a pleasure trip. "Pleasure" is not the adjective to qualify such a trip, where trees and flowers are decked with figures and where the mind sees phantoms of accumulated and accumulating work, waiting, waiting like Fate. Stories have been told of criminals carrying the body of a victim around on their backs until they stood on the brink of insanity. Hundreds of bankboys know what it is to feel the weight of corpse-like figures on their backs. One cannot get away from the horrible burden, it clings until the heart is sick and the stomach nauseated. And these monsters are not victims of the bankclerk's, either; the clerk is their victim; nor does he in any way merit the unnatural attachment—someone else digs them out of their graves (the bank "morgue" of accumulated back-work) for plunder, and saddles them on him.....

Evan's mind felt vacant; that was much better than having it loaded with worry, worry that could result in nothing but harm to the clerk and nothing but cold dollars to the bank.

The young ex-banker refreshed himself with a solitary sundae and then took steps in the direction of a theatre advertising the old drama, "East Lynne." He bought an economic half-dollar seat and entered while the orchestra was playing one of the reddest rags out. He had read "Mrs. Henry Wood's" great book, but he searched his memory in vain for a clue to the propriety of ragtime as a preface to the story.

A moment before the curtain lifted a girl came into the theatre and was ushered to a lonesome seat beside Evan. He was, gardener fashion, watching for his money's worth, and paid no attention to the person beside him until first intermission, when a squint told him that here was someone very like Hazel Morton of Mt. Alban. Then he looked fully into her eyes and held out his hand. She seemed surprised.

"Don't you know me, Miss Morton?"

"Why—I'm afraid—why, yes I do!"

They regarded each other a minute.

"You seem to have changed, Hazel!"

He was sorry he had said it. She blushed and did not look him squarely in the face as she replied:

"Hard work."

Evan sat wondering, in silence. Hazel had had a nice home in Mt. Alban. Had she run away from it? And how was it that she looked so subdued?—she used to be a vivacious creature, fond of dresses and gaiety. Now she wore a plain white waist and a skirt of cheap blue serge. The Mt. Alban color was gone, and pensiveness dusked her intelligent face.

It was, doubtless, to break the embarrassing silence creeping between them that Hazel asked Evan if he worked hard in Hamilton. How long had he been in that branch of the bank?

"I'll tell you after the show," he answered, "if you'll have dinner with me at the —— Hotel. We can go for a paddle afterwards."

She smiled and said it was very kind of him and that she would just love to spend the evening in that way.

In the second act Evan noticed that Hazel wiped her eyes frequently with a miniature handkerchief. He felt like doing it himself in the next act, and Hazel sobbed audibly. Of course, she was not the only weeping woman at that matinee.

At dinner a glow of the girl's old-time color came back, and with it a charm that Evan had noticed in her eyes at Mt. Alban dances, when a certain bankclerk was hovering near.

"Do you know what a boarding-house appetite is, Ev—Mr.—?"

"Did you say 'Mr.'? I've been calling you 'Hazel,' you know."

She laughed. "I meant 'Evan.'"

Evan suddenly recalled the last time he had bandied names with a Mt. Alban girl.

"Yes," he replied, "you bet I do. But I'm eating farm-meals now."

She looked surprised, and he told her about resigning from the bank, "because the work was too hard," and about coming to the Fruit Belt to recreate.

"You're what I call a sensible boy, Evan.... I wish....."

Hazel did not finish her wish. She blushed instead.

"You don't know how good it seems to meet you here like this, Hazel," Nelson observed, to relieve the situation. He knew perfectly well that her wish was about Bill Watson.

"I don't think you can enjoy it half so well as I."

"Why?" His question was curious, but thoughtless.

"Well—I'm lonesome," she hesitated; "I hardly ever go out—except when Billy comes over."

It was out at last, and then they became more intimate. As they walked down the street to the wharf, later, Hazel pressed his arm and cried softly:

"Did you see that? Don't you know her?"

"You mean the girl that just passed—the one in green? I was just thinking—wondering if that could be Sadie Hall, Alfy Castle's girl."

"That's who it was."

"Why didn't she speak, Hazel?"

The girl looked up into his eyes as she answered:

"I've met her on the street several times. First time I was with Billy, who had come over for a visit. Sadie nodded, and went on with the friend, at whose home here she is visiting. The second time I was standing in front of a confectionery talking to a girl who—well, who hasn't a very good name in Hamilton; but she works where I do, and anyway I would not snub her for the world."

"And Miss Hall has stopped speaking entirely, eh?"

Hazel smiled impishly.

"I gave her a fine chance to turn up her nose just now; I winked at her."

Evan laughed until his companion caught the contagion.

"They're well mated, Hazel—Castle and she."

"Yes, indeed."

When they were skimming through the bay in a canoe, Miss Morton's mind again reverted to Castle.

"Hasn't he always been a snob?" she asked.

"Don't mention him—it makes me sick to think of him. He takes it after his uncle, I think."

Nevertheless, Evan kept on thinking about the Castles, as he faced Hazel in the canoe, until at last and by degrees his story came out.

"Oh, the criminals!" cried Hazel. "Why do so many boys put up with it!.... Evan," she said earnestly, after a pause, "you have confided in me, now I want to confide in you." A canoe, it is said, affects people like that.

"It's something about Billy," she continued. "Will you tell me what I want to know?"

"If you ought to know, Hazel."

"Well, I should.... I—he—" The tears filled her eyes, and she seemed undecided whether to give them vent or wipe them away and be brave. She wiped them away.

"I left a good home and came here to work just so that I could be near him and help him. I've told him that I'll wait as long as I need to. I didn't want to go to Toronto, because I knew everyone in Mt. Alban would then say I tagged Billy. I'm willing to wait, but Billy seems so discouraged at times I am often afraid he'll run away or do something rash. Tell me, Evan, is he all right? Does he drink or—anything?"

Evan tried to recall something Bill had said that would cheer the waiting girl, but could not think of anything. He did remember the lectures Watson had delivered on the follies of clerkship; but to Hazel they would only indicate recklessness and dissatisfaction. And, too, Bill did take a drink frequently; in fact, Evan suspected that he made a night of it occasionally to "drown his sorrow."

"Hazel," he said seriously, "Bill is one of the finest fellows I ever worked with. I'm sure he's honest and true. He hates Castle and Castle hates him: that's something to his credit—but it may keep him back in the bank. But he'll never be false to a friend or a girl, I'm sure of that."

The girl in the canoe looked wistfully at Nelson. "Somehow I wish you were working in the same office with him. I always felt as though you were—a solid sort of a chap, Evan."

The last few words were accompanied by a little laugh, to counteract the suspicion of flattery that clung to them. But for that feminine interpretation Evan might not have so fully appreciated her meaning. He got a suggestion from her words: would it not be a good idea to write Bill and tell him of the evening spent with Hazel? It might give the slaving city-teller new vim for the eternity of figures and celibacy before him.

On Sunday Evan did write to Watson. He described Saturday's pleasure excursions with Hazel, dwelling on the enjoyment it gave himself and upon the sincerity with which she spoke of "Billy." Evan meant the letter to appeal. He knew that Bill knew him and would not resent perfect candor, when properly mixed with the right brand of sympathy. He thought, as he wrote, of the peculiar independence of character and cynicism of Watson; the combined traits amounting almost to recklessness. But he could not conceive of Bill's going wrong. He reflected that Hazel must love Bill, in spite of her fear that he was weak, and wondered at the tenderness of woman. Why was she so little considered in this world of business?

The Morton girl's companionship, quite naturally, took Nelson back to Mt. Alban, and Mt. Alban was only a few miles from Hometon and Frankie. He did not consider it likely that Julia Watersea or Lily Allen were still thinking of him; but he sighed when a vision of Frankie, with blue skirt and cheap white waist like Hazel's, rose before him. He wrote her a letter, the first in months, wishing her well, but saying nothing of love. A dollar a day with board wasn't much, truly, to apply against the great debit of matrimony, and why mention love at all if it could not be consummated?

To Robb, the vegetable-man also wrote, and to A. P. Henty at his home village.

Sunday night Lizzie Japers again fluttered her ribbons, and dropped a hint about church.

Afraid of losing his job, Evan accepted the bait and walked with the fair Liz toward the altar. It must have been hard for the organist to keep his fingers off a wedding march when he saw, in his mirror, the pair walking up the aisle.

Days sped again. June was come. Blossoms were falling and berries grew larger on the vines and bushes. A forwarded note came from Hometon, rejoicing in the promotion Mrs. Nelson had read between the lines of her son's letter, and in the miraculous recuperation spoken of. Lou had enclosed a slip of paper confiding to her brother the opinion that she should have a fellow, being now eighteen, and asking him to seek out an eligible and bring him home for the summer holidays. There was no word from Frankie. A fat, scrawly letter came from Henty.

Dear Evan,

After you left Banfield, old Penton was like a bear-cat. He tore around the office like something with the pip, took to chewing tobacco and spitting in the waste-baskets, and raised proper —— with the pups. He came up to me one day with Uncle Harry looking out of his eyes and gave me a short biography of myself. I stood it as long as I could, and then I seemed to be pitching in an exciting ball game. My right hand shot out, and before I knew it Penton was lying down at my feet. When he got up he almost cried, and tried to tell me he was just fooling. I noticed that night that the guns were missing from the cage drawer, and fearing that Penton had them in store for me, I packed my grip and beat it. A fellow's foolish to take a chance with a guy like W. W. My father was glad to have me home. He consulted a lawyer about my bond, and the lawyer said the bank wouldn't dare do anything about it under the circumstances; he said it would make too much of a stir and would hurt business. I imagine they'll fire Penton over the head of it; but I hope Filter doesn't lose his job—it would kill him. I wish you were farming like me; it feels mighty good after office work.

Write soon.

A. P.

When his muscles had grown until he felt the vigor of school days returning, Evan began to look higher than rhubarb and asparagus tops; he even looked beyond the Mountain, and saw himself in an easy chair with a telephone at his elbow and a stenographer in front of him. He wrote an answer to quite a few advertisements in Toronto papers; those to which he got a reply asked for references, as did those written in answer to his own insertions. Disgusted, he stopped advertising and answering ads.

"By Japers," he said to himself one day, "I'll beat it to Buffalo—there are no Canadian Banks over there!"

The idea took root in him. Also, he was counselled to leave the happy home of the Hamilton gardener by the actions of Elizabeth. She not only persisted in her cream-and-sugar attentions, but wheedled the "hired man" into taking her places, and finally began to speak of him as her "friend." Evan was willing to be friendly with most people, but the significant proprietorship implied in the tone with which Liz said "friend" was extremely discomfiting. The ex-clerk saw plainly that he must make a get-away.

Toronto offered nothing, neither did Hamilton; they were both bank strongholds. Buffalo, on the other hand, was in another country—a country to which almost every young Canadian turns his face, if not his steps, at one time or another. It was free from Canadian influence, a new world in fact, and yet only a short distance away. Inquiring at the ticket office as to fare, Evan learned that in two days there was an excursion to New York for only twice as much as the regular fare to Buffalo. New York! The name suggested adventure. Why not go there instead of Buffalo? It was only a night's or a day's journey from Toronto!

New York it would be! Evan sent the news sailing to Henty and Robb, but not home. Hometon would find it out when he had a position in the American metropolis. He called and bade Hazel Morton good-bye, and insisted on taking her out to the theatre. On their way home they dropped into a cafe for ice-cream. Again they met Miss Hall of Mt. Alban. She stared hard at Evan while he was not looking, and kept whispering to her lady companion.

"We don't care, Hazel, do we?" said Nelson.

Miss Morton smiled:

"What if she should go back to the Mount and tell Julia?"

Evan felt his heart sink.

"Hazel," he said, with awe, "you're not serious, are you?"

"Are you, Evan?"

"No. Why, I haven't heard from her in months."

The Morton girl looked at him in surprise.

"Do you think," she asked, wide-eyed, "that months mean anything to a woman?"

He showed his distress unmistakably. Hazel at last began to laugh, softly, with increasing merriment.

"My dear boy," she said, "what a serious fellow you are! The girl who falls in love with you for good and all, well—"

He gazed at her questioningly, gradually feeling a load leave him, a load that he did not know he carried. Hazel was speaking:

"Julia had a habit of juggling with bankers' hearts. She's married now, you know."

18

In the Country of Our Cousins

Hall's lawn was decorated with Japanese lanterns. The little Mt. Alban boys who passed in the dusk wondered if the time would ever come in their lives when they should be eligible for a real garden-party. Such a wondrous condition seemed very far off, like Heaven. And the little girls who passed peeked through the hedge, like fairies seeking admittance to a nymph gathering. There was no music as yet, for the evening had scarcely set in, but the tables were set and the lanterns threw a glimmer over the flower-beds and through the trees.

The party was, ostensibly, a welcome to the newly-married couple, James and Julia Watersea Simpson; actually it was to announce that Miss Sadie Hall had returned from Hamilton to accept the boredom of Mt. Alban again for a little season.

It is not for this bank story to enter upon details of that garden party; to spy on the sons of villagers behind dark balsams devouring cigarettes borrowed from the village cut-up; to play dictagraph to the gossips, or to hang around where the girls are chattering. However, there were characters at that lawn social more or less concerned in our story, and of whom we therefore ought to make mention.

Those characters occupied a place of prominence at the function, being seated close to Miss Hall herself. She was paying them flattering attention.

"Mr. Perry," she said, smilingly, "who would have thought you were going to turn out such a sport?"

Far from being offended, Porter grinned gleefully, and incidentally wondered where the money was coming from to pay the rent of the roadster that had brought him up to see his Hometon girl visiting in Mt. Alban.

"Well," he replied, "I never was what you'd call a willy, eh?"

"No," said Sadie, "but—well, you were so young, you know."

Porter's "girl" was talking in a low tone with a new bank junior who was beginning to realize what a juvenile and unromantic affair school had been. Sadie nudged Perry.

"You want to watch out," she whispered, so that the others could hear, "or you'll be losing your friend."

Frankie Arling blushed. The junior did too.

"N-n-no danger," he stammered, without knowing exactly what he said.

"Why no danger?" asked Miss Hall, anxious to say something interesting.

For answer the junior looked at Perry with the deference due a teller. Porter pouted—not like a child, but like a pigeon.

"Have some ice-cream, girls," he suggested, determined to convert the junior's respect into awe.

No one declining, the "porter" played a part long before assigned him in the Mt. Alban bank, and brought back a tray that had cost him eighty cents.

"Do you remember, Miss Hall," he said, to still a beating of the heart occasioned by the admiring glances of two strange girls in the circle, "the social we had here just two years ago?"

"Oh, yes," replied Sadie, after pretending to look backward through a great many sumptuous entertainments; "yes."

"All the boys were here. There was Bill Watson, myself, Mr. Castle, Nel—"

"Yes, that reminds me," interrupted Sadie, "I saw Mr. Nelson on the street in Hamilton the other day, and met him again in a cafe. Both times he was with—"

Sadie hesitated. Frankie was looking astonishedly at her.

"Why, Ev—Mr. Nelson hasn't been moved, has he?"

The question and the expression of voice behind it seemed to give Sadie an idea.

"I forgot—he comes from your town, does he not, Miss Arling?"

"Yes."

"Who was he with?" asked Perry, stupidly, "anyone we know?"

"Why—yes. Hazel Morton."

Frankie's question was not answered; but now she did not care to have it answered. She had been in Mt. Alban three days, therefore she had heard all about the Morton girl leaving a nice home to "be in a city where she can act as she likes,"—which, Mt. Alban females ruled, was wickedly.

It takes a girl, and especially one of Sadie Hall's stamp, to notice embarrassment or disappointment in another girl. Frankie was rather silent and downcast. She never talked much at any time, but even to Perry, with whom she was sometimes quite speechless, she seemed more than commonly quiet during the remainder of the evening. Of course, Porter may have been considerably on the alert.

"Is she related to him or anything?" Sadie asked Perry, on the side.

"Well—no," he hesitated; "their families are old friends, though."

"I could tell her something very interesting about him," replied Sadie; "he's been dismissed from the bank."

"What!"

"Sh-sh! Alfred wrote me about it. And that's not the worst of it—he's suspected of being a crook."

"For G—'s sake!" murmured Perry; and thought a while.

"Had I better tell her?" asked Sadie.

"I guess so; she'll soon find out, anyway."

Miss Hall found Frankie admiring a flower-bed, lonesomely, and approached her with the news she had. She knew that her Alfred hated Evan, who in his turn hated Alfred, and it was quite a satisfaction to circulate the truth about an enemy when it was unpleasant. To give her credit, Sadie was rather sorry she had done it, when she saw the effect produced on Frankie.

The following day Miss Hall met the girl whom Frankie Arling, of Hometon, had been visiting.

"Where's your friend?" she asked.

"Gone," replied the other girl. "She took it into her head to go home on the noon train, and we couldn't coax her out of it. I think she was lonesome."

"No doubt," replied Sadie, abstractedly.

Mrs. Nelson sat reading a letter, with tears in her eyes; another letter lay on the table. The one she read was from a woman-friend in Toronto. One paragraph of it puzzled Mrs. Nelson; it read: "One of the bankboys who boards here told me that your son had been discharged from the S—— Bank on suspicion. I think my boarder has made a mistake; he declares it was Evan Nelson of Hometon, though. Let me hear from you, Caroline, for I'm anxious to know that there has been a blunder."

The letter on the table was from Evan; one of those garden compositions sent through Sam Robb. It spoke about health, a good time and good board.

Frankie and Lou entered the kitchen where Mrs. Nelson sat in misery. She showed them the letter from Evan and the other one from Toronto. Frankie was silent, but Lou exclaimed:

"Why, mother! I'm surprised! Do you think for a minute that Evan would deceive us like that?"

"I can't believe it, dear; but what am I to do?"

"There's a mistake somewhere," replied Lou; "why, even if they have fired him it's all a mistake. 'On suspicion'—imagine! Why brother wouldn't take a—a—"

The thought was too much for Lou. What with lonesomeness for her brother and anger at the mere thought of anyone suspecting him, she gave way to a June storm.

Frankie was not free from signs of lamentation, either. She filled up more and more until there were raindrops from that quarter, too, and Sadie Hall's story came out.

Mrs. Nelson was overcome. Why had not her boy written about the trouble?

"Oh, Louie," she cried, "it's terrible! They suspect him of stealing! And he's discharged! Whatever are we to do?"

Lou raised her lovely face and forced a smile.

"Mother, dear," she said, "you know what a fellow Evan is. He doesn't want us to know about it until the thing is straightened out. It must straighten out, because we know he isn't guilty."

Such is a sister's logic. Mrs. Nelson telephoned her husband to come up at once. He came, and was told the news.

"Good!" he said.

"Why, George, how can you say that? They've ruined our boy."

Mrs. Nelson was taking it badly.

"Tut tut," said her husband, kindly, "don't get all worked up about it. He'll come around. There'll be an explanation from him some of these days. Jerusalem! but I'm glad he's out of it. I knew he'd get a lesson. Blast the banks!"

After this mild explosion Nelson walked to the water-pail and drank a dipper of water.

"But what's he doing in Hamilton?" asked the mother.

"That's only a fifty-cent trip from Toronto," answered Nelson; "the lad was probably over for a boat-ride."

"Well, what's he doing now?"

"I've got no more idea than you have, Carrie. But he won't do anything desperate, be sure of that. If he gets down-and-out he knows we're here."

At last Mrs. Nelson was consoled. She made her husband wire Evan at Toronto to come home. The telegraph operator surmised enough from the telegram to invent a story; it was supplemented by whisperings from Mt. Alban; and eventually the town gabs were wondering where Evan could have deposited the $50,000 he stole.

Besides the telegram, George Nelson sent a letter, telling his son not to worry, and enclosing a cheque for fifty dollars. Frankie Arling, in her little room at home, also wrote a letter:

Dear Evan,

We have heard that you are out of the bank. I think you were foolish to ever go into it. There are ridiculous rumors floating around that you were dismissed on suspicion. I know they're not true, and everybody else does; but still we are surprised you didn't write home something about it.

I don't suppose Hometon matters very much to you any more. The town is not so dull as it used to be, though. There is a new bunch of bankboys here, and we have plenty of good times. Mr. Perry rents a car occasionally and gives us girls a ride. He surely is a good-hearted chap. We all like him.

You will be surprised when I tell you that he has proposed to me. I don't think he'll ever make much money, but he'll always be free with what he has, and mighty good to a girl. He wants me to visit in London during summer vacation; he lives there. If I go he says he'll see that I meet a nice crowd. I haven't asked mother yet.

I guess you won't be coming home for vacation this summer, now you're out of the bank. It wouldn't be like you to come back a failure. It seems funny that you shouldn't have got along in banking as well as Porter: you are just as smart as he is. That fellow surprises me sometimes, though! I've been at him to quit the bank and go into something else. He shouldn't be proposing on six hundred dollars a year, should he? Well, good-bye.

Yours sincerely,

FRANK

After signing the letter Frankie dropped the pen and rested her chin on her hands. She gazed into space until the tears rolled down her cheeks; then she hid her face lest the looking-glass might see her.

"To think," she murmured, "that Evan sees girls like *that*!"

Girl-like, she had said nothing about Hamilton or Hazel Morton in the letter. She wanted to wound. Perry had helped her make Evan jealous once before. She was afraid mention of Hamilton would call forth explanations from Evan, and she didn't want him to explain. Even though he were innocent, she felt that she must hate him now, for she was jealous.

While the Mt. Alban garden party was in progress Evan attended one in New York—the Madison Square Garden party. There were no Chinese lanterns in evidence (although there were some Chinese), and the creatures who participated were not particularly young or care-free: there were the burning lights of Broadway and the Square, and wretched figures huddling on, beside, and under, the benches.

"And this is New York!" murmured Evan.

The melancholy sight fascinated him; he found it hard to leave Madison Gardens, although the White Way called to the youth and love of gaiety within him. He had never before seen so plainly the line of demarcation between sunlight and shadow. The startling proximity of riches to poverty, gladness to sadness, shocked him; he had a vague fear of something, he did not know what. Maybe it was the readjustment to come.

It is quite evident, from his loitering, that Evan was not worrying about himself. He had a job, therefore he sat and pitied those who did not have—and who did not want—work. Realizing at last that it was folly to pity without aiding, and that he was too poor to actually aid the wretches around him, he wandered across to Fifth Avenue and stared in the windows of a book store.

He had come to "town" (his room was in Brooklyn) with the intention of seeing a play, but the Madison garden party had taken away his breath, and left him without a desire to squander money on himself, when he had deliberately held it back from the hungry and the naked. Further reflection brought about a reaction in his mind, and eventually he compromised with himself by going to a ten-cent picture show. Afterwards he took subway and surface cars back to Eastern Parkway and found himself sitting thoughtfully in his little room.

Like a writer who gets "copy" on the streets and fixes it up in his garret, Evan thought the environment of his room would help him to arrange the impressions a trip to town had created, but—again like the writer—he found his head so full of notions that he could not think, and he understood perfectly that ideas apart from thought were poor things. So he turned in, bidding Madison Square and memories of Hometon good-night.

Quite early next morning he arose, fresh and eager, all vain philosophizing gone, prepared to hold his own in a big city. New York had not, from the moment he landed, frightened him. Like the child that looks into the fire, he saw only wonders. He had his health back, he knew he was a good bookkeeper, board in New York was cheap—why worry? He hadn't worried, and he had got work first crack! It is not hard to get a job in New York, unless you are in rags; but it is hard to get a good salary.

For a week now Evan had been engaged. The cashier, Phillips, told him he was going to be a good man for the firm. Phillips did not ask him where he had received his training: New Yorkers have no time for life-stories or autobiographies. Evan was surprised that they did not ask him more about himself, and for recommendations. Instead of saying: "What are your references, sir?" the boss had said: "What can you do?"

"I'm a bookkeeper."

"What experience?"

"Two years and a half in Canadian banking."

"Sounds good. What made you come over here?"

"Like every young Canadian," replied Evan, "I wanted to see New York."

Conscious of no guilt, he felt bold and spoke without fear.

"Well," replied the employer, "we'll give you a chance."

"Do you want a recommendation?" asked the Canadian.

"Nah," grunted the boss; "what good is that? If you can deliver the goods, all right; if you can't, out you go. As for your honesty, we depend on our ability to read character; after all, wouldn't you rather have your own opinion of a fellow than somebody else's? If ever you get to be cashier here we'll know you all right; not from Toronto references, but from daily observation. We learn to spot honesty here in Noo Yo'k: it's so dawn rare."

Evan smiled in spite of a desire to look solemn. He liked the "old man," and knew work with him would be pleasant. The office staff he liked, too, for they were free and easy, though mightily busy. It was a great change from the bank. No one seemed to be afraid of anybody else. The cashier was no bullier; although there was occasional friction, there was no subordination.

Everybody worked fast, but, for Evan, there was not the strain of a Canadian city bank. He knew there was no Alfred Castle watching him, and he knew that if a ledger went wrong requiring night work, the man who worked on it would be paid for every minute of overtime. Already he made fifteen dollars a week, and that was just as big as fifteen dollars would be in Toronto—it was bigger; it would buy more food and pleasure in New York than in any other city on the continent. Evan found it ample.

"If you keep on," said the cashier one day, "we'll be giving you more work to do."

Evan was surprised, and gratified. "I'll keep on," he said.

A few days after determining to keep on he asked for a half-day off to humor a headache. He was allowed an afternoon's leave.

On the way down to the ocean beach, where he hoped to soothe his palpitating cerebellum, he called at the Brooklyn room and found two letters and a telegram awaiting him. They had been forwarded by Sam, who had scribbled on the back of the telegram: "I knew you would have it in a few hours or I would have re-despatched the message." Evan smiled at his mother's anxiety—a letter had gone to her explaining everything; he had told her he was afraid his father would want to fight the bank in the courts, so he had kept the matter quiet until another position turned up. "No one ever wins in a suit against the bank," he said, "and Dad needs his money."

The cheque from home for fifty dollars looked good to Evan, but he hesitated before accepting it. Suddenly, however, he recollected a few little Ontario debts, and slipping the cheque in his pocket he thought what an unbusinesslike father he had. He sent a special letter of thanks, just as he would have done to any benefactor; he was not of the persuasion that everything is coming to the man who happens to be a son.

As a child saves the best bite of cake till the last, the New York clerk stowed Frankie's letter in his pocket until he reached Coney Island. He opened it as he sat on the sand, not far away from a group of attractive girls. Frankie's mention of Perry caused Evan to take note of a chilly breeze that was blowing over the surf. When the letter persisted and persisted in Porter, he suddenly thought the sun was mighty hot for June.

"Let her have him," the reader muttered; "she's welcome to him!"

Evan tried to make himself believe he had meant to say: "Let *him* have *her*," but that was not what he had said, and he knew it. He knew, too, that he could not coax himself to say it.

"She makes me mad," he muttered again; "what does she see in that mutt? Confound my head, what's the matter with it, anyway?"

Tearing the letter to bits, he ran into the surf. The girls had been watching him read and had been laughing over the expression on his face. They followed him into the water, and one of them managed to slip over the ropes beside him. The others made a fuss; and, not being used to swimming flirtations, Evan thought a real accident had happened. He bravely swam under the rope and rescued the water-nymph. An hour later, when they were all acquainted, he discovered that she could out-do him thrice over as a swimmer. But he was glad to know somebody in big, busy New York, and Ethel Harris was both pretty and smart.

Thus it was that the ex-bankclerk came to pass over Frankie Arling's letter, which had hurt him, and to take an interest in the pleasures of the present. Frankie and Perry, like the Past, were gone into eclipse.

In the course of months Evan became fairly familiar with New York, and with Miss Harris. The city stood scrutiny, and the girl—she was mighty fine. There was this difference between Ethel and New York, however: she was fathomable, as a girl should not be, and the city was not. Madison Square always reminded Evan of a dream he had dreamt in every fever of childhood—a nightmare in which a great wheel ran smoothly and little wheels crookedly; ran until the sleeper's brain was ready to burst with a sort of frenzy.

The people of New York turned out to be like the people of Toronto—and Hometon. Some were clever, and some were ignorant and dull. All of them were trying to make a living (except the predatory class) just as the farmers in Ontario were. Young men fell in love with girls and married them (occasionally), three meals a day were eaten, and sleep was popular.

And yet there was something about New York that was new and mysterious; its life was extraordinarily exhilarating. So many ten-thousands went to work and came from work every day at the same hours, it was like gazing upon the Creation to watch them. They lost their individuality, their human, insignificant (?) individuality, in the mass, and became a part of Adam's seed. Country people were less interesting than these New Yorkers, because country people were more independent. New Yorkers never looked at each other, but they felt each other; the atoms of the great mass, though separated by never-closing spaces, were held together by an eternal potentiality. There was a sympathy in the mass of city-folk, unspoken and even unobserved by many, but mighty—it was much more wonderful than the simple, verbal friendship between Jake Zeigler and Mat Carrol, neighbors at Bill's Corners. The power that held the atoms of the great mass together was the very same that gave each atom its individuality. Evan was impressed with the magnetism of New York, but he did not comprehend its strength. He came across atoms that had strayed off gradually, and been drawn back like lightning; but he understood but vaguely how the force operated, and why. In fact, who does understand?

The life he led, which was the New York life, kept the Canadian ex-clerk stimulated to a point beyond his power of physical resistance; he worked harder than the cashier wanted him to work. Those crowds that surged in every thoroughfare seemed to be behind him pushing him, and he could not take things easy. The strain was telling on him, though he tried to convince himself that it was not. Probably the lure of a great city would have held him up to the point of a break-down, had not a letter from his father set him thinking thoughts that changed his life once more.

When you build a house, Evan, you always want to have a solid foundation. So it is with a career. I hope you will, after a while, find your niche—I'm quite sure you have not found it yet. But don't worry—you'll get there: you have Grandpa Nelson in you.

P.S. I forgot to tell you that the bank's guarantee company and the general manager of the bank itself have dunned me for your part of the Banfield loss, fifty dollars. I laughed at them and told them to sue.

The postscript took Evan's mind back. It caused a burning in him that he knew must some day flare up. Unable to quench the resentment that filled him he bought some fruit and ate it as he walked along Wall Street, westward.

"Great heavens!" he muttered, waving his hand toward the marble halls of finance around him, "my country's got you backed into East River when it comes to a combination of Trusts!"

A few minutes after muttering this soliloquy he was in the crowds on Broad Street, directly opposite the Stock Exchange. A newsy thrust a paper into his hand, which he took and glanced at automatically. The first thing to catch his eye was a small headline over a news-item in one corner of the front page:

CANADIAN BANK CLERK SUICIDES

Evan felt his heart stop and a sickening shudder ran through him as he read:

Because he lost at the races and could not return money secretly borrowed from his cash, Sidney Levison, of the S Bank, Toronto, shot himself last night.

Of all the many thousands of New Yorkers who read that paragraph Evan Nelson, perhaps, was the only one who fully comprehended the meaning of it. He saw, as in a looking-glass, the gloomy series of steps down which the teller had come to where he lay, a suicide.

19

FAR-AWAY GREEN FIELDS

A germ began to work in Evan's mind. It must have been some relation to the garden-grubs that had infested Jim Japers' vineyard, for it showed a predilection for fresh air and outside work. Two incidents—the firing by the cashier of a clerk ahead of Nelson, and the receiving of a letter from A. P. Henty—did not help matters any.

Henty's handwriting had such a substantial appearance it seemed to indicate that some men were blessed with big fists to fall back on in case their fingers lost employment. A. P.'s composition, too, was solid and matter-of-fact; there were no flourishes, except occasional slang; the letter was plainly the product of a free mind and a steady nerve.

When the clerk who was discharged approached Evan with a smile and said: "Well, kiddo, you're next in line," Evan wondered why the fellow was so unconcerned about it. He asked him.

"Oh," answered the clerk, "we're used to that here, in New York. A fellow can always land another job. I usually manage to get the hook about twice a year; the work gets monotonous, and I suppose I lose ambish."

Evan wondered where one would get to under those circumstances. If he had stayed in the big city nine years instead of nine months he would have ceased to wonder about position hunters; they would have become a distinct element in urban life. As it was, the impression he received was quite true to the actual condition of affairs: a large city was a very precarious place.

However, the Canadian decided to stay in New York for the winter anyway; it was lively then, he was told, with the presence of returned "seasoners" and other summer absentees. He asked the cashier for promotion, and received it, along with two dollars increase in salary. He made up his mind to save five dollars a week; he could live and have considerable pleasure on the other twelve dollars.

Mardi Gras was over; not a straw hat was to be seen; the mornings grew chilly; theatres were in full swing. Then Miss Harris got Evan in with a "crowd"; the department stores hauled out their Christmas things; and with the first flurry of snow the whole town slid into winter.

The New York winter looked, at first, like a bluff. The man from Canada refused to wear an overcoat until one day a breeze came sweeping over the Atlantic and took him in hand; after that he had great respect for the climate.

Ethel Harris made good as a comrade. She knew how to keep things going. Evan was astonished at the ease with which he mixed in things; the boys seemed to have a way of fixing up that he could hardly catch, but they were a jovial bunch. An odd one was after the order of Castle, but most of them resembled Bill Watson in manner. The girls all expected to marry Riverside Drive property owners, but aside from that they were sane and congenial. Evan knew about how much money they made, and consequently took considerable delight in their exaggerations. They were practically all stenographers.

It takes New Yorkers to be friendly. The city is so big it resembles the world. In it there are as many countries as the world boasts, and when the members of a social set meet they come like so many travellers from the ends of the earth, bringing stories with them that Park Row reporters never hear about. There is real life and entertainment in a gathering of young Manhattanites.

Evan took great pleasure in those parties. Often he danced with some girl who had gone on the stage (for about one performance), and there was considerable romance in that. As the winter passed he wondered if he really wanted to leave those friends and that gaiety. Ethel treated him so well he was glad to spend all his spare money on her, at theatres, suppers and so on. But he always put away the five dollars a week just the same. He was led to believe that not many New York lads did that much for their future.

In February a Southerner came on the scene. The first night of his reception in the crowd he succeeded in breaking the hearts of half the girls; the other half succumbed the second night. The Southerner was not a flirt—that may have accounted for his elaborate success. He was so far from being a flirt that he fell in love with Ethel Harris and proposed to her.

Now, the real working-out kind of proposal is not so common in New York as, judging from the population, one might suppose. Ethel began to advise Nelson against spending so much money foolishly. For a while her objections to his "friendship" were overruled; but finally she got desperate and candidly told the Canuck he was up against Kentucky. He had to take the hint.

Thus, again, Evan was impressed with the uncertainty of things in the metropolis. He took Ethel's engagement to heart for a day or two, until an office-girl accidentally slipped while passing his desk and steadied herself on his neck. She proved to be a married woman, however, and Evan turned his attention to spring.

Appearances are against the ex-bankclerk, but he must not be judged too rashly on the head of his Manhattan experiences. It looks as if he had forgotten all about Toronto and Hometon; but he had not. He had never written Frankie, it is true, but he had heard about her from his sister and had a dim idea that some day he would go back and marry her. It is remarkable how a fellow sticks to his home-town girl! Through jealousies about other girls, like Ethel Harris, through the maze of a dance with actresses, he still sees the face that smiled on him across the school-room hack in the old town.

In March a very exciting letter came from Henty.

Dear Evan,

Wire me at once. Tell me if you'll come. I mean to British Columbia. The Nicola Valley is awaiting our arrival. There is a homestead there for each of us. My father will give me five hundred dollars, and I'll share with you, on a loan for life, if you'll come. A fellow only needs to pay ten dollars cash and hold down the land six months a year for three years, and make 'reasonable improvements.' I understand they are very lenient about improvements. Our five hundred dollars will look after that part of it. The soil is very fertile. I'm taking a cow with me and a clucking hen. In the winter months we can get a job bookkeeping or lumbering; or if our crop of onions turns out well this summer we won't need to work at all in winter. Wire. Don't let anything penetrate your nut for the next few hours but the word 'wire.' I must know. Don't let money keep you; if you need some, wire. What I have said goes, if you will come.

A. P.

Evan was sitting in the elevated when he read the letter. It had come as he started to work and he had not had time to stop and read it at his lodging. Again at the Bridge he read it. Around him the crowds were surging, rushing to work with that morning vigor that looks as though it would last forever. The merry throng about Evan seemed like his friends; the thought that he should leave them made him lonesome. What would he do without the morning paper? Where would he buy peppermint chocolates at twenty-five cents a pound? Even more trivial questions than these occupied his mind.

Stuffing the letter in his pocket, he boarded the up-town L, and got off at Twenty-third Street. The Metropolitan tower looked disdainfully at him: it was the New York flag-pole, and he was about to desert the colors. At noon-hour he sat in the little restaurant on Twentieth Street West. He had the letter memorized by this time, but he drew a bank-book from his pocket to make sure he was familiar with its contents. Yes, the eighty dollars were still there.

After work he was tired. He was always tired after a day's office work. The hour before supper was always one of yawning, of hurry, dust and reflection. Taking the subway down to the Bridge, he wedged up the steps between two foreigners who had been regaling themselves with garlic, and looked wistfully at Loft's. There was a candy-fiend in his stomach crying for food. He was half way to the candy-shop when he overcame the evil one with a sweet tooth; he turned back toward the Bridge, but seeing a crowd in one of the newspaper offices, stepped in. His ear caught the click of a telegraph instrument. He forgot the crowd gazing at new aeroplane models, and found himself again on Park Row. The ten-thousands faded from before his sight, the yapping of newsies died away, there was no dust and no yawning: he saw a green valley and heard the birds; he saw Henty in chaps astride of a pony; and a shanty loomed up. The blood of Grandpa Nelson bubbled in his veins; he was a proud son of Adam, doing business direct with Nature. There was no car to catch on the morrow, and no hash-house to patronize. His horses neighed to him, and he heard the sizzle of frying ham in a clean frying-pan.

The telegraph instrument continued to click in the young book-keeper's ears. He looked once more on the throng around him: it was the evening throng—tired, nervous, hateful. Men climbed in the cars ahead of pale, helpless girls; an old lady clung to the unwilling arm of a convict-faced son; and a little newsboy cried brokenheartedly in the gutter. Tiny girls wrestled with bundles of papers; a bald magnate cursed his chauffeur for refusing to run down a dog and save time; and a policeman chased half a dozen naked urchins who were puddling in City Hall Fountain. When one is tired these things jar on him. The telegraph still ticked in Evan's ear; the valleys still stretched before his imagination. He was aware, now, of a discord in the music of his dreaming: it was the noise around him, the shouting, the brutal rush. He turned toward Broadway.

Evan had made up his mind. He wired Henty that he would go to British Columbia. He asked A. P. to reply by day-message to Twenty-third Street.

About noon next day the answer came: "Meet me in Buffalo in two days, if possible. I will be staying at my cousin's, — Forest Avenue. If necessary I can wait a week for you."

But it was not necessary. Evan had no difficulty in getting away from his position. The cashier was disappointed, but he did his best to hide it; Evan heard him remark to the assistant cashier:

"When we do land a good man he gets offered more elsewhere. If I wasn't afraid of the boss I'd raise Nelson to twenty-five dollars rather than lose him."

Wondering, for a moment, if he had not done a foolish thing in resigning, Evan scratched his head, but the friction set his imagination aglow again—and he bade the office good-bye.

He met Henty in Buffalo the following night.

"What are you going by way of the States for?" he asked.

"So that the Canadian banks won't get you again," said Henty.

After sending his mother a silk scarf and Lou a pair of stockings and a box of candy, as a partial atonement for the wrong he was doing them in not visiting home, Evan bought a pair of corduroy breeches and heavy boots, subscribed for a farm magazine, and set out, with big A. P., for the far-away fields. They say those fields always look green; sometimes, perhaps, they *are* green.

Just as that "Overland Limited" sped along must this story speed. The boys fell asleep in New York State and awakened many miles from its border. And here in this story, as in a Pullman, only more obliviously, must the reader sleep—to awaken at a distance.

In a certain part of the Nicola Valley stood a cottage known as the "Bachelors' Bungalow." It, was alone except for the companionship of stables and out-houses. It was evidently not built in a land where lumber was scarce, for wide, heavy verandahs almost surrounded it.

From any of these verandahs one could get a splendid view of the mountains; to the south a green vista of valley stretched away.

A young man sat in the open, not listening to the greybirds or the meadowlarks sing of spring, and not revelling in the beauty before and around him, but working assiduously at a typewriter. On either side of his little table magazines and newspapers lay in heaps; there were Montreal, Toronto, Winnipeg, Calgary, Vancouver and other papers, and various Canadian magazines. Now and then he paused in his writing to pick up one of these periodicals and take note of a paragraph he had marked.

"I wonder if Alfy ever stops to read any of these articles?" murmured Evan, and laughed quietly. "Judging from the opinion he always had of my disability I doubt if he would attribute literary efforts to me."

Now that we know who the young man is and what he is doing at a typewriter in the Nicola Valley, it may be well to explain the situation.

Three years had passed since Henty and Nelson landed in the green fields of their dreams. They bought seed and other agricultural necessities on the way out, old man Henty shipped them two cows, two horses, a few hens, a pig, and some farming utensils. They ordered lumber from a Revelstoke company, erected a shack, a temporary shelter for the stock, and built a hen-house with a pig-pen annex.

A. P. showed that he was born to be a farmer. The way he handled the plow put Evan to shame; but Evan made up in willingness to work what he lacked in physical efficiency. He learned to milk cows and make butter; he went irregularly to the village for the raw food they needed, talked the merchant into giving him a line of credit, and surveyed the valley all the way home with the pride of Noah after the flood. He developed into so good a cook that A. P. declared there must have been a chef in the family away back.

The first crop the boys had was good because it was not very big. They sold their early garden-stuff at a big price to the C.P.R., and in the fall got twenty dollars a ton for their potatoes—on the ground. Every drop of milk they could spare found a ready market in the village; often they exchanged it for butter. And those hens of theirs made good; they made very good. A. P. insisted on eating all the eggs, but Evan managed to hide away enough each week to buy sugar, tea and bread. It must be admitted, however, that bread was more frequently absent from than present at the board; crackers and ginger-snaps made edible substitutes.

When the first winter set in the bachelors of "Bachelors' Shack"—it was not a bungalow yet—were prepared for it. They had money in the bank.

"It's me for a Jew's harp and a line of novels," said Henty; "no lumbering for mine this winter. I'm all calloused from wrestling with our valley."

Nevertheless A. P. could not content himself to read longer than a week at a time. He made irregular excursions into the village and juggled scantling in a new lumber yard. Evan wanted to go, too, but Henty grunted in disgust—and Nelson agreed to stay home and tend the stock. The sow old man Henty had given them raised a family. One of the pigs was killed for meat, and the others were dressed and sold to a butcher.

The winter was mild, and there was enough snow to protect and fertilize the ground. It was a good winter for the young bachelors; the wood-chopping they did gave them health abundant, their chores kept Henty's superfluous masculinity worked off and taught Nelson the practical way of things, and the simple food they ate gave their minds an appetite for knowledge.

With all their wood-cutting and chores, though, the boys had more spare time than they knew how to dispose of. Often in the evenings they played cards, sang duets from a book of old songs, or read. To say they were always content would not be true; many a time they felt the weight of the great Silence about them, and above all they longed for the fleeting image of a girl. If they could only just see one—it would be like a drink of water on Sahara!

At long intervals they hired a boy from the village to watch their flocks for a couple of days, while they made an excursion to some town. There they filled up on candy and picture-shows until they were glad to return home.

In many ways the first winter of their squatting in the Nicola Valley was a tester on the ex-bankclerks. They sometimes felt like giving up; not because they needed food or drink, but because of the youth in them. Young men are impetuous animals; they want to be forever shifting. Sometimes Evan had to walk in the beautiful winter night until he was tired out, so that he could forget his yearnings for city life, especially New York life. He felt the lure of the White Way at a distance of three thousand miles. Others had felt it from the ends of the earth, and had succumbed to it.

But Nelson did not succumb. He knew he must take his mind off the East, if he would succeed in the West, and he did so. He read more and more every week. When Henty was away at the scantlings Evan studied and thought. At last he began to write down his thoughts; he discovered that there was great satisfaction in expressing himself to a sheet of paper. He eventually sent to Vancouver for a typewriter, bought a book of instruction, and for twenty-one days studied the touch method. He practised six and eight hours a day, with his eyes on the chart before him. At the end of the twenty-one days he was a touch-typist, accurate and fairly rapid. The typewriter off his mind, he wrote and wrote. His heart was fast wrapping itself in vellum. Henty looked on in silence for a few weeks, then shook his head and said facetiously:

"I'm afraid you don't love me any more, Nelsy."

But spring soon came to A. P.'s relief, with the advent of which Evan had to set aside his typewriter and dream without writing down his dreams. Because of faculties newly awakened, however, he found more beauty and entertainment in Nature than he had ever seen there before. He began to think poems as he worked on the land. The plots of stories came to him, and articles grew upward from the horizon to the sun, or in columns like Oriental writings. At night he would sit up an hour longer than his big red-faced friend, and pour out his imaginings to the typewriter—the poor typewriter. The speed he developed was a detriment to composition; the faster he went the more hyperbolic and awful became his effusions, and so we repeat, the poor typewriter! It had brought about its own terrible punishment.

The summer passed, bringing its crops again, and another batch of pigs. A mare and a cow added to the animal creation, too. Old man Henty sent out a reaper and commanded his son to grow hay the following year instead of buying it from the Okanagan Valley. The boys built another out-house, bought some calves, and kept adding to their effects. The calves gave Evan copy for some humorous stories, several of which were good enough to be rejected by an Eastern magazine. The young "writer" thought the "not available" slip had been written especially for him, and its wording flattered him to further submissions.

The second winter was almost a repetition of the first—for Henty; but not for his companion. They made a trip to Vancouver at Christmas and sent bundles of presents home. A. P. loaded up with novels, and, to Evan's consternation, bought a guitar. But he learned to strum it, although it took him all winter.

Henty was a marvel in his way. Nelson put him in many a sketch and story. Not once during the long months had the Banfield ex-junior acted the part of a weakling. Evan reflected that it was easy enough for himself to keep within bounds, speaking after the manner of Physical Culture, being mentally engaged all the time; but Henty seemed to contain himself by force of will. His virility made a man of him instead of being a snare to him. Evan conceived a hope, founded on the respect he had for his companion, that was some day going to be realized.

A. P. took increased interest in the writings of his friend.

"Evan," he said, one day, in his sudden way, "I should think that a fellow with your habit of writing would tell the story a certain ex-bankclerk has to tell about the bank."

"By Jove!" exclaimed Evan.

He went right to work on a long bank story. He wrote it over and over, and submitted it over and over, but it did not meet with success. One editor told him it was too lurid; another said it was immature. Henty swore it was the best thing he had ever seen. Is it not unfortunate that our manuscripts cannot be finally edited by someone who can *appreciate* us? Gods of Literature! what a bunch of stuff would be printed. Typewriter companies would do away with the instalment plan entirely.

Between seeding and haying the third spring, the boys built a bungalow, enlarged their animals' quarters, and hired a man. They were blessed with a pretty good crop, and the market was growing. Other settlers had come into the valley, and there was talk of a village springing up near-by. Henty began to wear a smile.

After the fall rush Evan settled down harder than ever to his literary efforts. He wrote articles on the bank. As if his style had suddenly come up to the required standard, editors began to write short letters of excuse with returned manuscripts; then to accept. Why waste words on the thrills Evan, yes, and Henty, experienced when they read the breezy stuff of "X. Bankclerk" in print!

In his letters home Evan intimated that he would have a surprise for them before long, but that was as much as he said. He filled pages describing his and Henty's vines and figtrees, and his father came back with: "I told you your grandfather was in you!" His mother rejoiced in his health but longed for him home; Lou called him a "rube;" and Frankie—Frankie did not have a chance to say anything because Evan had never answered that letter she wrote to New York.

※

Now, as the young man sat on the verandah of his bungalow, not listening to the greybirds and meadowlarks around him, he felt happy. He and Henty were going to make a trip back to Ontario in the autumn, and then he could meet the editors who had congratulated him on his "good dope," as one of them had described his articles. He rattled over the keys of his machine, after making the observation about Alfy, and was so engrossed in his work that he did not notice the approach of Henty.

A. P. had been to Vancouver, and was back sooner than expected. He seemed excited.

"Evan," he cried, jumping on the verandah, "we're made men! A syndicate wants our land! They're talking of a townsite!"

"The dickens!"

"Yes, sir. They offered me $60,000, half cash."

"You're drunk, A. P.!"

"No, sir. You know the head of the syndicate; his name is William Watson."

20

High Finance and Promoting

It took Evan some time to recover from the shock association of Bill Watson's name with a real-estate syndicate naturally produced. Then he asked Henty bewilderedly:

"Are you going to accept the sixty thousand?"

"Am *I* going to?"

"Yes."

"Not unless my partner is willing," replied Henty. "Isn't one of these quarter-sections your own?"

"Yes, but you're manager of both; I don't know whether they're worth $60,000 or not. Would half of it look good to you?"

"You bet," said A. P. "I'd take a trip around the world, then come back and get married; I believe I'd settle down somewhere out here."

"Who would you marry?"

"Oh, anybody. I feel right now as if I could fall in love with anything."

Evan laughed, but soon sobered in thought,

"I think, A. P.," he said, after a pause, "that I can suggest a better trip than one around the world. I've often dreamed about it since my bank stuff has been well received. You know I've been drumming up the idea of Bank Union pretty strong. Why not bestow an everlasting favor on Bankerdom by travelling into every nook and corner of Canada and organizing the clerks? You and I could do it. They all know me by reputation, and I would give you credentials."

Henty ran his hands through his hair and looked wild.

"By the jumping Jehoshaphat!" he exclaimed, "what a hit that would make! Why, the boys would make a bronze image of you and a stone one of me to pickle our memory forever! Do you think we could do it?"

"Sure," laughed Evan; "haven't we got all the big newspapers in the country on our side? And aren't the banks in the legislative limelight? They couldn't pull off anything mean on us, because we would keep in touch with our editor friends. If they started firing the boys we could appeal to the public."

Henty grew more and more interested, not to say excited.

"You seem to have got the thing all cut and dried!"

"I have," said Evan; "I've been conning it over for months. At first I wondered if I couldn't get some rich man to endow such a movement, and make a real philanthropist of himself. But the trouble with rich men is that they want to get richer, and bucking the banks is no way to do it—in Canada, anyway."

A. P. let his eyes wander over the valley and up the mountain side. A smile gradually spread over his features.

"Nelsy," he said, "are you sure you haven't got an axe to grind?"

"You bet I have. Was there ever any sort of reform started by a man unless he had known the evil in his own experience? My grudge against the bank is going to be the boys' safeguard, and they will know it. They will know I'm out to organize a union because I want to show the banks that they are not supreme. Of course if it were for the satisfaction alone, I wouldn't spend a lot of money working it up. I know it will be a great thing for present and future bankclerks—that's really why I want it. But, you see, the boys will know I'm not out for graft when I have my own story printed and circulated among them. Besides, I won't collect any money; I'll merely carry the union up to a point where organization is possible, and then they can entrust the finances to anyone they choose.

The thing must appeal to them as a business proposition; I think they understand already that a union of clerks would be self-supporting. Some of them are suspicious because of past bunco games that have been pulled off under the guise of bank unions; but I will leave them no room for suspicion of us fellows. As to the moral success of the thing,—as soon as they realize it is past the dangerous stage they will be eager to join. Every effort so far made in the direction of an association of bankclerks has been squelched by the head office authorities. There was one instance in Toronto of a bank's firing quite a bunch of clerks who dared to defend themselves against the barbarities of the business. The press didn't even get wind of it. Things would be different now, and the boys would soon understand that; for the whole country is discussing those articles I have submitted, as well as the innumerable letters and articles of endorsation that have come from other clerks and ex-clerks."

"I'm ready to pack up," said Henty suddenly, half-jokingly. "But we haven't got the dough for our land yet. They want word at once; will I go to town and wire them?"

"Yes," replied Evan, mechanically, his whole mind on the bank.

"And how about the girl I'm going to marry?" asked A. P., as he led his horse up to the verandah.

"She's in my home town," said Nelson; "her name is Frankie Arling."

"Some name, too," observed Henty, dreamily; "you're not fooling me, are you?"

"No," replied Evan, smiling inscrutably.

Together they ate a bite of supper, and then Henty set out on horseback for the village. He returned before Evan was in bed. Next morning the hired man was informed that he would be left alone for a day or two, and to watch that the old sow didn't get any more of the hens.

Togged out like the homesteader sports they were, Evan and Henty left for Vancouver. They met the syndicate, who seemed to know every foot of land in the Nicola Valley, signed over their 320 acres, received a cheque for $30,000 and a note with security for another thirty, and refused to participate in a drunk.

"We must get back," said Henty; "I've got the live stock to sell yet."

Bill Watson and Evan excused themselves and went into a side office. It was their first opportunity to speak of old times.

"I can't tell you how glad I am you've made good, Evan," said Bill. "How did it all happen?"

Evan briefly related his experience since quitting the bank. Watson listened with interest until it leaked out who "X. Bankclerk" was, after which his silence changed to: "God love you for that!"

Without heeding the exclamation Evan continued with his story, and finally announced his intention of starting a bank union.

"You can do it," said Bill, enthusiastically, "and I'll back you if you need more money. I knew it would come. It had to come!" Then, "Won't you come down and see Hazel?"

"What, you're married!" cried Evan.

"You bet. I kept her waiting long enough, didn't I? But say—won't you come down and see her? I've got something more startling still to tell you about; two things!"

Evan wanted to see Hazel and to have a visit with Bill. He persuaded A. P. to stay over a day.

Hazel was a changed girl. There was the same old peculiar fire in her eyes, but she was now healthy and happy looking.

"How good it is to see you, Evan," she said, giving his hand a generous squeeze. "Look who's here!"—pointing to a cradle.

Evan got on his knees to the baby, who acknowledged the attention with a coo.

"I'll bet you have started already to spoil him! By the way, Hazel, the little chap reminds me: how did you win Bill all so suddenly?"

Hazel smiled happily:

"Only about a month after you wrote Billy he came down to Hamilton and informed me we were going West—together."

Bill turned and looked at Evan.

After supper, while Henty was dividing his attention between Hazel and the baby, Bill whispered to Evan:

"The boy is one of the surprises I had for you. I've got another—come in the smoking-room."

Nelson followed, excusing himself with Hazel and Henty.

"Haven't you been wondering, Evan," said Bill, puffing in his wonted fashion at a cigarette, "how I got—well, where I am?"

"I admit I have, Bill."

"Well, just listen to my story, and ask questions when I'm through.... Shortly after receiving your Hamilton letter I made up my mind to get some money somewhere and marry Hazel. She was working her head off and worrying herself to death about me; I couldn't stand it any longer. I made up my mind to *get money*. My chance came. The cash was short one thousand dollars one day—*my* cash. I explained that I must have paid out two hundred tens instead of fives. It was Saturday; they had transferred me to the second paying-box just a few days before. I figured that here was my chance to make a mistake. Now, being over twenty-one I was my own bondman, and the bank couldn't collect from anybody but me—or the guarantee company. I knew that, of course. Well, I pretended to worry myself sick over the loss, and checked my vouchers over about a dozen times. At last I pretended to give up, and told them I would look no more for it.

"'All right,' said Castle, 'you'll have to put it up.'"

"I said nothing just then, but before long I told them I would go to jail before I'd put it up. I went to the manager, then to the inspector, and hung the bluff around. At last they decided to kick me out of the bank and let the guarantee company make good the loss. I hung around Toronto for a little while, with two five-hundred dollar bills tucked under my shirt. Soon I made a trip to Hamilton, captured Hazel, and came to Edmonton, Alberta. I struck it rich there. I cleaned up ten thousand bucks in a few months. After that it was easy to get fifty thousand. I'm worth a hundred now."

Bill smiled around his cigarette, and waited for his friend to speak. It was no easy matter for Evan to find words, either, although he felt that Bill was telling the truth.

"Did you ever pay them back, Bill?" he asked, expectantly.

"Oh, yes," said Watson, drawing a registered-letter slip from his pocket. The receipt was made out to John Honig, for a thousand dollars. "Some assumed name that, eh, Evan?"

"Yes. How long did you hang on to the coin, Bill?"

"You see the date. I kept it as long as I thought it was coming to me. You know I labored like a lackey for five years on half pay in the bank. They really owed me every cent of the thousand, but I only pinched the interest on it for two years. That wasn't much, eh? It made me rich, though; and so I ought to forgive the bank. What do you think of me, Nelsy, as a one-time Sunday School teacher?"

"I wasn't thinking of the right or wrong of it, Bill, but of your nerve. Just imagine what would have happened if they had caught you."

Bill laughed disdainfully.

"Jail couldn't have been any worse than that office. My conscience troubled me a while—until I found that the thousand was making me more. Then I knew I could pay it back when I liked. When you come to figure it all out, isn't that exactly what the banks do with the people's deposits?"

As the train wound its way along gorges and through tunnels eastward from Vancouver, Henty and Evan were silent. Evan was thinking of what Watson had done, and said. It was a fact that banks gave three per cent. interest on deposits, which they used on speculations in Wall Street and elsewhere; those speculations netting them such high dividends that great buildings had to be erected to conceal them. And how was the customer treated who wanted to borrow a few hundred dollars in an emergency? Even though he had been a depositor for years, getting three per cent., what sort of accommodation was the bank willing to give him when he was temporarily up against it? Evan knew. He remembered too well the old excuse handed out to the customer, year after year: "We have to cut down our loans." Why did they *have* to? Why *do* they have to? Who makes them, who wants them to do it? The eternal answer is "Head Office." But who is Head Office?—the bank. The bank commands the bank to cut down its loans, just as it commands the bank to do many things detrimental to the country's good. And why not? Don't the people of Canada stand for it? Don't they give their money and sons to the banks, according to the traditions and idolatries of their fathers?

Evan's mind dwelt upon High Finance. He pondered and pondered on the thing Watson had done, and, in the light of common business morality, could find no fault with it; but in his heart he knew it was wrong. The argument he found against it was a trite one, but true: "The wrongs of others are no palliation of ours." If the banks did wrong in using depositors' money to earn dividends for the rich, that was not the clerk's business—that was the *public's business*.

What then was the clerk's business? It was the clerk's business to see that he received a decent salary. He did real work, oh very real! and he was entitled to a salary upon which he could both live and, at a reasonable age, support a wife. Why didn't he get it? Because the bank could, by intimidation and repression, by promising and bluffing, get him for less than a living wage. But "why" was not so much to the point as "how." *How* was he going to get it? How had other workers of every description obtained a bread-and-butter wage? By making themselves indispensable to their employers? Yes. And how accomplish that in banking? If any man thinks he can make himself indispensable to a bank *individually*, he is mistaken. But men in any trade or calling can make themselves necessary to an employer *collectively* by co-operating; and co-operation is the only way. Evan knew that it was the only way for bankclerks to obtain their rights. The banks would not do business with an individual because they didn't have to; it was easier to dismiss him. But their offensively arbitrary methods could not be employed where a great number of clerks were concerned. If the bankclerks of Canada were united they could talk as a body, and the banks of Canada would be compelled to listen. It did not occur to Evan for a moment that the boys would go on strike: but they would have the power to strike, and, if the banks were mad enough to resent business negotiations, they would show that they *could* strike.

Henty wakened out of his reverie and Evan began discussing bank union with him. They had money in their pockets and enthusiasm in their souls. They discussed the workings-out of the scheme, and youthfully pictured scenes that were brightest. Still, had they not dreamed of green fields and seen their dreams come true?

"How much are we going to spend on it, Evan?" asked Henty.

"I figure it will cost us two thousand dollars each to get the thing in motion. Then if the organization ever gets rich enough it may want to pay us back. Do you feel like affording so much?"

"Sure—I don't mind a couple of thou'."

Nelson laughed; he was happy. The spirit of the reformer had somehow got into his system and he thought only of the work before him. He tried to estimate the happiness it would bring to the worn-out clerk, the booze-fighting clerk, the forced-to-be-untrue lover clerk, the poor parents who spent their savings in fitting out juniors for the "glory of the bank," and the girls waiting in home towns.... His imagination came to a halt, for a space, and he very unimaginatively sighed over by-gone illusions. Then he forgot the bitterness of disillusionment in a picture that framed itself on the window of the observation-car, against a dark background of passing rock and pines. He saw himself walking beside Frankie on one of the streets of Hometon. Her dear eyes were downcast, but her hand was willingly in his, and they were speaking of the days when he should come back a manager! A longing made itself felt in his heart, a longing to go back and redeem his pledge; but he hesitated. He knew she was not married to Perry—Porter was no longer in Hometon—but Evan felt unworthy of her after a silence of over three years. He had often thought of writing her and asking forgiveness, but had not been in a position to marry her—until the syndicate came along. He had told himself all along that it was poverty that kept him from renewing his love; but now that poverty no longer stared him in the face, now that he could give her a home, he hesitated. Why?—Because he was afraid! He knew he loved her and he feared to run the risk of a rebuff by mail. Such is the cowardice of a guilty lover's heart. He realized that he had hurt her very deeply; hints from Lou had convinced him of that; and he felt that he would have to go for her in person and in earnest to fully demonstrate his all too mysterious affection. He had a strong impulse to stay on the train, with fifteen thousand dollars in his wallet, and make a run for Hometon; but he knew that would be rash. He wanted to go to Frankie with more than money; he wanted to go in all contrition and to carry news of his triumphs over the bank that had disgraced him.

"Where will we start in?" asked Henty, rousing.

For a moment Evan did not comprehend the question, then he smiled, remembering how readily Henty usually thought things out. A. P. must have been pondering very deeply to take so long a time in evolving that simple question. It was to the point, however; they might as well work from west to east, seeing that they were so near the Pacific and so far from the Atlantic. That consideration had caused Evan to hesitate when his impetuosity suggested Frankie at a single jump.

"Vancouver, I guess, A. P."

"That means," said Henty, grinning, "that I'll be a long time before I meet that Hometon girl of yours—of mine."

"Not so very long."

"What did you say her name was, again?"

"Arling—Frankie Arling. I'm sure you'll fall in love with her."

A. P. stretched, yawned and replied:

"I'm sure I will, too."

They sold out their stock and effects at a good profit—Henty always looked out for the profit. When the people of the village, fifteen miles away, heard that the boys of Bachelors' Bungalow were leaving they gave a dance, at which there were present lumberjacks as chief masters of ceremony and hotel-maids as belles. One of the village storekeepers was there, too, with bitter complaints against Fate.

"Dang you," he said, "how do you think a man's goin' to make a livin' out of these Chinks? Dang me if it ain't a shame as you're leavin'."

"Cheer up, Uncle Dud," said Henty, "I'll be coming back with a wife sometime, and then your sales will double."

In less than a month after they had closed the deal with the syndicate the boys took leave of their bungalow. They still owned it and the little plot of ground on which it stood, but they were loath to leave just the same. A meadowlark sang them a farewell, and the sweetness of his song affected Henty's eyes. Nelson saw it and liked his friend better than ever.

"I don't blame them for wanting to make a townsite of this valley," said A. P., as they drove to the station. "They won't be stinging anybody no matter what they charge for the lots."

Before doing battle in Vancouver the two "farmers" held a day's consultation. They warmed up on a matinee, digested a Chinese dinner of chop suey and foyung, rice-cakes and various uncivilized desserts, went to bed late, and next morning had a plunge in the ocean. By that time they had decided Vancouver was a bad place to begin operations in, and they took boat for Victoria. There they really went to work.

Selecting one of the largest offices, Evan sauntered in and took a view of the staff. Henty was waiting around the corner. Strange to say, two or three of the bankboys were taking a rest by one of the desks. Evan approached them and asked a general question about the town, as a stranger might. He liked the way one of the fellows looked at and talked to him, and made bold to reveal his identity. The clerk held out his hand:

"Put it there!" he said; "will you come up to our rooms to-night? We'll have a bunch there to see you that'll make your hair stand on end."

The ball was about to roll. Evan gave his promise and went out to rejoin Henty.

"A. P.," he said, "we've got them going. I've discovered the best way to proceed. Just spot some fellow who looks good to you and then lead up to the subject of X. Bankclerk. If he is not interested pass him up and keep on looking till you find someone who is; then leave the raising of a crowd to him. In cities like this we can afford to spend two or three days."

Henty was excited. He flushed as only he could flush, and closed his fists with nervous satisfaction.

The Victoria bankclerk got together a crowd, as he had promised; there were old and young fellows, tall and short fellows, but all good fellows. They forced Nelson into a speech, which they cheered and applauded. They insisted on ordering drinks, but Evan told them he would be disappointed if they started off a union that way. They were all anxious to have their names enrolled as first members of *"The Associated Bankclerks of Canada."* One of the boys went down to a bookstore and returned with a record book in which applications for membership were to be enrolled.

Nelson took the boys into his confidence, and their sympathy was aroused. He suggested that each man present do his best by letter or otherwise to enlist other clerks in the movement. Not only names but signatures were to be collected and pasted in the record book. Nothing was to be done that would put an instrument of destruction in the hands of head office. All letters were to be addressed to Evan Nelson, Hometon, Ontario. He wrote the post-office there to hold his mail for further orders.

The "organizers"—they grinned as they applied the term to each other—spent two nights among the Victoria clerks, who agreed to take charge of Vancouver Island, then departed for Vancouver. There it took them three days and nights to work things up. They got a heap of circulars printed, with the following titles: "What the Bank Did to Me;" "Why Are You a Bankclerk?"; "Bank Union"; "Why Does Head Office Resent Co-operation of Clerks?"; and others, all by "X. Bankclerk." Printed matter was left in the hands of every man who wrote his name in the record book. Head office might get hold of a circular, but what could they do about it?

After finishing Vancouver, Nelson and Henty turned their attention to towns and villages. They carried with them, after less than a fortnight's work, about fifty letters of introduction to clerks all over the Dominion; that bundle was going to increase twenty-fold before they reached Halifax.

Small towns were easy; the boys sometimes did two and three a day. A. P. proved to be a whirlwind talker when he got warmed up to it. He parted from Evan at Sicamous Junction, and went down the Okanagan Valley. Evan went on to Revelstoke and worked the Arrow Lakes. In two weeks they met at Penticton, as glad to see each other as if they had been separated for years. They had many funny incidents to relate and plenty of success to discuss. The ball was rolling even faster than they had expected.

It was Sunday. They walked through the pretty streets of Penticton, enjoying the splendor of an Okanagan day. By and by they passed a graveyard. A man and woman were standing beside one of the graves; they looked up at the boys, but seemed not to recognize either of them. Evan turned pale, momentarily, then walked up to the man and woman. She wept when he told her who he was, and she related to him the story of a girl who had loved too young; who had faded and contracted consumption, back in Huron County, Ontario. They had brought her out to the mountain valleys, hoping the air would cure her, but she must have been too far gone.

In the evening, while Henty was writing letters, Evan went out for a walk. He wandered along a back street until he came again to the cemetery. A greybird sang its sweet song to him—but not only to him. Evan was thrilled with the sad beauty of that song, and of the Song of Life. Until the sun's rays had disappeared and the little greybird's singing was done, he sat, alone, beside Lily's grave.

21

THE ASSOCIATED BANKCLERKS OF CANADA

I t was Labor Day morning. Massey Hall had been rented for the afternoon and evening to accommodate a mass meeting of bankclerks. The newspapers of Toronto, Montreal, Hamilton, London and Guelph, as well as the other big towns within a radius of four hundred miles from Toronto, had printed the news.

Notices had come in from over four hundred out-of-town clerks, promising attendance. Evan and A. P. were busy. Girl-friends of Toronto clerks had formed themselves into a club for the making of badges and pennants with which the boys and the assembly room, respectively, were to be decorated.

When the "organizers" arrived at Massey Hall already a score of young ladies were nursing bundles of bunting, anxious to have someone hold the ladders for them.

Before long city clerks began dropping in, bringing telegrams and letters bearing encouraging announcements. Evan called for volunteers to act on a reception committee, to meet all trains and to introduce the fellows. Everybody responded, and ten were selected.

A thousand seats were reserved for bankboys, five hundred for their friends, and the rest were free to the public. The newspapers had discovered two orchestras willing to serve gratis; both of them were accepted, and came in the forenoon for rehearsal under one leader.

During decorations Henty seemed to think that the girls required watching.

"I should think, A. P.," said Nelson, aside, "that when you survived Nova Scotia you ought to stand a few Toronto beauties."

"Believe me," replied Henty, "these are hard to beat. By the way, we ought to have a reception committee for girls. A good many of the fellows will bring their friends along."

"A good idea," laughed Evan; "you look after it, will you?"

"You bet. I wouldn't mind being that committee myself."

A. P. did look after it, and not vicariously.

Time sped. Every train brought in a bunch of town clerks. They came from far and near; from every city and almost every hamlet in Ontario.

Nelson and Henty themselves went down to the Montreal train. Two hundred and fifty boys came in on it. They hailed from Quebec, Montreal, Kingston, Peterborough, and points along the line. When they recognized X. Bankclerk, whose common-looking face had been reproduced in most of the big Canadian dailies, they cheered and shouted until holiday travellers stood aghast.

The Windsor train came in about eleven o'clock, shortly after the Montreal, bringing a delegation larger than the Eastern. Union Station was crammed with bankclerks, and a band was waiting for them on Front Street. After a fair display of noise and confusion the boys formed in quadruple line and marched up town. Two men in the van carried a gigantic streamer bearing the inscription: "The A.B.C.'s."

As they marched up Yonge Street Evan saw a figure with a pointed beard and a hand-bag disappear around the corner of Temperance Street, as though afraid to face the music. It is hardly probable the Big Eye was going to the Moon Theatre to buy tickets for an afternoon performance. Nelson would not have been at all surprised at that, but he thought it more likely that Castle would forego the pleasure of a burlesque performance, on that day of his defeat, and crawl into the gallery of Massey Hall.

By noon seven hundred bankclerks were assembled. Henty drew Evan's attention to the fact that it was chiefly the country chaps who brought their lady-friends; the city fellows probably had had a strenuous time of it paying their own fares. Nevertheless, there was present a good representation of the fair sex.

A. P. and Evan had lunch with Mr. and Mrs. Nelson and Lou, from Hometon. It was a happy reunion.

Mrs. Nelson cried with joy; Lou blushed at the look of admiration her brother gave her; and George Nelson's eyes twinkled.

"And this is Mr. Henty!" cried Mrs. Nelson, after her first little cry.

"Yes," said Evan, looking at Lou, "this is the other rube."

Lou's face burned.

"I didn't include Mr. Henty," she explained, "when I used to call you a rube, brother. In fact, you both look like real sports now."

"Oh, we're sports all right," said A. P., laughing with peculiar animation.

Was there nothing lacking at that lunch-party? Why then did Evan, for brief moments, seem absent-minded? Probably it was the bank union that engaged his thoughts. His sister had so many questions to ask him he could not get a chance to formulate a sufficiently sly question about Hometon, and the people there. When he observed that he was going up, with Henty, to rest a while, his mother said:

"You'll see everything the way you left it; nothing new to tell you, son. Except—oh, well!—How many thousand miles have you travelled?"

"We estimate them in millions," said Henty, soberly.

Noon-hour passed away very rapidly, and the boys escorted the Nelsons over to the Hall. Henty was informed that somebody waited to see him. It was the old gentleman.

He was dressed in typically farmer style, and wore a merry smile. After a brief greeting with his son he turned for an introduction to Lou, and was soon chuckling at everything she said.

One of the reception committee came hurrying up to Evan and whispered that the assembly was waiting.

"We've got a box for your folk," said the bankclerk.

The other boxes were filled with ladies, none of whom were more attractive than Lou Nelson. Old man Henty pushed her chair out where a thousand bankmen might admire her, and it took her several minutes to master the color in her cheeks.

The two "organizers" came on the platform together, and the audience applauded generously. Evan sat down while Henty, his face aflame, announced in quavering voice:

"Ladies and gentlemen, and especially boys of Bankerdom, instead of introducing you to Mr. Nelson and myself we will ask you all to stand and sing the Canadian National Anthem."

The orchestra leader faced the audience, with his baton poised, and one of the players led in the singing. The sound of the pipe organ itself was drowned in the strains of "O Canada" that swelled from so many young Canadian throats.

Thoroughly thrilled, when the singing was done Evan arose to speak. There was a demonstration of a few minutes, then the speaker's voice rang out vibrantly:

"Dear friends,

"I thank you for such a welcome. I am going to make a short speech, but not because I want to: the occasion demands it. There are many people here, who want to know what this is all about. I shall tell them and then we will get down to business.

"Perhaps if I had not been fired from one of the banks in this city, about four years ago, I should not be here now trying to organize a bank union. But I don't want any of you to think it is revenge I am after; I am really here to make it impossible for any clerk to be discharged and disgraced as I was, without a trial. You all know my story, how I was denied the right to plead my own cause, and all the rest of it. It is hard for me to forgive—I never can forgive them; but let us forget them. Those days of tyranny are over—dating from to-day."

Nelson was smothered in cheers and clapping of hands.

"The great necessity for clerk union," *he resumed,* "is based on a condition of affairs, still prevalent in the business, which made it easy for the bank to fire and blackball myself. I represented the clerk who had no protection; the insignificant individual. He is—rather I should say, dating from to-day—he has been clay in the potter's hands; but the potter has got to go out of business, and we're here now to see that he does." *(Here, the bankclerks expressed their endorsement of the idea in clapping and laughter.)* "Heretofore, my friends, we have been the mere tools of a combination of rich institutions; they have hired and fired us how and when they pleased. We are sick of it; it's bad business."

"You bet it is," cried someone in the crowd; and the galleries enjoyed the show.

"I see a great many girls here to-day," *continued the speaker,* "and they look like the friends of bankclerks. Now what is going to become of them unless we can make enough money to support them? An engagement never made any girl happy, after it was more than two or three years of age. How many of us have been engaged for five and ten years, and can't even yet afford to make good our promise? I'm glad you take it as a joke, instead of growing angry with me; but, my bank friends, it is not a joke, particularly to the girl who is waiting for you and me."

The seriousness of Nelson's tone had its effect on the audience, and the silence that followed his last sentence was tense.

"There are many other crows," *he went on,* "to pick with head office, the majority of which will have to be plucked in committee meetings of the A.B.C.'s." *(Applause.)* "We are here to get the organization of that association under way, rather than to entertain our friends. So with your permission I will conclude my introduction and begin business by asking you to form a *pro tem.* organization. Who will you have for temporary chairman?"

Before Evan had sat down several bankmen were on their feet nominating him for chairman. Henty tried to elicit some other nomination but failed: they shouted and whistled for Nelson. He thanked them and took the chair. A. P. was chosen secretary, a committee to draft resolutions and by-laws was selected, and a full temporary organization effected.

To relieve the monotony of business the orchestra was asked for an overture, and while it was playing Evan was called behind the scenes. A gentleman, whom he took for a bank official, was waiting to speak to him.

"My name is Jacob Doro," said the gentleman; "I am a friend of your movement. Let me congratulate you on this splendid success. I want to make a suggestion, Mr. Nelson, and hope you will not misunderstand me. Will you accept an endowment for the establishment of a sort of club here in Toronto, where bankclerks can congregate, have a library, a gymnasium, and recreation of every kind? I am president of a loan company, and if you will not accept a donation, you will at least accept a loan on a long note."

Evan was, of course, surprised.

"That is a good scheme of yours, Mr. Doro," he said, "but why should you want to throw away money on us bank-fellows?"

"It won't be thrown away, Mr. Nelson," replied the stranger; "I was not always rich, but now I am, and it would give me great pleasure to endow this bankclerks' association. In the days when I was struggling I had a son enter the banking business, and they killed him with work. Now perhaps you understand?"

No one could have doubted the sincerity of a man who spoke with the feeling Doro evinced. Evan held out his hand.

"We will be needing friends," he said; "may I use your name, Mr. Doro?"

Mr. Doro thought a moment before replying.

"I'm not afraid of the banks," he said, finally; "and, besides, by telling my name and why I give the money, you will attract other contributions. I know you will. Tell the boys I donate $25,000, and that I know others who have several thousands to spare."

Feeling a bit unsteady, Evan offered Doro a seat on one of the wings of the stage, then went back to the platform. When the overture was finished he stood before the assembly again.

"I have great news for you," he said, and related the newly-found philanthropist's offer. There was perfect order while he spoke, but it was evident the clerks were restraining themselves.

"Let us see Mr. Doro," one fellow shouted. Everyone clapped the suggestion.

"He will appear at our meeting to-night," said Evan, answering for Doro, "when we convene to elect permanent officers."

They were satisfied with that. Mr. Doro's suggestion was talked to informally by different men from Montreal, London and other cities, all of whom were in favor of some such institution as the one proposed. The general opinion was that it would be a fine thing for the boys; would serve as a rendezvous for transient clerks, make a good club for city men, and promulgate the spirit of sociability. Toronto was thought to be the most convenient city in the Dominion to have as headquarters for the A.B.C.'s: there Hague conferences with head office would take place.

At a signal from the chairman the orchestra began to play a song entitled "Bankerdom." It was sung by a quartette of clerks, and afterwards by the Assembly, who were provided with printed copies. The refrain went:

> *O Bankerdom, dear Bankerdom,*
>
> *We sing to thee a freedom-song;*
>
> *The years have gone that knew us dumb,*
>
> *The years we found so hard and long;*
>
> *And here to-day is taken from*
>
> *Our aching wrists the silver thong*
>
> *That bound us to a monied wrong,*
>
> *Our Bankerdom, free Bankerdom!*

About five o'clock the afternoon session was adjourned.

A. P.'s father, who was quite a plunger when he came to town, persuaded the Nelsons to dine with him at a first-class hotel. Evan could not go along; he had accepted an invitation to dine at Mrs. Greig's.

Sam Robb was ill—that accounted for his absence from the mass meeting in the afternoon. Evan had been to see him a few days before, but Robb was too sick to talk. Now he was downstairs in carpet slippers, and looked pretty well.

"How did it come off?" was his salutation.

Evan described the whole affair, to the ex-manager's extreme satisfaction. Before they had been conversing long he asked frankly,

"Are you still slaving away?"

"Yes," sighed Robb; "but the union will help us boys."

"Why do you smile, Mrs. Greig?" asked Nelson, himself smiling. She looked at Robb before answering.

"To hear an old married man call himself a boy."

"Married!"

The ex-manager laughed and blushed.

"Yes," he admitted, "our landlady's name is Mrs. Robb; I hadn't the nerve to tell you before."

Although the same landlady objected to "Sammy's going out in the night air," Sam accompanied Evan to Massey Hall after dinner. As they walked down University Avenue Evan could scarcely realize that his position had altered so greatly in four years. He thought of the day after he had been dismissed and how dejectedly he had sat, with a swelled head, on one of those avenue benches.

"Do you know," said his old friend, replying to a reminiscent observation of Evan's, "that spree of yours cured me; that and Ede."

At Massey Hall, Robb was introduced to Mr. Henty's party, and took a seat in their box.

The hall was filled again. At the front of the balcony a bevy of suffragists were seated, ready to approve of a movement that appealed to their adventurous spirits. Evan noticed their colors and gave them a public welcome. He said he was proud of their support, and hoped they would win in their fight against Man as satisfactorily as the bankclerks were winning against Money.

After a few general remarks the chairman exhibited a record book in which he said there were written and pasted about one thousand two hundred names of applicants for membership in the association. Not more than two hundred of those present, of whom there were one thousand, were enrolled; so that, to start with, the A.B.C.'s would have a membership of two thousand. He held up an armful of mail which had been forwarded from Hometon, to illustrate the enthusiasm with which bankclerks everywhere were responding to the call.

"Now let us proceed with permanent organization," he said, using a bank ruler for a gavel; "we must first have a resolution to form an association; after that decide on a name; then elect officers and appoint committees."

A man arose in the audience. "Mr. Chairman," he said, "might I speak a word?"

Evan recognized the speaker. "Come on up to the platform," he invited; "I was forgetting about you, Mr. Doro."

The audience shouted "Platform!" and Doro reluctantly obeyed.

"Ladies and gentlemen," he said, "and you boys in the banking business, I hope you will understand that I am not looking for notoriety here to-night. I merely want to boost a good thing along. Now I don't want to force a donation on this society, but if you will accept it you are welcome to it; if you cannot see your way clear to accept it, I beg of you to borrow from my trust company as freely as you wish. I will accept the signatures of your executive without security."

There was a terrific demonstration. After it had quieted, Evan whispered to Mr. Doro that they were not yet organized, but as soon as they were they would entertain his offer. In the meantime he was given a seat on the platform.

Motions began to circulate. In a few minutes it had been decided to organize a union; a name was chosen; a brief constitution was adopted; and the election of officers began.

The name of president came up first. The bankclerks would have nobody but Nelson. He thanked them briefly, assuring them he would look after their interests with all his might. It was thought advisable not to have a vice-president. For secretary-treasurer A. P. Henty was nominated. In a short speech he declined, and finished by suggesting Mr. Sam Robb, whom he said would know how to handle the banks because he had been a manager.

"Does anybody know him?" called someone, during a silence.

"Yes," replied the president, coming to the front of the stage. "If any man is competent of handling the work, and worthy of the honor, I know Mr. Robb to be. He is one of the best friends I have, and I know him to be both clever and honest. Added to his ability and integrity, he has experience; and the ways of big business are plain to him. My friends, we need just such a man as Mr. Robb for secretary-treasurer."

Their gratitude to Evan for his long efforts in making a bank union possible would not permit the assembly to reject the man whom the president so strongly recommended for the position of secretary. They elected Robb to the office, on a good salary.

Why go into further details of the organization? It was in good hands, and behind it were the brains of two thousand young Canadian businessmen. Why should it not work out? And with the initiation fee and monthly dues, why should it not pay as it grew?

A committee on finance was chosen, to thoroughly canvass any endowments offered. Mr. Doro's offer was refused, but the association made him honorary-president and adopted a resolution to borrow money from him for the erection of a Bankclerks' Retreat in Toronto. The financial committee saw to it that Nelson and Henty were refunded their expenses from Victoria to Halifax.

The hour was late before the evening session adjourned. A. P. delivered a farewell address, in which he declared he was "not cut out for office work," and Sam Robb convinced the assembly that he was the man for the office they had conferred upon him.

Evan cut his closing sentences short. As the orchestra played "God Save the King" he looked down into the audience and saw someone pushing toward the platform. It was the Bonehead.

"Hey," said Perry, beckoning to Evan, "I want to speak to you." He dragged his yielding victim to a corner. "This union'll just about bring my salary up to the marriage mark. Fine, ain't it? I suppose you know that Frank and I are——"

"No, I didn't know," replied Evan, coldly. Then, absently, "Did you bring her down with you?"

"Sure. I've been working in Orangeville; she came down on the late afternoon train and I met her on the way. Why don't you congratulate me?"

Nelson acted as though he had not heard. "Where is she?" he asked.

"Oh, she beat it with a friend just before the thing was dismissed. She's staying with her cousin on Jarvis Street. We're going back together on the morning train."

Never in his life had Perry been so objectionable to Nelson as he was during those few minutes. The egotism of him to aspire to Frankie's love! And yet there came to Evan the stinging realization that he, himself, had failed to cherish that love. It was not the Bonehead's fault that he was engaged to her—who could blame him? That was a matter for Frankie to decide, and apparently she had decided.

Evan had no heart for further handshakes. He sought out Robb and taking him by the arm left Massey Hall by the stage entrance. Rain had fallen in torrents and the gutters were full of water, but the sky had cleared, and the air was fresh and cool.

"Let's walk home," said Robb, "I'm all worked up; this thing has taken away my breath—I need the air."

Evan did not smile; he walked along in silence.

"What's the matter, old man?" asked his friend when they had reached University Avenue; "has something disappointed you?"

"No," said Evan, ashamed of his moodiness, "I was just thinking of one night similar to this when I was on the cash-book. Doesn't it seem a long time ago, Sam?"

Robb took a deep breath at the word "Sam."

"Old friend," he said, vibrantly, "you can't understand what you've done for me to-night. I was almost at the breaking-point."

Evan's eyes were turned up a side street, an unpaved street where the mud was deep and slimy.

"For heaven's sake!" he whispered, "look who goes there! When I whistle," he continued excitedly, "you fall back and watch for cops. I'm going to spoil that blue coat and those flannel pants."

"I recognize him," said Robb; "go easy; remember you've been a farmer."

It was past midnight. The avenue was deserted. Large chestnuts clothed the side street, down which the person designated walked, in darkness.

Evan fairly panted as he trailed his quarry. Within a few rods of It he began to run noiselessly upon the grass. Then he pounced upon it, like a jaguar upon a fawn. Sam was a short distance behind.

Down in the mud went the blue coat and flannel pants, and there echoed a cry much like that of a frightened girl. Smothering that cry with a handful of mud, Evan proceeded to plaster every part of his victim, except the ears, into one of which he facetiously whispered:

"Alfy dear, this is Evan."

All but howling, Castle scrambled out of the gutter and ran for his life.

Sam tried several times to speak, as they walked up to his home, but his eye fell on Evan's muddy raincoat and he failed. Through the night Mrs. Robb was startled by certain silent convulsions.

"Sammy," she whispered, "are you ill?"

"Yes, Ede," he said jerkily, "a pain in the side."

22

She Waits for Us

Early next morning Evan was at Henty's hotel.

"A. P.," he said, "all aboard for Hometon."

The old man looked up.

"Take him with you if you like, Mr. Nelson," he said; "but mind you bring him back, and come along yourself. I've got a cook down home I want you to taste."

Evan accepted the invitation and expressed hope that the cook was not from Western Canada. A. P. jumped into his clothes.

"I'm ready," he said, soon; "have I time for breakfast?"

"No; get a banana on the way down town. Our folks will meet us at Union Station."

They missed the Teeswater train, in spite of their hurrying, or, perhaps, on account of their hurrying; and had to wait for the Owen Sound.

"You couldn't guess who went out on the first train, Evan," whispered Lou, looking wise.

"Frankie and Porter, I imagine," replied Evan, casually.

"How did you know?"

"Met Perry last night," answered the brother, briefly. "What are you looking so queer about, Sis?"

"Oh, nothing," said Lou, disappointedly; "only I thought you would be more interested than you are."

He made no reply, again to his sister's astonishment, but turned to Henty.

"A. P.," he said, "we'll meet the girl you're going to marry, when we get to Orangeville. We'll have to change from this train to hers."

A. P. blushed ridiculously, and so did Lou. Evan pretended not to notice, and turned his attention to the luggage.

On the way to Orangeville father and son found each other interesting. There was still a sparkle in George Nelson's eye. Back in a double seat Henty was bravely endeavoring to take care of two ladies, mother and daughter.

At Orangeville, as Perry was saying his farewells to Frankie, Lou caught her eye and beckoned to her. Not having to pass the seat where Evan and his father were, Frankie obeyed the summons. She was introduced to Henty, and deliberately sat beside him. "The porter" looked sourly around and disappeared. Evan caught a girl's eye in a mirror and left his seat. Not having seen Frankie for three years and a half he was somewhat prepared for a change, but not for the change that had taken place. Her cheeks were no longer round and girlish, her voice had changed, her eyes were older and more womanly-comprehending.

"Frankie," he said, taking the little hand she offered, "it seems mighty good to get a look at you after—all that has happened."

He fully expected that she would show embarrassment—he was inwardly excited himself—but she answered him calmly, while Lou looked on in wonder:

"I've been looking at you for hours, Evan—on the platform; you are quite famous *now*, you know. Everyone waits to get a peep at you."

There was a potent rebuke in her words. Evan felt it keenly. He made an excuse to get back to his father.

Hometon was out with the town band to meet the Nelson party. Some of the bankclerks had driven to the depot in hacks to meet him they called their "New G. M."

The excitement did not appeal to Evan, but he readily forgave dear old Hometon this one excess. There was a concert arranged in the town-hall for the evening, which, of course, had to have a chairman.

Just before the concert began old Grandpa Newman nudged John, the grocer, sitting beside him, and whispered huskily:

"It do beat all, John, the way people carry on nowadays. Now, in my day—"

Luckily for the grocer, the band began to badly play a march. The chairman grinned in his seat—in fancy he was transported to Albany Avenue, Brooklyn, and listened again to the saloon bands of that benighted street.

The day after the village dissipation Evan loitered around home playing catch with Henty and Lou. He found they liked to have the ball tossed midway between them, and did his best to be accommodating.

"Well, A. P.," he said, when Lou had given up the game to help get lunch, "what do you think of Miss Arling?"

Henty blushed from his adam's-apple to the tips of his ears, one grand and final blush.

"Evan," he said, "I'm in love."

"I thought you'd fall in love with her, A. P.," was the reply. "Frankie is the finest girl in town."

"For you, maybe," said A. P., "but not for me. Nelsy," he continued in confusion, "we have known each other a long while. What would you think of me if I told you I loved your sister?"

A smile, happy yet troubled, was the answer Henty got.

In the afternoon Evan sat reading beneath the old maple trees that had shaded his school-books from the sun in the beloved school-days gone by. Lou came out and stood beside him a moment, and when he looked up she bent over him, with the lovelight in her eyes.

"Brother," she said, "I knew you would bring him to me, but I never dreamed he would be so grand!"

The brother laughed and teased her. When she had gone he sat musing on the wonders of a girl's heart. There came to him, as there had often come, the sure knowledge that he possessed such a treasure; but this time came also the fear that that treasure might unwillingly be given to another, for reasons that puzzle men.

"What foolish creatures we are," ran his thoughts. "I know that Frankie is waiting for me to come. I have known it for years, and she made me see it again yesterday on the train. I don't know why I can't get up the courage to face the girl I love. I must. I must go now and make good my promise. She is waiting for me in spite of all!"

More serious, perhaps, than he had ever been, he walked down the back street along which a schoolboy and schoolgirl had so often strolled together. When he came to the Arling residence he ascended the steps with a palpitating heart. The front door was open. He rapped timidly and waited, but there was no response. He peeked in, believing that someone must be there.

Yes, Someone was there. She lay on the couch asleep, tear stains on her cheeks. He moved toward her and knelt beside the couch. Her eyes opened in wonder.

"I've come for you," he said, quietly.

She studied him as if he puzzled her. There was the mystified expression of a baby's eyes in hers. For a while they gazed at each other; then came the tears that must stain her face forever with marks of happiness, and she murmured:

"I can't believe my dream has come true!"

No questions were asked. What mattered the past, now? Porter Perry and Hamilton episodes were no longer of any consequence. The only significant thing was love; love that had endured and was therefore true.

About the Author

As part of our mission to publish great works of literary fiction and nonfiction, Colour the Classics Publishing Corp. is extremely dedicated to bringing to the forefront the amazing works of long dead and truly talented authors. Connect with us!

instagram.com/colourtheclassics

facebook.com/colourtheclassics